EMPLOYMENT RELATIONS IN CAMEROON

EMPLOYMENT RELATIONS IN CAMEROON

Irene FOKUM SAMA-LANG

GALDA VERLAG 2022

Bibliografische Information der Deutschen Nationalbibliothek
Die Deutsche Nationalbibliothek verzeichnet diese Publikation in der Deutschen Nationalbibliografie; detaillierte bibliografische Daten sind im Internet über http://dnb.ddb.de abrufbar.

ISBN 978-3-96203-227-2 (Print)
ISBN 978-3-96203-228-9 (E-Book)

TABLE OF CONTENTS

Chapter 3

Chapter 4

Chapter 7

Chapter 8

Chapter 9

FOREWORD

I am absolutely delighted to write this foreword to the book "Employment Relations In Cameroon", for, I have known the author Irene Fokum Sama-Lang since her infancy and watched her evolve from a cheerful, inquisitive little girl to a voracious reader and unsurprisingly an erudite, articulate teacher, an avid researcher and a prolific writer.

From the title the author eschews the sombre commonly used term "Labour Law" in favour of the more engaging "Employment Relations", approaching the subject from a humane and rights-based paradigm. Then, in her perceptive style, she orientates the reader with the history of employment relations and the right to work from the pre-colonial, through the colonial, to the post-colonial era. Irene Sama-Lang aptly articulates the concept of the worker and the right to work positing that productive work in any society is important not only because of the resources which they create for the community, but also because of the income they bring to workers, the social role which they confer and the feeling of self-esteem which workers derive from them.

The 1992 codification of labour law might have constricted labour law and paralysed practice by putting a torniquet on damages, making practitioners often unable to think out of the box, but one of the hallmarks of the book is that it is inclusive, holistic comprehensive and comprehensible. The author regenerates creativity by bringing fresh wind to the different avenues of redress and institutions which administer labour law such as the little-known National Labour Advisory Board, the role of trade unions and the right to unionise the right to collective bargaining, collective disputes and arbitration proceedings, remedies such as specific performance and reinstatement. The book then does justice to the many International Labour Conventions ratified by Cameroon, great sources of redemption, which practitioners and grievors often ignore.

The author has done justice to caselaw by the ample and diverse cases which she uses to accompany and explain concepts, for example, the case of Simon Tamanjong & 6 others v. Cameroon Tea Estates to illustrate the absence of independence on the part of the Labour Inspector; Tatah Ndiwa

Faison v. Cameroon Development Corporation a welcome example of specific performance and reinstatement.

True to her foresight and visionary leadership, Irene Sama-Lang dedicates the closing chapter to the protection of migrant workers, a topic we can no longer avoid, for indeed, pandemics, crisis, calamities and conflict have forced millions to migrate in search of a livelihood with implications on labour relations of receiving states.

EMPLOYMENT RELATIONS IN CAMEROON is a must-have and must-read handbook for practitioners, students and teachers. It is conceived with sensitivity and sensibility, thoroughly researched, and articulately executed.

I heartily recommend this book with great enthusiasm!

Sincerely,

Lady Justice Vera N. Nkwate Ngassa
(LLM Georgetown University, Washington DC)
Justice, Supreme Court of Cameroon
Lecturer, University of Buea
International Faculty, Haggai Institute for Leadership, Hawaii, USA
LAWA (Leadership and Advocacy for Women In Africa) Fellow
Author: "Gender Approach to Court Actions", "Gender Law Report", "Cameroon Women's Land Rights Handbook" and "Victim-Friendly Court Manual"

ACKNOWLEDGEMENTS

This book would not have been completed without the concerted effort of some persons whose invaluable encouragement and support require my profound gratitude.

I am deeply indebted to Dr. Monkam Cyrille for his in depth comments, criticisms encouragement and insistence to write this book. Thank you Professor Djieufack Roland for your profound criticisms and comments. I am especially indebted to Dr. Patrick Akamin for his contributions, especially the ninth chapter of this book.

I acknowledge my colleagues of the Then Department of Law which has been split into four other Departments in the newly created Faculty of Laws & Political Science, University of Buea.

I cannot thank Lady Justice Vera N.Nkwate Ngassa for wriing the foreword to the book

I thank my husband Dr. Patrick Sama-Lang and our children, Ruud, Adolphine and Lena Desiree for their ceaseless encouragement and for understanding when I could not be available.

TABLE OF CASES

Cameroonian Cases

Foreign Cases

Printing & Numerical Registering Company v. Sampson (1879) LR 19 Eq 462	56
Priestly v. Fowler (1837) 3 M & W 1	71, 75
Qualcast (Wolverhampton) Ltd v. Haynes [1959] AC 743	72
R v. Secretary of State for Transport, ex parte Factortame Ltd (No. 2) [1991] 1 AC 603	188
R v. Lord Chancellor's Department, ex parte Nangle [1992] 1 All ER 897	
Rose v. Plenty [1970] 1 All ER 97	75
Ready Mixed Concrete (South East) Ltd v. Minister of Pensions [1968] 1 ALL ER 433	37, 40, 91
Reid v. Rush & Towkins Group PLC [1989] 1 RLR 265	75
Reynolds v. Shipping Federation Ltd [1924] 1 Ch 28	200
Rigby v. Ferodo Ltd [1988] 1 CR 29	147
Roberts v. Dorothea State Quarrers Co ltd [1948] WN 246	114
Robb v. Hammersmith and Fulham London Borough Council, [1991] 1 RLR 72	188
Rudd's Case [1933] 1 KB 566	75
Scally v. South East Thames R.H.A [1987] 1CR 700	60
Secret*ary of State for Employment v. ASLEF No.2* [1972] QB 455	85
Shepherd & Co Ltd v. Jerrom [1986] 1 RLR 358	86
Short v. Henderson [1946] SC 24	38, 76
Singh v. British Steel [1974] 1 RLR 131	214
Simmons v. Heath Laundry Co [1910] 1 KB 543	30
Smith v. Baker & Sons [1831] AC 325	71
Smith v. Crossley Brothers [1951] 95 Sol. Jo. 655	71
Squib UK Staff Association v. Certification Officer [1980] 1 RLR 431	200
Stavely Iron & Chemical Co Ltd v. Jones [1956] AC 627	76
Steveson, Jordan & Harrison v. MacDonald & Evans [1952] 1 TLR 101	50

TABLE OF STATUTES

International Statutes

Foreign Legislation

Regional Legislation

Cameroonian Legislation

Subordinate Cameroonian Laws

ABBREVIATIONS

ADR	-	Alternative Dispute Resolution
All. E.R.	-	All England Reports
BCA	-	Bamenda Court of Appeal
CASWP	-	Court of Appeal South West Province
CCJA	-	Common Court of Justice and Arbitration
CCLR	-	Cameroon Common Law Report
CDC	-	Cameroon Development Corporation
CGT	-	*Confederation Generale du Travail*
EAMI	-	*Exploitation Agricoles de Moyenne Importance*
FCFA	-	Franc, *Communaute Financiere Africain*
HCF	-	High Court Fako
HCK	-	High Court Kumba
HIPC	-	Heavily Indebted Poor Country
ICESCR	-	International Covenant of Economic Social and Cultural Rights
ILO	-	International Labour Organisation
IMF	-	International Monetary Fund
ICFTU	-	International Confederation of Free Trade Unions
JCA	-	Judge Court of Appeal
NEF	-	National Employment Fund
NUCW	-	National Union of Cameroon Workers
OHADA	-	*Organisation De L'Harmonisation de Droits 'Affaire*
SC	-	Supreme Court
SYNES	-	*Syndicat des Enseignants du Superieur*
UNDHR	-	United Nations Declaration of Human Rights
USCC	-	*Union des Syndicats Confederes du Cameroun*

INTRODUCTION

Over the years, civilisation and societal development have been a function of work. According to Rifkin,[1] from the Palaeolithic hunter/gatherer through the Neolithic farmer, medieval craftsman to the assembly line worker of the present century, civilisation and development have remained intrinsically linked to work[2].

Section 23 (1) of the Labour Code of 1992 defines employment contract as resulting from an 'agreement by which a worker[3] undertakes to put his services under the authority and management of an employer against remuneration.' Although under this provision a contract of employment involves service under the control of another, its performance must be under conditions that foster the development and dignity of the worker. Indeed, both within the country's domestic legal framework[4] and obligations assumed under international treaties[5], the worker is entitled to certain minimum standard of treatment in the course of the performance of his/her service.

---

1 Rifkin, J., *The End of Work, The Decline of Global Labour Force and the Dawn of the Post Market Era*, A Jeremy P. Tachner/Putman Book, 1999, p, 3. See also the South African Human Development Report, 2003, UNDP, p. 144.

2 This is buttressed by the preamble to ILO Convention No. 168, 1988 which points out that productive work (employment) in any society is important not only because of the resources which they create for the community, but also because of the income they bring to workers, the social role which they confer and the feeling of self-esteem which workers derive from them. The central nature of work in Cameroon, is reflected in the motto of Cameroon: "Peace, Work, Fatherland."

3 Section 1(2) Labour Code 1992 defines a worker as any person irrespective of sex or nationality, who has undertaken to place his services in return for a remuneration, under the control of another person, whether an individual or a public or private corporation, considered as the 'employer'.

4 The 1996 Constitution as revised, the Labour Code 1992 and the several Ministerial decisions relating to labour relations.

5 Cameroon has been a member of the ILO since 1960. Cameroon ratified The International Convention on Economic, Social and Cultural Rights on June 24th 1984. The Universal Declaration of Human Rights contained in the preamble of the 1996 Constitution of Cameroon as revised and according to article 65 of the same constitution, preambular provisions are part and parcel of the constitution. Cameroon has ratified 49 ILO Conventions amongst others: Labour Inspection Convention, 1947 ratified in 1960, Abolition of Forced Labour Convention 1957 (No. 105) ratified in 1962, Right to organize and Collective Bargaining Convention 1949, ratified in 1962, Equal Remuneration Convention 1951, ratified in 1970, Employment Policy Convention 1964, ratified in1970,Termination of Employment Convention 1982 ratified in 1988.

Article II Paragraph (a) of the International Labour Organisation (ILO), Philadelphia Declaration 1958[6], provides that: 'all human beings are entitled to pursue both their material well-being and their spiritual development in conditions of freedom and dignity, of economic security and equal opportunity.'[7] This principle, which is binding on signatory states like Cameroon, is possible only in a society, which is development-driven[8], where the basic equitable doctrine of good faith[9] the bedrock of all modern contracts (including employment contracts) is respected and preserved. It is inherent from the construction of section 23 of the 1992 Labour Code that such a principle apply better, where contracts are truly consensual since freely negotiated contracts tend to create an atmosphere and spirit that facilitates scrupulous respect of the terms of the employment contract.

Work, the subject matter of a contract of employment, is a socio-economic right secured by section 23 paragraph 1 of the Universal Declaration of Human Rights 1948.[10] This provision recognises everybody's right to 'just and favourable conditions of employment.' That work is a (socio-economic) right is further confirmed by article 6 paragraph 1 of the International Covenant on Economic, Social and Cultural Rights (ICESCR)[11] that obliges parties to the convention to give the opportunity to gain his/her living through work, freely chosen[12].

Justice Forbang in the High Court of Fako case of *Akamangwa Martin v. SONARA*[13] described the right to work as 'sacrosanct'. It follows from this

---

6 Cameroon ratified this Declaration on 7th June 1960.

7 In this light, the World Summit for Social Development 1995 adopted a commitment to promoting full employment as a basic priority for economic and social policies of states and to ensure the attainment of sustainable livelihoods through freely chosen productive employment and work. This impacts on security of service (employment) during the period of crisis since workers are usually under employed or inadequately employed with attendant consequences.

8 This is because the passing of laws per se do not protect and ensure the right to development. It is only a state that has the political will to foster such rights that can be said to be development driven.

9 Good faith here is not in the *uberrimae fidei* sense but is conceived as the moral obligation to keep ones side of the contract agreement.

10 The Universal Declaration of Human Rights and all duly ratified treaties are part and parcel of Cameroonian law as it has been incorporated into the preamble of the 1996 Constitution, the grundnorm of the country. According to Art 65 of this Constitution, provisions of the preamble are part and parcel of the constitution.

11 Ratified by Cameroon on June 24th 1984.

12 This does not enjoin all and sundry with work. It rather require state parties to create an enabling environment to ensure that businesses that provide employment thrive so that all persons willing and able to work should be able to engage in gainful employment.

13 Suit No. HCF/ L.011/2000-2001 (unreported).

categoric ratio that there is a firm obligation on the government to provide work and guarantee its security[14] and performance by the contractual parties under acceptable conditions.

In this regard, in the event of redundancies or terminations, workers should be paid-off in time and/or appropriate remedies be awarded according to stipulated rules in the Labour Code, Ministerial orders and the contracts of employment. The preambular provisions of the Cameroon Constitution of 1996[15] as revised and section 2 of the Labour Code 1992, both of which reflect the country's treaty obligations, explicitly secure for the country's nationals the right to work,[16] which is central to employment.

The right to improve on oneself either under an apprenticeship contract of vocational education training is becoming the more relevant in a world that is moving from theory to professionalism and skills gaining to improve on the competitiveness of workers and their mobility. Cameroon caught this fever in 2018 with the passing of the Law on Vocational Training.

Although the labour Code is not generous in its handling of migrant workers, it is a fundamental aspect of Labour relations that cannot be swept under the carpet especially with the ILO convention of 1998 on the fundamental rights of a worker, which makes migrant worker's right a core right in Labour relations.

The right to collective bargaining and the right to unionise is a core labour right that has been secure in the bill of rights, different ILO conventions, the constitution of Cameroon 1996 as revised and sections 3 *et seq* of the labour Code 1992.

---

14 It has been argued by some human rights scholars like Wellman, *Welfare Rights,* Rowan and Little, Totowa, New Jersey, 1982, that the right to work is an abstract which is impossible of realisation by the state because of lack of funds. However, granted that the right to work does not necessarily impose a duty on the states to provide all and sundry with work, states are nonetheless enjoined to draft policies and strategies that will ensure job creation and create an enabling environment for its security. General comment No.3 (1990) on States parties' obligations makes Art. 6 IESCR a core obligation of the state and so no state can derogate from this responsibility in the guise of lack of funds. See ILO Covenant No. 111, 1958 on Discrimination (Employment and Occupation), which is instructive on this.

15 Art. 65 of the Constitution of 1996 makes preamble provisions part and parcel of the constitution.

16 The right to work as conceptualised in Article 6 of the ICESCR 1966 is the right to productive and gainful employment which he/she freely chooses, enabling the employee to live in peace, justice and dignity free from discrimination. To this effect, the conditions of employment, basic labour protection, technical and vocational training of the worker to ensure their career development and the benefits upon redundancy or retirement becomes central to this right.

A. The Historical Evolution of Employment and Labour Relations

This section traces historical evolution of labour and employment relations from the period before the coming of the colonial powers into Cameroon to post-independent Cameroon to ascertain the extent to which these might have affected the labour scene and employment security of Cameroon today.

A.1 Labour Relations Before the Arrival of the Colonialists

By the 16th century, before the colonialists arrived and introduced cash economy in what is now known as Cameroon, trade in labour was alien to the native inhabitants. Indigenous communities were self-sustaining societies engaged in subsistence agriculture, supplemented by ocean and river fishing[17], trapping and hunting. Since there was no monetary economy for that reason, trade then was by barter. What semblance of working for others existed in the present day West Region of Cameroon where custom demanded that people out of love and respect devote some of their time to work in the fields of their rulers whom they considered God's representative on earth.[18] Wives and children in each household, which in the most were polygamous, considered it part of their routine obligations to offer their labour freely to their spouses and fathers. It was sacrilegious for a free born to give out his labour to another against remuneration.[19] There were however unregulated *njangi* systems involving groups of friends pooling their labour and working in the fields of persons belonging to the groups on a rotatory basis.[20] Some form of slavery however existed where conquered tribes were converted into the slaves of their conquerors.[21]

---

17 Le Vine, V.T., *The Cameroons From Mandate to Independence*, Berkeley and Los Angeles: University of California Press, 1964, p. 46.

18 Ebune, J.B., *The Growth of Political Parties in Southern Cameroons 1916-1960*, Kumba: First Impression, 1992, p. 40.

19 Yanou, M.A., *Labour Law, Principles and Practice in Cameroon*, Buea: REDEF, 2009, p.1.

20 Yanou holds that labour services were also rendered in a form of collective co-operatives where families and friends helped to do work for no pay apart from food that was provided during work. Labour could also be rendered by a standing association for help which required members to work for other members when called upon to do so. This relationship unlike the former is founded on reciprocity. Yanou, M.A., *Labour Law, Principles and Practice in Cameroon*, Buea: REDEF, 2009, p 2-3.

21 These "slaves" were whole clans conquered. They had a degree of basic freedom except that that mandatorily had to render services and pay allegiance to their 'master'.

A.1.1 Labour Relations Under the German Rule

The coming of Europeans to the coast of Cameroon introduced changes in labour relations in the region. The Portuguese who had established sugar plantations in Sao Tome and Fernando Po, badly in need of slave labour turned particularly to Bimbia and Douala in Cameroon, which at the beginning of the 19th century had become centres of slave trade.[22] Negative as slavery is in contemporary labour relations, the subsequent idea of payment for labour rendered in the context of Cameroon must be traced to slave trade around present day Douala. The contact with Europeans, the subsequent trade in raw materials and the setting up of plantations led to the commercialisation of labour. These in turn led to the growth of a monetary economy effecting in the process a shift from a wholly subsistence economy based on co-operative bonds of lineage to a dynamic money economy based on cash nexus and wage employment.[23] This was captured by Rudin[24] who observed that, without native labour, nothing could be done, since the weather condition was unfavourable for white men, making it impracticable to transport them to Cameroon to work.[25]

With the abolition of slave trade in Kamerun[26] in 1902, slave collectors and intermediaries had to find new forms of employment. Some became intermediaries in trade for oils, ivory and other products while others were employed as human porters to carry goods to the coast from the hinterlands. By 1913, the coastal economy had employed over 80.000 men, women and children.[27]

It was not until 1908 that a law was passed[28] regulating the employment of porters. This law which forbade children carriers limited such contracts to able-bodied adults. The amount of load per carrier was fixed at 30kg.[29] There was to be one reserve porter for every ten porters. Decrees were also passed regulating the hours of work for the porters fixed at 3-4 marching hours for a

---

22 Le Vine, *op. cit.* p. 17

23 *Ibid* at p. 46.

24 Rudin,H., *Germans in the Cameroons 1884-1914, A Case Study in Modern Imperialism*, London: Jonathan Cape, 1938, pp.316.

25 Indigenous population was thus needed as porters, for clearing the jungle for the railroads and as plantation labourers.

26 This is the German appellation of Cameroon a territory founded by Portuguese explorers who had named it *Cameroes*.

27 Rudin *op. cit.* at p. 316 and Le Vine *op. cit.* at p. 47. Apart from being porters, natives who were employed as gatherers of rubber, palm products, ivory and other commodities were rewarded for work done with gun powder, arms, liquor and other European goods.

28 The *Kolonial Gesetzgeburg*, xii, Doc 67; *Kolonialblatt 1908*.

29 An allowance of 5kg was given per career for their personal needs.

day's work[30]. In the same light, in 1907, a law was passed[31] that regulated the employment of native rowers for water transportation.[32]

The fertility of the soil around the coast (especially around the foot of volcanic Mount Cameroon) encouraged plantation agriculture necessitating the recruitment of natives as plantation labourers. The native Bakweris would however not work in the plantations because of the policy of payment in kind by means of arms, liquor and gunpowder instead of money. The shortage of volunteers made the colonialists to resort to using slave labour from the hinterland. The slaves seized by the German colonialist from rebellious areas were compelled to work without pay for their freedom.[33] That forced labour fast replaced voluntary recruitments was clear from the report by Mansfield, the officer in charge of Ossindige (Mamfe) that:

> "there can be no question of recruiting voluntary labourers...... Only by executive measures such as the punishments of chiefs, threats of burning down villages, and forcible dispatching under military escorts, can one attain the results of obtaining from 1500-1800 men to go to the coast and moreover, to labour centres which are universally hated."[34]

As early as 1896, the German government in Cameroon made a significant move towards introducing security of employment of workers[35] by passing a decree,[36] which governed the recruitments of natives as employees. This law required white traders or planters seeking recruitment of labourers first to obtain permits from the governor. The authorisation, which had to be presented to the local administrators was to include a list of proposed recruits with whom contract, had been made. To ensure enforcement of recruitment regulations, labour commissioners who were appointed for each district could inspect plantations without prior notice to ensure that the labour regulations put in place to safe-guard the security of service were adhered to.

---

30 Rudin *op. cit.* at p. 331-332.

31 *Kolonial-Gesetzgebung*, xi, doc.219.

32 *Ibid* at p. 333

33 Konings. P, *Labour Resistence in Cameroon*, Leiden, African Studies Centre, 1993, p. 59. Also see Rudin, H.R., *op. cit.* at p. 321 who explained that, slaves from conquered tribes like those from Adamawa area were sent with their families to the coast where they could obtain work as free labourers. Free borns recruited from the hinterlands and transported to the plantations had to work under harsh and difficult climatic conditions and contract terms.

34 Konings, P. *op. cit.* at p. 60, Delancey. *Dependence to Independence*, 1978, *op. cit.* at p. 162

35 *Denskschrift, 1896-7*, doc.94, *Anlajen zu den Reichstagsverhandlugen*, 1897-98, in Rudin *op. cit.* At p. 324.

36 The *Kolonial-Gesetzgebung*, vi,doc. 308.

Rudin explained that[37] under this agreement, recruits had to be informed about the terms of their contracts, the kind of work, the place, the period of service, the number working hours per day, wages and the method of payment, provision for food, shelter and aid in times of ill-health. Work was forbidden on Sundays and no employee was allowed to work for more than ten hours. The wages paid to the natives varied according to the length of service and the type of work done. The labourers received on average 8-9 marks per month if they worked for one year or 6 marks per month if they worked for six months.

More often than not, the natives were paid only 50% of their wage to keep them from running away. In case of death, the accumulated wages were paid to their next of kin.[38] In spite of these measures, the natives were still taken advantage of as their ignorance was abused by some employers who used alcohol to encourage the natives to sign contracts whose terms they did not fully grasp. Although these measures made employment secure for the natives, its rather oppressive nature eroded the security of service it was trying to give to the native employees to the extent that many of them died.[39]

A.1.2 Evolution of Labour Relations Under the French

On becoming a French mandated territory,[40] French Cameroon witnessed the introduction of two regimes of laws by the French colonial administration. French laws were applicable to the *assimiles* who were educated natives from

---

37 *Ibid* at p. 321.

38 *Ibid* at p. 325.

39 Because of unhygienic living conditions, poor meals, the shame of trekking for long distance to the point of employment, home sickness as a result of separation from familiar environment, friends and families, the hard and long hours of labour and poor medical conditions contributed to the high death rate amongst the labourers. Most recruits seldom returned home to their families. The death rate was as high as 60-70 per thousand although officially the death rate was less than 0.1%. See generally Rubin *op. cit.* p.25.Since the only means by which the colonial government could raise money was through taxation, natives were not exempted. On October 20th, 1908, a decree the *Kolonial-Gesetzebung, xii, docs. 293-294* on tax was passed imposing taxes on all able bodied grown up males of 6marks per year which was taken up to 10 marks in February 1913 or perform tax work of thirty days on public works. Tax was thus used as an indirect method of forcing natives into selling their labour.

40 The British and French Allied Forces defeated the Germans in Cameroon during the First World War (1914-1918) in 1916. The League of Nations then granted this territory to these countries as a Mandated territory and later on after 1945 as a Trust Territory when the United Nations was formed. In an Anglo-French Declaration of March 4th, 1916, these Mandatory powers partitioned Cameroon with each power ruling its part of Cameroon. These Mandatory powers were enjoined by Art 8 and 9 of the Mandate Agreement to promote to the utmost the material and moral well-being and social progress of the inhabitants of the territories, and required them to make regular reports of their work.

France who had acquired the French culture, while local laws were applied to *sujets indigenes* made up of the rest of the indigenous population. However, in spite of the existence of these laws, forced labour was used extensively for public works particularly for the construction of rail and trunk roads. This policy was put in place in violation of the terms of Article 3 of the French Mandate prohibiting the Mandatory Power from all forms of forced labour or compulsory labour.[41]

In 1920, the French introduced the *prestation* or *corvee* labour compelling all men to supply government with ten days free labour a year.[42] Natives who sought to escape from such forced labour recruitments were man hunted and forcefully taken to work under deplorable conditions. Le Vine has noted that some local chieftains took advantage of the state of affairs to forcefully conscript workers to work in their private plantations.[43]

The main decree that regulated labour relations was that of 4th August 1922. It bothered on labour relations and administration between colonialists and African indigenes[44]. This decree also introduced an Arbitration Council to settle labour disputes[45]. Following mass exodus of natives from agricultural zones, a decree was passed on 9th July 1925 limiting freedom of movements of Africans to other zones. Such movements were permitted only if the indigene presented a *laissez-passez*[46] or duly signed employment contract in the destination point of the employee. A decree was passed on 17th November 1937 forbidding employment of children under 12 years and proscribing night wok for women and children between 12and 18 years.

After the Brassaville Conference of 1944, a mile stone Decree of 7th August 1944 was passed fascilating the application of French Labour Code in Cameroon although with some modifications. On 29th August, 1946 The labour Inspectorate were created through a metropolitan order in Nkongsamba, Yaounde, Garoua and Douala as an independent corps to

---

41 Ebune, *op. cit.* at p. 41.

42 Le Vine *op. cit.* at p. 105 and also Ebune *op. cit.* at p. 41, Rubin. N., *Cameroon: An African Federation*, London: Praeger Publishing,1971 p. 57.

43 See generally, Le Vine, *op. cit.* at p. 106-107.

44 The conditions of work were no way near the labour relations that prevailed in Europe at the time. It was a window dressing shielding the true prevailing labour relations which was in the main forced labour.

45 This board entertained disputes from indigenes whereas non Africans brought any such litigations before competent civil courts.

46 The spouses and children of such grantees were not allowed to accompany their father/wife. Defaulters were forcefully brought back and subjected to imprisonment of from 1-15days under hard labour.

check labour excesses and administration. In 1952, the French overseas Labour Code[47] was considered as a code that guarantees the protection and blossoming of native workers since it abolished forced or compulsory labour (section 2), its section 3 to section 28 approved the creation of professional syndicates even if it was merely for the study and defence of economic, industrial, commercial and agricultural interests; established social and well as the creation of trade unions after due procedure. It further permitted to a certain extent the free negotiation of employment contracts and the different forms that the contract can take as well as probationary contracts. It spelled out the time of work per week which was limited to 40 hours. The statute also instituted certain social benefits, health and safety of (sections 133-144) workers including paid leave. It laid the basis for the termination of labour contracts by either party after the service of appropriate notice. Further more it made provisions for wrongful terminations in its section 42-45. It also laid down basic laws for apprenticeship contracts. Most of these provisions were subsequently reproduced in the first harmonised labour code of the Federal Republic of Cameroon of June 1967.[48]

A.1.3 Employment Relations Under the British[49]

Although the British declared after taking over the administration of "Southern Cameroons" that forced labour will be replaced with a policy encouraging voluntary labour migration to plantations. Konings argues that in spite of this, forced labour lingered on even after the British took over the administration[50] with attendant negative effect on security of service. In a bid to gain the confidence of potential voluntary recruits the British encouraged, plantation employers to increase food rations, sanitation, pay, and sometimes reimbursement of transport expenses.

Article 9 of the Mandate Agreement embodying the terms of reference of British Administration in the Cameroons, authorised the British

---

47 Law No. 52/1322of December 1952 which was promulgated into law by Arrete No 8214 S. et du 24th December 1952.

48 Law no. 67/FL/6 of 12th June 1967.

49 As explained above, the British began its rule over Southern Cameroons with the defeat of the Germans by the Allied forces during the First World War. The league of Nations Granted Cameroon to Britain and France as a Mandated Territory and later on as a Trust Territory after the Second World War. In the Anglo-French Declaration of March 4th 1916, Britain officially stated its administration over Southern Cameroons.

50 Konings, *op. cit.* p. 60, quoting from BNA, file Qd/a (1917) 65.

administration to apply British laws directly in Southern Cameroons. Based on this, the administration passed a series of laws meant to ensure the security of service of the employees in the territory. The mandate agreement gave permission for Britain to rule Southern Cameroons through Nigeria. For this reason the common law and statutory laws in force in Nigeria were exported to Southern Cameroons. A series of such laws (which touched on labour and employment relations) were exported to British Cameroons.

The passing of the Trade Union Ordinance No. 44 of 1938 which laid down rules and regulations for the functioning of trade unions trade unionism gained roots[51].

The Trade Disputes (Arbitration and Inquiry) Ordinance No. 32 of 1941 laid down procedures for amicable settlement of disputes between management and employees' unions. Under this procedure, where there is a failure to reach amicable settlement, the Department of Labour will intervene. The Workmen's Compensation Ordinance No. 51 of 1941 regulated compensations for injuries suffered by workers, arising out of and in the course of employment. If the worker suffered temporary incapacity periodic payments were paid to him whereas, in the case of death, the dependents of the deceased received the compensation.

In 1945, the Labour Code Ordinance No. 54 was passed. Chapter V spelled out conditions for the recruitment of workers. It required that all labour recruitments must be under licence following specified procedures, with each contract specifying terms of engagements, duration, remuneration, rest, particulars of clothing, crockery, health, sanitation and accommodation. Specifically, the Code fixed the hours of work at 44 hours for industrial workers including labourers and 34 hours for clerks. Industrial workers were supposed to work for 8 hours from Monday to Friday and 4 hours on Saturday.

Chapter IX of the Labour Code regulated the terms and conditions for the employment of women, with particular reference in Part 11 of this chapter dedicated to provisions regarding maternity leave. The commissioner

[51] In 1947, there was the founding by the Late Dr. E.M.L Endeley of Cameroon Development Corporation Workers' Union which eclipse from the Cameroon Plantations Workers' Union (CPWU). The trade union's primordial aim was the protection of the general welfare of workers and conditions of employment. Others like the Likomba PlantationWorkers'Union, Tombel Banana Union and the Bakweri Corporative Farmers' Union followed in tow with practically the same interests. Konings has observed that, the British Trusteeship Authority introduced a model of 'free but responsible trade unionism' aimed at controlling the militancy of trade unions. This in a bid to ensure that the unions pursued a moderate, productionist and a-political policy especially with the emergence of nationalist movements and political parties.

of Labour had authority to specify contracts which a woman could enter into particularly or generally. Chapter X regulated the employment of Children. It prohibited the employment of children under the age of 15 in industry, although they could be employed on a daily basis. The major feature of security of tenure was found in the fact that contracts covering child-workers must be in writing and for not more than eight hours a day. Furthermore, such contracts could be terminated if so required by the child's parent or guardian.

The Factory Ordinance No. 35 of 1955 made provisions for health, safety and welfare of persons employed in factories and other places. In 1957, the Wages Boards Ordinance No. 5 replaced the Labour Advisory Boards. Its role was to fix the minimum wages and condition for industries in which wages were low. Wages were fixed through joint regulations or collective agreements following trade disputes.

A.1.4 Employment Relations in the Post-Colonial Era

After the independence of the Former East Cameroons in 1960 and that of Southern Cameroons in 1961, leading to the formation of a Federal Republic of Cameroon, there was need to harmonise the labour laws inherited from the colonial past. The union of the two Cameroons led to considerable hike in the cost of living as the salary scale of workers west of the Mungo was relatively lower than those in the Former East Cameroon.[52] Workers under the West Cameroon Trade Union Congress which had been formed in the mean time agitated for harmonisation of wages and salaries which should benefit foremost the lowest paid worker in order to reduce the gap between the income groups. This was achieved after a thirteen days strike ended with the revision of the wage and salary scale.[53]

After the re-unification of the two Cameroons as a result of the plebecite of 11th February, 1961, the government made persistent attempts at controlling the autonomous trade unions in West Cameroon. After the birth of the Cameroon National Union (CNU) in 1966 as the lone political party, the government was bent on subordinating trade unions to the party.[54] To achieve

---

52 Konings, P., *Labour Resistance in Cameroon, op. cit.* Chapter Three.

53 Konings, P., *Labour Resistance in Cameroon, op. cit.* p. 126.

54 As Konings points out, the role of the trade unions as conceived by the government ought not to be contentious but construction. In this wise, labour could only make demands according to available resources,, since mutual sacrifice was required for economic progress.

this, there were emphatic demands for the unity of trade unions.[55] This was attained when in October 1969, the West Cameroon Trade Union Congress founded in 1962 joined the *Federation Syndicale du Cameroun* and the *Union des Syndicats Croyants du Cameroun* to form the *Union des Travailleurs du Cameroun* (National Union of Cameroon Workers). This new trade union was supported from the background by the government which placed it directly under the control of the state.[56] This regrettably signalled the birth of a new model of trade union (state controlled trade unionism) aimed at ensuring that trade unions pursued a moderate, productionist and apolitical policy.[57]

A major landmark in the country's labour history occurred in 1967 when the Federal Labour Code[58] was passed to harmonise employment and labour relations in the Federal Republic. The Code was significant for improving on security of tenure for it introduced staff representatives,[59] which before then had not existed in the former West Cameroon. The Code introduced arbitration, a peaceful out of court settlement of labour disputes, making the court a last resort in situations where other dispute settlement mechanisms fail. This procedure to a certain extent improved security of employment since apart from being cost free, it gave the parties the opportunity to peacefully settle employment disputes without putting a strain on the employment relationship as a court process would do.

The unification of the two federal republics of Cameroons in 1972 resulted in a need to revise the law governing employment relations under a unitary state. However, the Labour Code of 1974, Law No. 74/14 of November 1974 enacted during this period was criticised for the wide discretion given to judges in the award of damages for wrongful termination. This amongst other short comings negatively impacted on security of tenure as well as destroyed investor confidence in the country. Labour relations in Cameroon are now regulated by Law No. 92 /007 of 14th August 1992, which was passed to address and handle labour relations during the economic crises that bedevilled the country in the 1990s. This Code is the principal statute that regulates substantive and procedural employment laws in Cameroon.

---

55 Konings, P., *Labour Resistance in Cameroon, op. cit.* p. 126.

56 See generally Konings, P., *Labour Resistance in Cameroon, op. cit.* at p. 137.

57 Konings, P., *Labour Resistance in Cameroon op. cit.* pp. 155. The trade unions were moderate in the sense that they were not suppose to be militant. Productionist in the sense that they were to help the government to achieve the maximisation of capital accumulation.

58 Law No. 67/LF/6 of 12th June 1967.

59 These were elected to look after the interests of the workers.

B. Importance of Labour Law

Labour law has a uniform and specific purpose which is the protection of workers and employers obligations. Its primary obligations are to provide equal opportunity and pay to all workers, industrial peace and stability that ensures productivity and development, worker's mental and physical wellbeing, workplace safety and diversity.

Labour relationships are power relations in which the employer has dominance over the employee who in economics is a factor of production. In recognition of this, checks and balances are put in place to enforce the employer's rights while securing, protecting and guaranteeing the rights of the workers. The history of labour movements are laden with lobbying for the protection of workers before an all-powerful employer with the sole aim of leaving the workers satisfied as productivity is bound to increase where there is industrial peace.

Labour laws preserve the dignity of the worker from being exploited as a mere factor of reduction as these laws go beyond contracts and embrace human rights since labour is resident in a human being whose person is inviolate.

These laws also contribute in the honing of the skills of the employees as it makes provisions for professional training which improves on the value and quality of the worker. It facilitates gender equity and fairness by elaborating anti-discrimination laws as well as protects the vulnerable especially children and migrant workers.

Labour laws also gives structure to organisations and businesses which otherwise would not have been inclined to keep the laws. The laws are useful in the preservation of organisational integrity and workplace ethics.

By ensuring that the workers are afforded protection there is improved industrial relation, the prospects of employees being exploited it limited and industrial unrest is minimised, there is social and labour justice.

Since labour is a factor of production necessary for development in any given society, industrial peace is also necessary to increase productivity y. In this regard, although labour relations are private, state interventions by way of laws is justified to reserve not only the workers right and the profits of the entrepreneur but also to guarantee the smooth functioning of the society. That is why in the global plain, the ILO ensures not only the employers and employees but also the national economic investment through its laws, programs, recommendations, guidelines and policies.

C. Sources of Labour Law

The sources of labour law are divided into domestic or national sources and international sources.

C.1.1 International Sources

i) The Bill of Rights which comprises the Universal declaration of Human Rights, The UN Charter, the international Covenant of Civil and Political Rights 1966, the International Covenant of Economic Social and Cultural Rights 1966 as well all ILO conventions and the African Charter are fundamental hard and soft laws on Labour relations. All other treaties, conventions and protocols with provisions on Labour matters.

ii) Suggestions in the form of recommendation as the best course of action made by the ILO for states. They are non-binding. But they are minimum standards of expectations of states by the ILO.

iii) ILO Declarations which are resolutions of the International Labour Conference used to make formal and authoritative statements and reaffirm the importance which constituents attach to certain principles and values. Though not subject to ratification, they are intended to have a wide application and contain symbolic and political undertakings by member states. E.g The ILO Declaration on Fundamental Principles and Rights at Work 1998 is an expression of commitment by the governments, employer's and employee's organisation to uphold basic human values that are vital to our social and economic lives

C.1.2 Domestic Sources

These are divided into formal and informal sources

C.1.2.A Formal Sources

C.1.2.A.i These include the constitution, the local legislation and case law. The main source of statutory law in procedural and substantive matters regarding labour law is the Labour code - Law No 92/007/14 August 1992. This is complimented by decrees and orders on labour matters. Case law on labour law and labour related matters especially from the appellate courts are important sources.

C.1.2.A.ii In addition to this, we have the professional sources of law like the Collective Agreements which are negotiated agreements between one or more trade unions and employer or employers' association regarding conditions of employment and wages (family benefits, training, working hours, health, retirement, time-off, insurance, work environment and equipment, pay, leave)[60].

C.1.2.A.iii Internal Rules and regulations are work rules concerning safety, over time, sick leave, social security and general conditions of employment drawn up by the employer alone or with the assistance of the assistance of the worker's representative. As per s. 29 LC provides that even if it is unilaterally drawn up it becomes binding source of law once it receives the fiat of the labour inspector as well as proof that it has been relied upon previously as was held by Mokwe J in the Buea High Court case of *Eboa Moukery. v. S.G.B.C.*[61]

C.1.2.A.iv Labour contracts which is the will of the parties expressed in hard are the primary source of law concerning the type of relationship that has been contracted. Although labour contracts can take any form, the written contract is a very important source.

C.1.2.B Non-Formal Source

1). Customs, codes of conduct, practices and Employment Usage which are unwritten but which are used by workers and employees in their different employment are the non-formal source of labour law.

D. Legal and Institutional Frameworks of Employment Law in Cameroon

The checks and balances of employment relations in Cameroon are kept within the ambit of both the legal and institutional frameworks. In this light, the study of the legal and institutional frameworks on the regulation of employment relations in the country becomes necessary in ascertaining the contemporary labour and employment relations of the country. We shall therefore under this chapter examine the available legal and institutional frameworks on the regulations of employment relations in Cameroon.

---

[60] See 18 (1) (e) of Labour Code.

[61] Suit No. HCF/L.20/98-1999 (unreported)

D.1 Legal Framework

D.1.1.a The Cameroon Labour Code

This Code first saw the light of day in 1967 when the Federal Labour Code was adopted by the then Federal Parliament. The 1967 Code was later revised in 1974 and 1992.[62] Yanou[63] on the revision of this Code argued that the present Labour Code remains essentially a product of the 1967 legislation, in that some of the 'patently obnoxious provisions' in the present labour code such as sections 28 (6),[64] 29 (4)[65] and 37 (2)[66] giving the Minister of labour powers to make what amounts to executive legislation covering a wide range of important areas can be traced to the 1967 legislation[67] which to this scholar is pro-administration. However, the 1992 Code remains the fundamental legislation that governs the substantive and procedural rules covering employment relations in the country.

The 1992 Labour Code of Cameroon is gradated into eleven parts covering diverse aspects on employment relations. For instance, Part one provides for the general provisions on employment relations in the country. It defines concepts like workers, employers, employment amongst others. Part two addresses trade unions and employers' associations, part three examines the contracts of employment, part four covers wages, part five looks at the conditions of employment, part six focuses on safety and hygiene at work, part seven dwells on administrative bodies and measures of implementation, part eight covers professional institutions, part nine provides for labour disputes settlement, part ten covers penalties and part eleven looks at special transitional and final provisions.

---

62 See Law No. 92/007 of 14th August 1992.

63 See Yanou *op. cit.* at P. 4.

64 Which provides that 'an order of the Minister in charge of labour issued after consultation with the National Labour Advisory Board shall fix the conditions of probationary hiring'.

65 It provides that ' an order of the minister in charge of labour issued after consultation with the National Labour Advisory Board shall prescribe the procedure for communicating, registering and posting up the internal regulations as well as the number of company workers above which the existence of such regulations shall be compulsory'.

66 Which equally states that 'an order of the Minister in charge of labour, issued after a recommendation by the National Labour Advisory Board, shall prescribe the conditions for granting and calculating the severance pay'.

67 To this scholar, these provisions must be situated within a civil law context of the supremacy of the executive arm of government.

From the above structure of the Labour Code, one can affirm that the Code is indeed an embodiment of the country's substantive and procedural law on employment relations. This is true as save for the authoritative position of relevant ratified international instruments on the subject; the Code remains the most authoritative legislation that informs employment relations in the country. To this end, recourse is always made to the Code on the conclusion of employment contracts, resolution of employment disputes, formation of trade unions, annual leaves, amongst others. The Code, therefore, can be conceptualized as the informative legislation on employment relations in the country.

D.1.1.b The 1996 Constitution of Cameroon

Though there is no single portion of the Cameroon constitution dedicated to employment relations as in elsewhere[68], at least it addressed silent aspects of employment relations of the country. In this connection, paragraph six of the Preamble to the 1996 Constitution ofCameroon provides that '... The State shall provide all its citizens with the conditions necessary for their development'. If we were to add a second voice to a portion of this preambular phraseology namely; 'all its citizens', we will simply say 'the State shall provide all its citizens especially workers' with the conditions necessary for their development. This reasoning is informed by the fact that 'workers' constitutes an integral part of States citizens, 'work/service' which they rendered and 'the remuneration/pay' they received are veritable catalysts of development in any nation. Thus, it is only through the proper regulation of employment relations that workers can attain the necessary conditions needed for their development.

Paragraph six further states that 'the freedom,...of association, and of trade unionism, as well as the right to strike shall be guaranteed under the conditions fixed by law'. This preambular provision is particularly relevant in the analysis offered in this research in that it touches on essential labour rights. The rights to freedom of association and strike as captioned therein, are trade union rights which constitute an aspect of what is known in classical labour law as core labour rights.[69]

The Cameroonian constitutional position on freedom of association for trade union purposes is that the enjoyment of the right to freedom of association

---

68 See Section 23 of the 1996 Constitution of South Africa which is dedicated to labour relations.

69 See ILO Declaration on the Fundamental Rights of Workers, 1998.

for trade union purposes is tied to the requirement of conditionality.[70] Unlike the situation in Cameroon, the constitutions of most African[71] as well as some European[72] States provide for the direct respect of freedom of association for trade union purposes.

Though the constitutional provisions on employment relations in Cameroon can be inferred from the preamble to the 1996 Constitution of Cameroon, this remain a no issue since as the preamble constitutes an integral part of same constitution by virtue of Article 65 of same. It follows that the provisions of the preamble remain authoritative as the substantive provisions of same constitution.

D.1.1.c Ratified International Instruments

The place of ratified international instruments on the regulation of employment relations in the country cannot be undermined. These instruments takes their authority from Article 45 of the country's 1996 Constitution which states that 'Duly approved or ratified treaties and international agreements shall, following the publication, override national laws....'

---

70 The condition that freedom of association and trade unionism shall be guaranteed under conditions fixed by the law. The condition fixed by law in the understanding of this researcher simply mean 'the condition under the Labour Code' to the effect that freedom of association and trade unionism can be guaranteed only if the relevant conditions under the labour code are observed; namely when these trade unions are properly registered with the registrar of trade unions in the Ministry of Labour and Social Security as contained in section six of the Cameroon labour code 1992.

71 For instance Article 21 (1) (e) of the Constitution of the Republic of Ghana of 1992, provides that 'all persons shall have the right to freedom of association, which shall include freedom to form or join trade unions or other associations, national and international, for the protection of their interests.' On a similar note section 80(1) of the Constitution of the Republic of Kenya of 1963, provides that 'except with his consent, no person shall be hindered in the enjoyment of his freedom of assembly and association, that is to say, his right to assemble freely and to associate with other persons and in particular to form or belong to trade unions or other associations for the protection of his or her interests.' That of Nigeria, that is Section 40 of the Constitution of the Federal Republic of Nigeria of 1999, expressly guarantees to the citizens the right to associate with other persons, in particular, to form or belong to trade unions. Section 31 (2) of the Constitution of the Republic of Malawi 2000, equally protect workers right to freedom of association for trade union purposes by stating that 'every person shall have the right to form and join trade unions or not to form or join trade unions.' Article 16 of the Constitution of Lesotho of 1993 (order No. 16 of 1993) equally safeguards freedom of association without any conditionality what so ever. It provides that 'every person shall be entitled to, and (except with his consent) shall not be hindered in his enjoyment of freedom to associate freely with other persons for ideological, religious, political, cultural, recreational and similar purposes.'

72 For instance Article 9 of the German Constitution of 1949 as amended. Referred to as the Basic Law of the Federal Republic of Germany (Grundgesetz) protects the right to freedom of association by stating that 'the right to form associations to safeguard and improve working and economic conditions shall be guaranteed to every individual and to every occupation or profession.'

A close examination of these instruments is almost impossible since as their list can go *ad infinitum*. It suffices to note that these instruments are largely ILO, UN[73], and AU instruments[74]. In the ILO context, prominent instruments regulating employment relations in Cameroon are gradated into three major categories; the fundamental conventions, the governance conventions and the technical conventions. Cameroon has ratified 8 out of the 8 fundamental conventions in existence, 3 out of the four governance conventions and 39 out of the 178 technical conventions, making a total of 50 ILO ratified Conventions applicable to employment relations in the country.[75]

D.2 Institutional Framework

For an industrial relations system to effectively function, the intervention of industrial actors which consists of; employers, employees and their representatives as well as external agencies is indispensable. It is in the context of these external agencies that institutions charged with the furtherance of employment relationships in the country are situated. These institutions are; administrative,[76] professional,[77] judicial,[78] and consultative in nature.

D.2.1 Administrative Institutions

The regulation of employment relations cannot be left exclusively in the hands of employers and employees. To ensure that there is some degree of serenity, the State often directly intervenes at certain levels. Administrative institutions such as: The Ministry of Labour and Social Security and the Labour Inspectorate placed under the tutelage of the Ministry in charge of Labour and Social Security, the Ministry of Employment and Vocational Training have been instituted to help regulate employment relations in the country.

---

73 See the Universal Declaration on Human and Peoples' Rights 1948 and International Covenant on Economic, Social and Cultural Rights 1966, ratified in 1984.

74 See specifically the African Charter on Human and Peoples' Rights 1986

75 https://www.ilo.org/dyn/normlex/en/f?p=NORMLEXPUB:11200:0::NO::P11200_COUNTRY_ID:103038 accessed on the 26th of September 2021.

76 Administrative institutions such as the Ministry of Employment and Vocational Training, the Ministry of Labour and Social Security and the Labour Inspectorate are responsible for labour administration in Cameroon.

77 Professional institutions such as trade unions.

78 Such as the Court of First Instance, the High Court, Appeal Court and the Supreme Court.

D.2.1.a The Ministry of Labour and Social Security

The Ministry of Labour and Social Security (MINLSS) is in charge of the development and implementation of government policy in the fields of professional relationship, workers' status and social security. As such, it is responsible for: developing and implementing the social insurance and social security policy; enforcing the Labour Code and international agreements ratified by Cameroon in relation to Labour; connecting Government, trade unions and employers' organisations; connecting institutions of the United Nations system and African Union specialised in the field of work, in conjunction with the Minister of External Relations.[79]

In addition, MINLSS plays an indispensable role in the formation and registration of trade unions and employers' associations in the country.[80] MINLSS careters for temporal, occasional or seasonal employment,[81] the regulation of the contract of employment of foreign workers,[82] the conditions for probationary hiring,[83] the modalities of communication, and the drawing up of the Internal Rules and Regulations of an organisation[84] amongst others, are equally largely under the jurisdiction of MINLSS. From the foregoing, it cannot be contested that the Ministry of Labour and Social Security plays a crucial role in the regulation of employment relations in the country.

This institutional support in the regulation of employment relations takes a dual form. The Ministry of Labour and Social Security acts in the field of labour relations as a legislator and administrator. As a legislator, it creates substantive and procedural rules, established basic employment conditions

---

79 It liaises between the Government and the International Labour Organisation as well as international agencies in its jurisdiction, in conjunction with the Minister of External Relations. For example, during the presentation of Cameroon's Report on the implementation of the International Covenant on Economic, Social and Cultural Rights, to the Committee on Economic, Social And Cultural Rights on 21 February 2019, the delegation of Cameroon consisted of representatives of the Ministry of External Affairs, the Ministry of Public Health, the Ministry of Education, the Ministry for the Promotion of Women and of Family, the Ministry of Justice, the Ministry of Labour and Social Security, and the Permanent Mission of Cameroon to the United Nations Office at Geneva. See Committee on Economic, Social and Cultural Rights reviews Cameroon's Report, available at https://www.ohchr.org/displaynews, accessed on 27/09/2021.

80 See section 9 of the Cameroon Labour Code 1992 and Decree N° 93/574 of 15 July 1993 fixing the form for the registration of professional associations and its annexes.

81 Section 25(5) of the Labour Code and Decree N°. 93/577/PM of 15 July 1993 fixing the modalities for the employment of temporal, occasional and seasonal workers.

82 Section 25(2) of the Labour Code.

83 Section 28(6) of the Labour Code and Order N° 017/MTPS/SG/CJ of 26 May 1993 fixing the maximum duration and modalities for probationary hiring.

84 See section 29 of the Labour Code 1992.

as well as processes of labour relations.[85] Through its legislative role, a legal and institutional framework is thus established, within which various forms of social dialogue take place. As an administrator, the Ministry of Labour and Social Security promotes the smooth functioning of labour relations by providing various kinds of services, tools and administrative mechanisms, inspecting compliance with laws and by guaranteeing enforcement of legal provisions. For instance, by facilitating judiciary and extra-judiciary conflict resolution mechanisms (through the Labour Inspectors) or by facilitating resolution of industrial conflicts, providing macroeconomic data, mediating between the parties, facilitating communication and negotiation through the establishment of negotiating bodies,[86] and equally facilitates collective bargaining. It also provides support (administrative or material) to tripartite bodies.[87]

However, despite the broad mandate of the Ministry of Labour and Social Security in the regulation of employment relations, workers' rights are still violated. Mfondo[88] argues that in Cameroon, the Ministry of Labour and Social Security through its Regional Delegations of Labour is responsible for implementing Labour Regulations and ensuring the smooth functioning of the labour market, but lacks enough capacity to carry out its mandate. There is a shortage of personnel to carry out inspection visits to organisations.[89]

85 See for example, sections 52(4) and 53(1) of the Cameroon Labour Code 1992.

86 See for example, section 29(4) of the Labour Code, 1992 which provides that: An order of the minister in charge of labour issued after consultation with the National Labour Advisory Board shall prescribe the procedure for communicating, registering and posting up the internal regulations as well as the number of company workers above which the existence of such regulations shall be compulsory.

87 The tripartite body is made up of Representatives of the Government, Employers' and Employees' representatives. ILO standards require that the government elaborates its labour-related measures in consultation with social partners. In the field of employment policies, governments are required to consult representatives of the people who will be affected by the measures to be taken, especially representatives of workers and employers "with a view to taking fully into account their experience and views and securing their full cooperation in formulating and enlisting support for such policies". Article 3 of ILO Convention No 122 concerning Employment Policy, 1964.

88 Mfondo, M., "Assessing the Implementation of Labour Regulations in Public organisations of Cameroon", *Journal of Entrepreneurship and Organisation Management*, Vol. 8, No 1, 2019, PP. 1-6, P. 3.

89 The ILO contends that inadequate human resources policy is a great drawback in the protection of the fundamental rights of a worker. When employees of labour administration are of insufficient numbers, are poorly motivated, lack necessary qualifications, workers tend to suffer from violation of their rights, as there is no effective monitoring mechanism. See Bamber, G.J., "International Labour Standards and Decent Work: A Critical Analysis of Thailand's Experiences, with Suggestions for Theory, Policy, Practice and Research", *Asia Pacific Journal of Human Resources*, Vol. 56, No 4, 2018, PP. 539-565, P. 540.

This situation is further compounded by weak capacity to enforce labour laws and the poor functioning of labour inspection. In fact, the weak capacity to enforce legislation arises from bureaucracy, lack of the political will, poor human resource capability and inadequate financial resources.

In carrying out the herculean task, the Ministry of Labour and Social Security is assisted by its Regional Delegations of Labour (found in each regional headquarter), and the Labour Inspectorates which are found at the divisional levels. The Labour Inspector provides strong incentives towards compliance with laws, preventing unnecessary conflicts at the workplace and contributing to better relations between the contractual parties. Advising both employers and workers on their mutual rights and obligations often implies helping them to find mutually agreeable solutions. Labour inspectors thus contribute to better communication and cooperation at the enterprise level. In fact, many inspection visits and other inspection activities are done as a follow-up to complaints from workers often through their trade union organisations or occupational safety and health representatives. As a result, their role in the regulation of labour relations cannot be minimised.

D.2.1.b The Labour Inspectorate

Referred to in the 1992 Cameroon Labour Code as the Labour and Social Insurance Inspector, the Labour Inspector is a civil servant of the labour administration corps placed at the head of a labour and social insurance inspectorate. A Labour Inspector, though a partner in work relations is not a party to the contract of employment. His role is enormous in the regularisation of employment relations which range from: representation, control, reconciliation, and pursuit reason why he has been described by an author as a "*magistrature sociale d'influence*."[90] He is a judge when he decides on the dismissal of a worker; an agent of the labour police when he records in his official reports labour offences; a prescriber when he closes a work site or gives warning; a pedagogic officer when he informs the administered on the rule of law; and an internal speaker or contributor when he participates in certain discussions in view of finding appropriate solutions to certain difficulties.[91] With all these attributes, the Labour Inspector contributes in employment relations.

---

90 Anazetpuou Z., *Le système Camerounais des relations professionnelles, op. cit.* at P. 321.

91 *Ibid.*

The Labour Inspector considerably influences labour relations as he controls the regularity of certain contracts and the respect of collective conventions and labour legislation within an enterprise. The Labour Inspector further ensures the technical control of labour relations by ensuring that working conditions, safety and the basic rights of a worker such as the right to freedom of association and the right to be free from forced labour are respected. To ensure the proper respect of these basic rights, he is empowered, as per section 108(1) of the Labour Code 1992 to: enter any establishment liable to inspection, freely and without warning at any time of the day or night, for the purpose of inspection; enter for the purpose of inspection any infirmary of an establishment or any canteen, sanitary installation or any facility supplying workers with water; carry out any examination, control or inquiry which he/she consider necessary to ascertain that the regulations in force are strictly complied with and, in particular: to interrogate, alone or in the presence of witnesses, the employer or the staff of the enterprise on any matters concerning the application of the laws and regulations in force.[92]

From the provisions of section 108(1) above, the Labour Inspector under the auspices of the Ministry of Labour and Social Security is charged with the responsibility to ensure compliance with all national and international labour standards connected with terms and conditions of employment. To ensure that the Labour Inspector effectively carries out these duties as contemplated in section 40(6), he must be independent and have no interest in the enterprise controlled.[93] Under article 6 of Labour Inspection Convention No 81, 1947 and article 10(1) of the Labour Administration Convention No 150, 1978, labour inspection staff must be composed of public officials whose status and conditions of service are such that they are assured of stability of employment and are independent of improper external influences. Nonetheless, in Cameroon, some Labour Inspectors lack the means to visit enterprises in their jurisdiction and others are influenced and corrupted by very powerful

92 See section 108 of the Labour Code for more on the functions of the Labour Inspector. He is equally empowered to ask for any books, registers and documents the keeping of which is prescribed by laws or regulations relating to conditions of employment, in order to ensure that they conform with the laws and regulations in force and to copy such documents or make extracts from them; to enforce the posting of notices where this is required by the laws and regulations in force; to take and carry away for purposes of analysis samples of materials and substances used or handled, subject to the employer or his representative being notified of any samples taken and carried away for such purpose.

93 See section 105(3) of the Labour code which provides that: "In order that their independence may be ensured, the said inspectors shall have no interest whatsoever in the enterprises under their supervision".

employers to have a blind eye on the infringement of labour legislation. The case of *Simon Tamanjong & 6 others v. Cameroon Tea Estate*[94] illustrates the absence of independence on the part of the Labour Inspector in effectively carrying out his functions. Here, workers of the Cameroon Development Corporation (CDC) who were transferred from Ndu and Djutissa to Tole saw their employment contracts terminated on the 17/04/2004 and 26/2/2006 respectively. Though they were paid off in September 2006, the terminated workers continued to stay in the accommodation at their CTE camps in Tole since their employers had not put at their disposal the usual lorry to transport them back to Ndu and did not pay their repatriation dues as required by section 94 of the Labour Code.[95] Even though they complained about this to the employers, no reply was received.

After they were driven out of the camps where they did not pay rents, electricity and water, these impoverished workers complained to the local Labour Inspector. The matter went to the arbitration board which awarded the complainants 200.000 FRS each for their transportation. Rather strangely and contrary to section 94(4) of the Labour Code,[96] the Labour Inspector failed to award them their remuneration up to when the transport was to be provided.

In a subsequent letter written by the workers to the representative of the International Labour Organisation in Yaoundé-Cameroon, dated 19th September 2010, the ex-workers complained that not even the Regional Delegate of Labour and Social Security (a Labour Inspector) could make the employer respect the arbitral award. It is indeed fascinating to note that the workers concluded that the Labour Inspector was afraid to submit any claim against CTE to any court in Cameroon because any official who does so is penalised by the powers that be. In desperation, they urged the Cameroon government, which ordered the privatisation of CTE to pay them otherwise they will not receive justice.[97] The fact that the Labour Inspector in exercising

---

94 Suit No CASWP/L.8/2007 (unreported)

95 Section 94(1) of the Labour Code provides that "where, because, of the employer, performance of the employment contract requires or has required a worker to move from his usual residence, the employer shall be responsible for the travelling expenses of the worker, his spouse and minor children normally residing with him, as well as for the transport of their luggage".

96 Section 94(4) provides that "A worker who has terminated his service and is waiting for the means of transport selected by the employer in order to return to his usual residence shall retain the right to benefits in kind and shall receive from the employer an retain the right to benefits in kind and shall receive from the employer an allowance equal to the remuneration which he would have received, had he continued to work".

97 See Sama-Lang, I. F., "The Role of a Labour Inspector in Labour Dispute Resolution in the Private Sector of Cameroon: A Critique", *Labour Law Review NJLIR*, Vol. 8, No 4, 2014, PP. 47-56. P. 53.

his functions is remote-controlled by the government makes it difficult for social justice to be adequately dispensed to an aggrieved worker. He may, for non-altruistic reasons refuse to commence a worker's case against employers in which the government has a substantial interest since he is a civil servant bankrolled by the State.[98]

D.2.1.c The Ministry of Employment and Vocational Training

A sound employment relation requires that the State prohibits all forms of interference, mismanagement and exploitation of a worker. In this light, The Ministry of Employment and Vocational Training considerably intervenes in the domain of employment relations in Cameroon. This ministry is responsible for: the elaboration of work policies; the defence and promotion of employment; carrying out studies on the evolution of work and the labour market; the definition of norms on the organisation of probationary hiring and control their respect; the organisation and follow-up of trained youths in the professional milieu and the organisation of activities relating to social reinsertion for employees who have lost their employments.[99] In carrying out these functions, the Ministry of Employment and Vocational Training is accompanied by the Ministry of Labour and Social Security.

Though the Ministry of Employment and Vocational Training plays a limited role in the execution of a contract of employment, its practical involvement during the formation of the contract cannot be neglected. It plays an indispensable role, through its regional and divisional delegations, in ensuring that the rights of a worker to a valid contract of employment is respected and that the terms of the contract are carefully drafted in order to shield the worker from exploitation. However, in carrying out its functions, the functioning of the Ministry of Employment and Vocational training is marred by certain difficulties. A major difficulty arises from the recalcitrance of some employers who are reticent to declare the number of workers in their enterprises and as a result the reports which are forwarded from the Delegations to the Ministry are not a true reflection of the practical realities on the field. This practice does not augur well for the protection of the fundamental rights of a worker, as violations of workers' rights usually go

---

98 *Ibid.*

99 See Article 1(2) of Decree No 2005/123 of 15 April 2005 on the organisation and functioning of the Ministry of Employment and Vocational Training.

unnoticed. Moreover, the divisional delegations which are the key actors in ensuring compliance with workers' rights lack both material and financial resources for their smooth functioning. Office stationaries are inadequate and the available few are not properly maintained. The unavailability of service vehicles for some divisional delegates who have very vast divisions to cover and poorly constructed and equipped offices have greatly hampered the activities of the Ministry.

D.2.1.d National Council for Career Guidance and Vocational Training[100]

Section 42(1) of the 2018 Law on Vocational training in Cameroon provides clearly that the role of this institution is to assist the state in developing and implementing the vocational training policy of the state.

D.2.2 Judicial Institutions

The main role of the judicial institutions in furthering employment relations is visible in the domain of conflict resolution. labour disputes can occur in any area of work concerning the rights and interests of workers and employers and may arise from a variety of reasons including the violation of the rights of workers such as ; the non-payment of wages, wrongful dismissals and breach of a section of the Internal Rules and regulations, amongst others. When this occurs, section 139(1) of the 1992 Labour Code mandatorily requires the disputant(s) to seize the competent Labour Inspector, who shall attempt a settlement through conciliation. However, if conciliation fails, the parties can precede to litigation. The failure of conciliation, therefore, ushers in judicial institutions (the Courts of First Instance, High Courts, Courts of Appeal and the Supreme Court) which play a great role in preserving the right of an aggrieved party seeking justice.

In this regard, for these institutions to fulfil their respective roles effectively, some basic requirements of fairness, thoroughness and objectivity must be met. These judicial actors are therefore, required to execute their duties in a "fully independent manner" and have to be impartial and objective not only in fact, but must also be perceived as being so, since this is essential to ensure that the law is enforced impartially and consistently no matter who

100 One of the drawbacks is that the text of implementation is still awaited.

is in power, and without undue influence from any source.[101] Therefore, an aggrieved worker who is not satisfied with the outcome of a conciliation decision[102] can approach: The Court of First Instance or High Court. Nevertheless, if not satisfied with the decision arrived at first instance, he can proceed with an appeal to the competent Court of Appeal and then on further appeal to the Supreme Court.

D.2.3 Professional Institutions

Aside the administrative and judicial institutions, there are also professional institutions charged with the mandate to regulate employment relations in the country on specific subjects. To this end, the Cameroonian legislator recognises two institutions, which play exclusively, the consultative role in labour matters. These institutions include; The National Labour Advisory Board and the National Commission on Industrial Health and Safety.

These institutions are directly under the jurisdiction of the Ministry of Labour and Social Security. They exercise both administrative and legislative functions.[103] There are pivotal in labour administration of the country, this justifies why the Ministry of Labour often make recourse to them in the exercise of its functions when it concern certain subjects.

D.2.3.a The National Labour Advisory Board

The National Labour Advisory Board, (the Board), is a consultative organ with national competence established under the ministry in charge of

---

101 Judicial independence is the idea that the judiciary needs to be kept away from the other branches of government. That is, courts should not be subject to improper influence from the other branches of government, or from private of partisan interests. Simon, T.T., "Reflections on judicial Independence in Cameroon's Public Administration", *Law and Politics in Africa, Asia and Latin America Journal*, Vol. 44, No 3, 2011, PP. 422-437, P. 422.

102 As earlier indicated, the Labour Inspector may after conciliation issue a statement of: conciliation (where through his intervention, the parties agree to the terms of settlement); partial conciliation (where the parties accept or reject some of the terms proposed by themselves or the Labour Inspector); or non-conciliation (where the parties do not reach an agreement). In a situation of partial and non-conciliation, the dissatisfied party can proceed to litigation for a settlement of his/her claim.

103 In their legislative role, they make recommendations and suggestions as far as labour legislation is concerned. With regards to technical and professional functions, they examine matters relating to working conditions, hygiene and safety.

labour.[104] Its organisation and functioning has been guaranteed by Decree No 93/084 of 26 January 1993. In effect, the Board has two important functions. First, it plays a consultative role in matters relating to working conditions, employment, vocational guidance and training, placement, manpower movements, migration, improvement of the material conditions of workers, social insurance, trade unions and employers' associations. This board is equally consulted in matters relating to: the conditions for the application of collective bargaining agreements;[105] the conditions for the housing of workers who have been displaced from their residence;[106] derogations relating to the legal duration of work and the modalities for remuneration of additional hours of work done;[107] the period of rest for women and children;[108] the conditions for leave;[109] and the conditions for the transportation of a worker and members of their family in the case of a transfer.[110]

The second function of the Board relates to making recommendations and proposals relating to laws and regulations to be made in the above areas, where such recommendations are provided for by the law. The necessity of this measure is to ensure the participation of all the social partners who are likely to be affected by any decision which is arrived at concerning working conditions by encouraging the highest level of consultation possible.

The composition of this Board is laudable given that it falls in line with article 2 of Convention No 144 on Tripartite Consultation (International Labour Standards), 1976, which encourages members of the ILO to operate procedures which ensure effective consultations between representatives of the government, of employers and of workers with respect to matters concerning the activities of the ILO.[111] Nevertheless, what is interesting about the composition of the Board is the fact that, although an equal number of

---

104 Section 117(1) of the 1992 Labour Code.

105 See Sections 53(1), 54(2), 56(2) and 60 of the 1992 Labour Code.

106 *Ibid.* Section 66(1).

107 *Ibid.* Section 80(4).

108 *Ibid.* Section 82(4).

109 *Ibid.* Section 89(40 and 93.

110 *Ibid.* Section 94(3).

111 Tripartism on its part is defined in the ILO Thesaurus as: "the interaction of government, employers and workers (through their representatives) as equal and independent partners to seek solutions to issues of common concern". It refers to institutions, mechanisms and processes for consultation, negotiation and joint decision-making, depending on arrangements agreed between the parties involved. These arrangements may be ad hoc or institutionalised. See ILC, Social Dialogue and Tripartism: A recurrent discussion on the strategic objective of social dialogue and tripartism, under the follow-up to the ILO Declaration on Social Justice for a Fair Globalization, 2008 Geneva, ILO, Report IV, 2018, P. 3, available at www.ilo.org/publns, accessed on 27/9/2021.

substantive and alternate representatives of workers and employers participate in the process of the Board, they are appointed by an order of the Minister of Labour at the proposal of the most representative workers and employer's organisations.[112] The wide powers accorded to the Minister of Labour at the level of selection of members of trade unions to be represented in the Board, defeats the very purpose of trade union autonomy. In practice, trade union independence is jeopardised as the prerogative to choose their representative to the Board is swerved in favour of the Minister of Labour. This is further compounded by the fact that such proposals might not be followed by the Minister as he may select those he wants to be represented in the Board, especially to examine employment conditions and trade union opinions, to the effect that the decision of the Board may be partial in favour of employer.

In effect, this means that the decisions of the Board can be arrived at with little or no consultation of trade union representatives. On 30 August 2016, the CSTC (*Confédération Syndicale des Travailleurs du Cameroun*), affiliated to the ITUC, denounced the authorities' interference in its internal affairs following the Labour Ministry's recognition of a faction claiming to have been elected as the confederation's executive, despite a court ruling invalidating the election in question. The CSTC also criticised the Labour Ministry's unilateral appointment of workers' representatives to national collective bargaining commissions, without regard for the representativeness of the organisations in the sectors concerned.[113]

The existence of independent trade unions on paper is only a perfunctory sign that associational life is flourishing in Cameroon since the 1990's. Unfortunately, the practice regarding trade union matters is far from being liberal. The laws on freedom of association and on trade unions still contain clauses that undermine real trade union autonomy. In trade union matters, much has to be done and only proper consultation between the various stakeholders with a view to producing truly and genuinely acceptable liberal laws on the matter seems a viable solution. Trade union right to free and voluntary negotiations should be respected with the full support of administrative institutions in place.

112 Section 119 (1) of the Labour Code provides that The National Labour Advisory Board shall be presided over by the minister in charge of labour or his representative. Section 119 (1)(d) of the Labour Code provides that: "an equal number of substantive and alternate representative of workers and employers appointed by an order of the minister in charge of labour on the proposal of the most representative workers' and employers' organisations.

113 See Cameroon-ITUC Survey of violations of trade union rights, available at www.survey.ituc-csi.org/Cameroon, accessed on 27/9/2021.

In order to enable the National Labour Advisory Board to effectively play its role, giant arsenals of personnel have been placed at its disposal. The Board is composed of: The Minister of Labour and Social Security, a permanent member and an alternate representative of the Economic and Social Council. A permanent and alternate representative of the Supreme Court, an equal number of permanent and alternate representatives of employers and workers nominated by an Order of the Minister of Labour and Social Security with approval the most representative trade unions and experts designated by an Order of the Minister of Labour and Social Security.[114] Despite the powerful composition of the Board, workers still suffer from violations of their rights. However, this can be justified by the continuous struggle to enhance stability in the social, economic and political facets of labour law which remains a daunting challenge.[115]

D.2.3.b The National Commission on Industrial Health and Safety

The National Commission on Industrial Health and Safety is a consultative body with jurisdiction over the national territory. It is setup under the Ministry in charge of Labour and Social Security.[116] The National Commission on Industrial Health and Safety has as chairperson the minister in charge of labour or his representative. It is composed of technicians or experts of unquestionable competence in the fields of industrial medicine and industrial hygiene and safety. Representatives of workers and employers are represented in equal number within the National Commission.[117]

This commission is charged with the study of problems related to industrial medicine and the hygiene and safety of workers. In this capacity, it is responsible for: making suggestions and recommendations concerning laws and regulations to be made in the above fields; making recommendations for the benefit of employers and workers, insurance bodies and various ministries concerning the protection of the health of workers; making proposals concerning the approval of dangerous machinery and manufacturing processes likely to endanger the health of workers; carrying

[114] See Anazetpouo, Z., *Le Système Camerounais des Relations Professionnelles*, PUA, Yaounde, 2010. at P. 326.

[115] *Ibid.*

[116] Section 120-121 of the Labour Code 1992.

[117] *Ibid.* Section 121(1).

out or participating in any work of a scientific nature falling within its sphere of activity.[118]

The National Commission on Industrial Health and Safety gives advisory opinions which influence the national policy on hygiene and security in the work place and consequently the type of relationship that should be maintained between the employer and the worker. In carrying out its mission of consultation, this Commission works in collaboration with administrative as well as professional organs.

Despite the provisions of article 2(1&2)[119] of Order No 39/MTPS/IMT of 26 November 1984 fixing the general measures of hygiene and security at work, the effective implementation of these measures leave much to be desired as some workers in Cameroon continue to work under precarious and life threatening conditions. For example, in the Lom Pangar project, there was the near absence of basic health care facilities and basic amenities for the employees, including, the supply of water, adequate sewage and garbage disposal system, appropriate protection against heat, cold, damp, noise, fire and disease-carrying animals, adequate sanitary and washing facilities, ventilation, cooking and storage facilities and natural and artificial lighting, and in some cases basic medical services.

---

118 Section 120 (2) (a-d) of the 1992 Labour Code.

119 Article 2(1) obliges the employer to take all the necessary security and hygienic dispositions to ensure the protection of his employees.

CHAPTER 1

CONCEPT OF A WORKER

The question of who is a worker is fundamental in ascertaining whether the relationship is that of a contract of service or for services. The former relates to the contract of employment while the latter involves the engagement of an independent contractor. Uvieghara[120] has observed that, work may arise in familial or quasi-familial milieu where one offers his services for no remuneration even though he is under the control of the other[121] as well as where one receives remunerations and orders but is not regarded as a worker.[122] This has made the need to identify who is an employee within the contemplation of Cameroon's employment laws absolutely imperative[123].

In the first instance, it is only an employee in fact that can benefit from employment protection including vitally the requirement to be served a notice before termination under section 34 (1) of the Labour Code 1992. Besides, compensation for redundancies and dismissals, annual and maternity leaves all depend on whether the person engaged is an employee and not an independent contractor.[124] The existence of the employer /employee relationship is a critical determinant of the rights and obligations involved in the engagement and accordingly the extent of security that the parties enjoy.[125] It is only in cases of contract of services that the employer can deduct taxes and national

---

120 Uvieghara, E.E., *Labour Law in Nigeria*, Lagos : Malthouse Press Ltd, 2001, p.3.

121 Whincup, M., *Modern Employment Law: A Guide to Job Security and Safety*, 8th edition, London: Butterworth, 1995, p.18.

122 *Ibid.*

123 It should be noted that there is no consensus as to the meaning of a worker. Worker beibg used here as a synonym to employee. See generally Davidov, "who is a worker?" (2005) 34 *Industrial Law Journal* 57; Waas, B and Van Voos, G., "Restatement of Labour Law in Europe" in *The Concept of Employee*, Vol. 1. Oxford: Hart Publishing, 2017

124 In the old, social security entitlements depended on whether the individual is an employee. This position changed in Cameroon with the passing of the 2014 Social Insurance law reform which has given independent contractors the opportunity to do voluntary contributions to National Social Insurance Fund for such purposes.

125 See Guest, A.G.,*Chitty on Contracts (Specific Contracts)*, 26th edition, London: Sweet & Maxwell, 1989, p.721.

social insurance from the employees on the basis of pay as you earn.[126] It is, for instance, only in an employment contract that the employer is vicariously liable for the acts of the employee in the course of lawful employment which provides some sort of security to the worker.[127]

In *C.D.C v Akem Benbella*[128] Bawak CJA cited *Fisher v. Oldham Corporation*[129] as the basis for his conclusion that the employer in this context is vicariously liable pointing out that a master is vicariously liable for the torts committed by his servant while acting in the course of employment, which does not avail independent contractors. Yanou,[130] drawing inspiration from the English Case of *Ferguson v. John Dawson Partners*[131] is of the opinion that whether an individual is an employee or not rests on the substance rather than the form adopted, in the employment relationship.

1.1 A Worker: Definition and Analysis

Section 1(2) of the 1992 Labour Code defines a worker (otherwise known as an employee or servant) as; 'Any person irrespective of sex or nationality, who has undertaken to place his services in return for remuneration, under the direction and control of another person, whether an individual or a public or private corporation, considered as the employer...."[132] The salient features of this

---

126 See Whinchup, M., *Op. Cit.* at p. 18. Rideout, *supra* opines that an independent contractor pays social insurance at a lower rate, he/she is not subject to deductions of income tax at source and other tax benefits, see especially Ackner L.J. in *Young and Woods Ltd. v. West* [1983]I.R.L.R. 201 and. To an extent his safety at work is guaranteed though it is not as protected as those in a contract of services who have both statutory and common law protections. See for example Megaw L.J. in *M.J. Ferguson. v. John Dawson and Partners (Contractors) Ltd* [1976] I.R.L.R. 346.

127 See section 173 of the Labour Code 1992 which makes the head of an enterprise civilly liable for the torts of his subordinates in the course of employment. See also Rideout, R.W., *Principles of Labour Law*, 4th edition, London: Sweet & Maxwell, 1983, p. 597-612 for more details.

128 Suit No. CASWP/67/96 para 10-15.(Unreported).

129 [1930] 2. KB. 354.

130 Yanou., M.A., *op. cit.* at p. 8.

131 [1976] 3 All ER. 517.

132 Compare with the definition in Britain where a worker is defined in section 230(1) of the Employment Rights Act 1996 as an individual who has entered into works (or, where the employment has ceased, worked under) a contract of employment. A contract of employment is defined in section 230(2) of the same act as a contract of services or apprenticeship, whether express or implied, and (if it is Express) whether oral or in writing. In Nigeria, section5 of the Labour Act, Cap. 198 Laws of the Federation of Nigeria, 1990, defines a worker as any person who has entered under a contract with an employer, whether the contract is for manual or clerical work or is expressed or implied or oral or written and whether it is a contract of services or a contract personally but does not include...persons employed for purposes of business, public servants, family members of employers agents or representatives of the employer who work outside the permanent work place, persons working in a vessel or aircraft and persons who are given articles

definition include the fact that the one engaged (i) offers his services, (ii) the payment of remuneration (iii) and is controlled by the employer. The element of control is defined[133] in terms of the power of the employer to instruct the worker on what and how to work. This element of control makes the relationship almost slave-like, since the worker is totally subordinated to the employer with the latter having authority to discipline the worker at his convenience.[134]

The existence of these conceptual features in the definition of a worker is significant for obvious reasons. It weakens the security of employment by ensuring superiority of the employer as well the inequality between the parties in the employment. Kahn-Freund[135] has for this reason observed that the employment relationship is concerned with social power at the elementary level. Kahn-Freund notes that it involves command and rule-making on the one hand and obedience on the other.[136] Employment is from the above conceptual analysis a relationship between the bearer of power and one who has none. That control and total subordination is central in the employment relations has been judicially affirmed. This position was clearly explained by Dervish J.[137] in *Secretary of State, West Cameroon Development Agency v. M.N. Wole*,[138] where he said that:

> "I am of the opinion that the Labour Court was wrong in asserting that the respondent was an employee of the appellants. In as much as not only his appointment but also his salary, other emoluments and termination of his appointment were at the discretion of the Prime Minister, it cannot be said the respondent was under the direction and control of the agency as envisaged by sub (2) of section 1 of the Labour Code.[139] It is true that the respondent served the agency and received his remuneration for services, rendered to the agency in so far as the execution of duties assigned to

---

to clean, alter, repair, wash for sale in their homes or premises under the control of the person who gave out the article. From these two definitions the element of total subordination and control have been left out which is how modern employment relations ought to be.

133 *Yewens v. Noakes* (1880) 6 QBD 530.

134 Yanou, *op. cit.* at p.10-11.

135 Khan-Freund, O., *Labour and the Law*, London:Stevens, 1974, p,4.

136 *Ibid.*

137 In Tabe, S.T., "Enhancing the Protection of Female Workers under the 1992 Cameroonian Labour Code," *Analles de la Faculte des Sciences Jurisdiques et Politiques*, Universite de Dschang, Cameroun, Tome 5, 2001,p. 169-170.

138 Civil Appeal No. CASWP/17/76 (unreported).

139 Now section 1(2) of Labour Code 1992.

him were concerned; but I am of the opinion that these alone do constitute him as an employee of the agency within the definition of the sub section the Labour Code."[140]

This principle was followed in the Supreme Court's decision in *Nanga Emile Honore v. SCTA*[141] where the Court insisted that remuneration and supervisory control were essential definitive element of employment. The Court equally held that the master's ability to discipline was a major feature of the definition of a worker in the context of the Labour Code in Cameroon. It is thus clear that an employment relationship is subject to the ultimate power of the employer to discipline.[142]

However, it is worth noting that the definition of worker is subject to the provisions of section 1(3) of the Labour Code 1992 which provides that: 'this law shall not apply to staff governed by:

- The General Rules and Regulations of the Public Service;
- The Rules and Regulations governing the judicial and legal Services;
- The Special Rules and Regulations of the National Security;
- The Special Rules and Regulations of Prison Administration Civil Servants:
- The Special Provisions applicable to auxiliary staff.

By this provision, those engaged pursuant to the above are not workers under our employment dispensation.

By this provision, civil servants do not fall within the definition of a worker as defined by section 1 of the Labour Code. In spite of this, it was held in *Regional Head of P&T Buea v. Samuel Ndima*[143] that a daily paid staff of the Ministry of Post and Telecommunication is not excluded from the definition of a worker under section1 (3) of the 1974 Labour Code (now Section 1 (2) of Labour code 1992). But, it does not imply that the number of hours or days work necessarily affect ones status as an employee as section 25 (1) (a) of the

140 It is from this premise therefore, it is necessary to ask whether an apprentice can be said to be an employee since he is under the control and direction of his master. Despite the fact that it is regulated by the Labour Code, with the specific requirement that it should be in writing and notwithstanding the fact that a special decree as to form, substance and the effect of apprenticeship contracts has been passed, it is submitted that they are not employees. See also Whincup, M., *op. cit.* at p.26. For general purposes an apprentice may be so regarded since the terms of the relationship may be regulated by collective bargaining and is regulated by employment protection legislation.

141 Arete No. 48/S of 01/04/82.

142 See also the Case of *Assurances des Provinces Reunis v. Tiogum David* (1999) CCLR 462 where the Bamenda Court of Appeal expressed a similar principle.

143 Civil Appeal No. CASWP/14/1976 CA (unreported).

Labour Code 1992 contemplates this kind of employment contract which may not be for up to two years.[144]

1.2 A Worker: The Common Law Approach

At common law, the definition of a worker was based on certain tests. These tests evolved with the industrialisation and sophistication in the work place.

1.2.a The Control Test

The single control test, which was the first to emerge at the scene was expounded by Lord Brownwell in *Yewens v. Noakes*[145]. It became the take-off point in ascertaining who a worker or servant is at common law. According to the promoters of this test, a worker was one who was not only given work to do but told how the work is to be done as well as the time and place of the work. The test made it imperative to ascertain the nature and degree of control that was exercised over the staff engaged before the conclusion about his/her status can be drawn.[146] The test is invariably relative particularly in employments where the employer may not be skilled or even knowledgeable in the employee's job and so may not be apt to direct and control the employee as contemplated in the *Yewens* case above.

It is obvious from the Cameroonian context that control is a primary feature in the employment relations because sections 1(2) and 23 of the Labour Code 1992 read together stress on control as a defining feature of the contract of employment[147]. Indeed, *Dorothy Wotani v. Cameroon OIC*[148] and

144 This notwithstanding, the length of service is very important as it now enables a worker to earn

145 (1880) 6Q.B. 530. Conversely if one is given work and is not directed or told how to do it could be said to be an independent contractor? To an extent the answer could be in the affirmative but is not conclusive as other issues have to be put into context to reflect the labour relations of this century which are quite different from the one in which the test was propagated where lowly placed domestics and commoners were who were the 'workers' were regarded as servants while the rich and aristocrats were seen as the masters /employers of those who performed the unsophisticated and menial jobs of that time.

146 Per McCardie J. in *Performing Rights Society Ltd v. Mitchell and Booker*[1924] 1K.B. 762. Notwithstanding the single factor control test, Mackenna J. in the *Ready Mixed Concrete Case* [1968] 2QB 497 is of the opinion that 'control includes the power of deciding the thing to be done, the way in which it shall be done, the means to be employed in doing it, the time when, and the place where it shall be done.'

147 Anderman argues that with advances made in education, training and industrial/technological development, such assumptions can no longer be tenable. See Anderman, S.D., *Labour Law*, *op. cit.* at p. 112.

148 (2003) Suit No. HCF/IL.7/987-99 (unreported).

CDC v. Akem Besong Benbella[149] clearly exemplified this view. Bawak JCA in the latter case,[150] after citing with approval the decision of Fletcher Moulton C.J in *Simmons v. Heath Laundry Co.*[151] held that:

> traditionally, it has been said that the relationship of master and servant exist between A and B if B agrees to work for A and under the contract, A has the right to determine not only what work B does but also how he does it. The contract is thus said to be a contract of service or a contract of employment.[152]

The court continued in the above case by identifying what Bawak JCA felt were benchmarks for contracts of services which are same like Lord Parker C.J. in the House of Lords decision in *Short v. Henderson.*[153] These include:

i) the master's powers to select his servant;
ii) the payment of wages or other remunerations;
iii) the master's right to contract the method of doing the work and
iv) the master's right of suspension or dismissal.

Following the above reasoning, it was held in the *Akem Besong Benbella Case,*[154] that security officers employed by the Cameroon Development Corporation to protect their products from theft were employees of the

149 CCLR RART 3 p 313-319. Also, Suit No. CASWP/67/1996 (unreported). The direct facts of the case were that the respondent had commenced a suit in the court of First Instance Tiko (Suit No. TM/64/1993 unreported) claiming damages for injuries suffered in the course of employment as a vigilante working for the appellant. The cause of disagreement was whether the respondent was a worker.

150 See in the same light, the North West Court of Appeal decision in *UNVDA Ndop. v. Ange Mando* BCA/ch/ 1988 (unreported) which followed the Cameroon Supreme Court decision in *Nanga Emile Honore.v. SCTA* Arête No. 48/s of 01/4/1982, *Jurisprudence de la Cour Supreme, Deuxieme Semestre Annee* 1981-82, p. 16. As well as *Henock Bih Fon v. Ako Fru* BCA/1321/78 (unreported).

151 [1910] 1. K.B. 543 at p. 550. Who pointed out that 'the greater the amount of direct control exercised over a person rendering the services by the person contracting for them, the stronger the ground for holding it to be a contract of services'.

152 At p. 313-314.

153 [1946] SC. 24 at p. 33.

154 As evidenced in exhibit 'F' tendered which was part of a letter from Mr. Mbandi the Group Palms Manager to the Acting Harvesting Manager dated 19th November 1992 which point to the fact that ; i). the appellants engaged the services of the committee; ii) the payment of wages or remuneration from the harvesting of the fruits by them; iii) they controlled the method the respondent and his friends were to use in the performance of their duties; iv)the contract could be abrogated if they failed to stop fruit theft within the area thereby indicating that there was a contract of employment.

appellant and not independent contractors as contended by the appellants who had failed to protect the respondent employee against risks of physical injuries.

Jani JCA in the North West Court of Appeal decision in *Assurance des Provinces Reunis. v. Tiogum David*[155] in citing the Supreme Court's interpretation of section 1(2) of the Labour Code 1974 in the *Nanga Emile Honore v. SCTA*[156] case, held that to ascertain whether the plaintiff (respondent) in the instant case is a worker and not a broker for SOCIETE ORGASSUR/ASSURANCE (now *Companie d'Assurance des Provinces Reunies*) the court must establish (1) the subordination and control of the worker by the employer and (2) the payment of remuneration by the employer.[157] The learned judge extended the control test to include the power of the employer to discipline his employee where the latter is in breach.[158]

The disciplinary power of the employer, which is often not regulated by the Labour Code or work rules, conditions of employment or negotiated by the parties under the auspices of trade unions, may become abusive if not contained. Can a teacher who fails to follow a specific teaching method as instructed by the employer be said to have erred because he failed to follow instructions even if such instructions have long outlived their usefulness? Whatever the answer may be, the question shows the effect of an unreasonable reliance on control on the employment relationship. Although control underpins the employment relationship, it should not be the dominant factor for ascertaining the existence of employment. It is obvious that the reality of control cannot be total although the employer has a supervisory role, certain jobs require the worker be allowed considerable discretion in carrying out their work. Each employment has a certain degree of discretion within which the workman may act.

---

155 (1998) 1CCLR 1-125 Part 4, 62-66.

156 Arête No. 48/S of 01/04/82, *Jurisprudence de la Cour Supreme, Deuxieme Trimestre Annee* 1981-1982 at p.16

157 Since a document marked exhibit 'C' tendered in court show that the respondent was recruited as one of the personnel to work as sub director in the B amenda branch on a monthly salary of 75.000FCFA plus a motivation commission of 7%, the courts held that for all intend and purpose the respondent was a worker.

158 See Yanou *op. cit.* at p. 10-11. See also Lord Thankerton in *Short v. J. and W. Henderson Ltd* [1946] L.T 174 at p. 421 of which Jani JCA's decision in the *Tiogium Case* is in line with. He specifically spelt out that one will be a worker amongst others if the master has rights 'of suspension or dismissal.' This clearly spells out the limits of power of the employer and it is not as vague as the power to discipline an erring staff.

1.2.b The Integration Test

The shortcoming of the single control test especially in technical and sophisticated jobs, led to the elaboration of the 'organisation,' or 'integration' test as expounded by Denning L.J (as he then was) in *Stevenson, Jordan and Harrison. v. Macdonald and Evans.*[159] The erudite judge put the issue thus:

> "...under a contract of service, a man is employed as part of a business, and his work done as an integral part of the business; whereas, under a contract for services, his work, although done for the business, is not integrated into it but is only accessory to it."[160]

Based on the above, Lord Denning argued that once the employment function is an integral part of an organisation or enterprise, one will be considered an employee even if control is minimal[161]. The organisation test has been apparently adopted in Cameroon[162] as was seen in *CDC.v. Akem B. Benbella.*[163] Here, the activities of vigilantes engaged to protect CDC crops were seen as integral to the operations of CDC. An attack on them when they were searching for produce stolen from CDC was considered as having occurred in the context of the business of the company. Although providing security is neither central to the functioning of the appellant, nor ancillary to it, the Court noted that it was an integral component of the organisation's work because it leads to the protection of agricultural produce which is the main stay of CDC.

1.2.c Multiple Factor Test

This test also suffered from the fact that it was based on a single factor, that is, how integral the function is to the organisation. The integration test became unsuitable with Mackenna J. in *Ready Mixed Concrete (South East) LTD v. Minister of Pensions*[164] moving away from it. In the above case, the Minister of Pensions claimed that the plaintiff company had to pay national

159 [1952] 1T.L.R. 101.
160 [1952] 1T.L.R. 101 at p. 111.
161 *Ibid.*
162 See also Yanou *op. cit.* at p, 12.
163 Supra
164 [1968] 2Q.B. 491. See also *Cassidy v. Ministry of Health* [1951] 2 K.B. 343; *Whittaker v. Minister of Pensions* [1967] 1 Q.B. 156

insurance contributions for a driver it had employed to transport concrete even though the contract between the two stated that the driver was an independent contractor who for the duration of their contract will carry nothing else other than the plaintiff's concrete in a vehicle he would hire purchase from the company. The driver was to wear the company's uniform and the said vehicle painted with the company's colours and emblem and in case of his ill-health or otherwise, the driver could hire another driver for the vehicle. All of these he had to do at his expense and he was being paid a rate per mile for the quantity which he delivers. The question arose as to whether the driver was an employee with the company for the purpose of the National Insurance Act 1965. It was held that the fact that the contract called the driver an "independent contractor' was immaterial to the true nature of the relationship which is determined by the contractual rights and obligations. In this regard, a contract of service exists between the two if i. the driver agrees against a remuneration to offer his services to the company; ii. He agrees expressly or otherwise to render such services under the control of the company; iii. The contractual provisions are consistent with the requirements of an ordinary contract of service. Mackenna J in this case asked the rhetorical question that - 'what is meant by being part and parcel of an organisation? Are persons who answer this description servants? If only some are servants, what distinguishes them from the others if it is not their submission to orders?' After these questions, the judge made the very significant argument that since employment is evidenced by several factors, these must be included in determining whether a person is an employee as elaborated above. Base on the facts, since the driver had independence in the performance of the contract. e.g, maintain the vehicle in working state, repairing the vehicle's worn out parts, make the vehicle available all throughout the contract, hire another driver to take his place if at any state he is unable to drive, paid a rate a mile for the quantity he delivers, etc, it was a contract of carriage and not of service. Mr. Latimar had freedom to choose to perform these obligations, which is not the case with workmen. Ownership of assets, profits and the financial risks of loss was all in the hands of Mr. Latimer and not Ready Mixed Concrete. For this reason, he was a 'small businessman' (independent contractor - self employed) and not a servant.

Based on this approach, what has become known as the multiple factor or composite test was elaborated incorporating control, the extent of financial risks and other factors in the definition of a servant. Cooke J in the *Market Investigations Ltd. v. Minister of Social Security*[165] then proffered a non-exhaustive guideline, which inter alia must include: the degree of control, the degree to which the worker risks loss/ stand to gain for profit, ownership of tools and equipment, the degree to which the worker's work is an integral part of the business, the regularity of payment, the mutuality of obligation, the ability to delegate the performance of the contract, the terms of the contract (substance and not the form), the hours of rest and social insurance benefits.[166] Where all or most of these guidelines are present then at common law such a person is a worker[167]. It has been observed by Anderman[168] that a proper understanding of the characteristics of the contract of employment is a virtual pre-condition to an understanding of labour law as a subject.

In deciding whether one is an employee, Henry LJ in *Lane v. Roofing Co. Ltd*[169] rightfully observed that the overall context of employment has drastically changed from that most of these leading cases expounded above were decided as there are more self-employed now than those in employment with most of them being temporal and shared employment in addition to the fact that there are some perceived advantages for both parties if the relationship is that of a self-employed (raging from more benevolent and less prompt tax regimes on part of the workman to disincentives if the employment is long term from the employees perspective). Mindful of all of these, the learned judge averred that there are many factors to take into consideration in deciding who is a worker at Common law. This should be so decided on the facts of the individual case which each have as different priorities. Although control test is pre-eminent in deciding who a worker is, in the light of what and how work is done and who provides materials for the work, etc, it may not be the case in skilled work where discretion is with the workman as to how the work is to be done. Better

---

165 [1969] 2 Q.B. 173.

166 Yanou *op. cit.* at p. 12-13 opines that this composite test is part of the labour relation as sections 1 (2) and 23 L.C 1992, has a multiple factor flavour since it embodies in its definition of a worker not just control and management but also remuneration as determinant of employment relationship.

167 See generally on this Rideout, *op. cit.* at pp. 6-16. Furthermore, although the composite tests and the non-exhaustive checklist were confirmed in *Lee v. Chung and shun Sing Construction and Engineering Co Ltd* [1990] 1RLR 236. The Court of Appeal in *Hall (HM Inspector of Taxes) v. Lorimer* [1994] 1RLR.171 warned against the mechanical application of the checklist as it is not an all purpose definition but just guidelines to ascertain the status of an individual in an employment relationship.

168 Anderman, S.D. *Labour law: Management Decision and Worker's Rights*, 3rd Edition, London: Butterworth, 1993, p.3.

169 [1995] 1RLR 493.

still, was the workman doing his own business or that of his employer?[170] Who bears the financial risks and who stands to profit from the business? All of the above as pointed out by Henry LJ must be seen from the spectacle of who is responsible for the overall safety of the workmen which should be a strong indication of the type of relationship entered into.

1.2.d Who is a Worker in the Technological World?

The economic melt-down and the telecommunication revolution has probably changed the traditional notion of who a worker is. This is especially so as machines are fast taking over the places of a human worker. Should the definition then of a worker include humans and abstracts?

In addition, What about the status of platform workers? Are they employers of independent contractors? If the later view is adopted subsequently in Cameroon it will mean that such a worker will be denied the benefits that flow from being a worker and by implication will not be able to benefit from for example, the social security that the ordinary employment contracts import into the relationship.[171]

1.3 A Worker: The Public Service Approach

Section 2(1) and of Decree No. 94-199 of 7th October 1994[172] defines a worker in the context of the public sector as a civil servant who fulfils conditions of entry into the civil service as contained in sections 12, 13 and 15.[173] A civil servant is according to section 3(1) of this decree any person who occupies a permanent job position and is confirmed in a cadre[174] of the

---

[170] In the United States of America Supreme Court case of *United States of America v. Silk* [1946] 331 US 704, the question was whether the employment was as a matter of economic reality.

[171] See generally ILO: Digital Platform and the future of work: towards Decent Work in the on line world (Geneva: International Labour Office, 2018); Shibata, S., "Gig Work and the Discourse of Autonomy: Fictitious Freedom in Japan's Digital Economy" (2019) 25 new Political economy535-51.

[172] To establish General Rules and Regulations of the Public Service in Cameroon.

[173] To qualify as civil servant the applicant must enter through a competitive examination like those recruited into the teachers training colleges or qualify through special and specifically defined conditions like those recruited into the Higher Education as teachers.

[174] A cadre as defined in section 6 of Decree No 94-199 of 7th October 1994, is the body of job positions reserved for civil servants recruited at the same level of education or professional qualification and subject to the same professional conditions. Each of such cadre has one or two grades. The grades which are also comprised of several classes (each with several incremental positions) define the position of a civil servant in his cadre.

government service. The civil service itself is subdivided into four categories in descending hierarchical order identified by letters, to wit; A,B,C and D. The definition of a worker from the public service perspective does not stress elements of control and disciplinary supervision as is the case with the private sector.

It is possible for a staff to work in the public service and be subject to public service control and pay without necessarily being a civil servant. Though one surrenders one's labour under the control of the public service, such a person is regarded only as a state agent with negative consequences on the security of their employment. Assistant lecturers recruited in the state universities though paid and controlled by the government are not civil servants. The assistant lecturer cannot ask for a suspension of the contract of employment or for a long leave of absence[175] in order to take up other functions. Furthermore, an assistant lecturer can be summarily terminated, as was the case with three assistant lecturers of the University of Buea.[176]

Section 10 of the Rules and Regulations of the civil service, excludes from the definition of civil servants the following:

- personnel recruited and administered by the National Assembly,
- Employees of local authorities, semi-public bodies and public establishments of an administrative, cultural, scientific, industrial and commercial nature who are not civil servants,
- State employees governed by the Labour Code;
- Auxiliary administrative employees;

---

175 Although such may be granted for further service on condition that the assistant lecturer will resume duty upon completion of the further studies. Because there is no cut and dry rule for the award of such leave of absence, the grant of permission becomes discretionary and depending more on the relationship with the university hierarchy, to the extent that fortunate assistant lecturers are granted leave with their salary not suspended while others who are less fortunate go without their salary. This adversely affects the security of employment as not only are likes not treated alike (propounded by Aristotle) they are not given the same opportunities in contravention to universal norms particularly article 2 of ILO Convention No. 111 which requires state parties to not only declare but also pursue a national policy designed to promote, by methods appropriate to national conditions and practice, equality of opportunity and treatment in respect of employment and occupation, with the view to eliminating any discrimination in respect thereof. If such lecturers do not have a scholarship, they take longer to finish up school and may not find any need or better still do not owe it to their employers to return to their previous jobs, increasing the number of academics in the diaspora, when the technical man power is needed back in the country.

176 If however the assistant lecturer is promoted to the rank of lecturer after the age of 35, he/she does not become a civil servant because he /she has passed the age of recruitment into the civil service. This is the position notwithstanding the fact that he /she gained employment before attaining 35 and might have been delayed by the want of publication and/or terminal degree.

- Judicial and Legal officers;
- The Armed Forces; and
- The civil servants of the National Security and Prisons.

It is clear that there is no single labour statute that regulates all employment relations as even in the civil service, different laws regulate the different employment relationships with each determining employees for its purposes. The mere fact that an employee is seen differently depending on the specific statute regulating their employment contract, does not in our context suggest that such an employee is not a worker. However, as observed by Uvieghara,[177] the only difference is that such an employee will not claim the benefits provided for in the statute that excludes them. The existence of the multiplicity of statutes on employment law with each defining an employee for its purpose has to be criticised for contributing to the weakening of security of service in Cameroon.

1.3.1 Civil Servants on Secondments

It is clear that public servants are not workers as defined in the Labour Code. However, it appears from the Court of Appeal Bamenda decision in *CARFOP v. Kan Elroy Moses Payne,*[178] the Buea Court of Appeal decision in *Local Government Training Centre v. Bobuin John Gemandze*[179] and section 24(2) of the Labour Code, 1992, and Articles 12 and 13 of Ordinance No. 95/003 of 17th August 1995, that civil servants sent on secondment to private enterprises are regulated by the Labour Code and not the Civil Service Rules and Regulations. The soundness of the decisions has been challenged in the Supreme Court decision in *MIDENO v. Nyanga Emmanuel.*[180] It was in this latter case categorically held that a civil servant does not lose his/her civil servant status upon secondment to a private service.

However, it seems that while on secondment, a civil servant's career is suspended and during this period, he becomes bound by his contract with the new employer and the statutory rules,[181] for example, the Labour

177 Uvieghara, *Op. cit.* at p. 11.
178 2001 CCLR Part 67.
179 HCF/L20/98/IM
180 Appeal No. 113/S/02/03
181 This seem to be the position in England as was held in *R v Lord Chancellor's Department, ex parte Nangle* [1992] 1 All E.R 897. Here although Nangle a civil servant was employed as an Executive officer in the Lord Chancellor's Department, he was engaged under a contract of service which gave him right to seek relief in contract rather than public law for loss suffered after allegation of

Code that supplement the contract. At the end of his secondment, he resumes civil servant status and goes back to the civil service under the civil service rules and regulations. This is so as one can be on secondment to an international organisation, where he will not insist on imposing his/her terms of contract on the organisation. This is because by accepting to be under the authority of the international organisation, such a worker becomes bound by the terms of the contract that sent him on secondment and the treaty obligations between international organisation and the Cameroonian government.

Although a civil servant on secondment is paid by the private enterprise he is seconded to, section 78(1) of Decree No 94-199 of 7th October 1994 is categorical that a civil servant on secondment shall continue to be regulated by the civil service law. The situation remains confused because section 78(2) rather provides that mindful of section 78(1) a public servant shall be subject 'to all the regulations governing the body to which he is seconded, subject to the exceptions provided for by the law in force, the general principles of the law and by jurisprudence.' It would seem that in spite of the *MIDENO case* a civil servant seconded to a private enterprise is governed by the labour Code notwithstanding section 78(1) of the 1994 Decree on Civil Service Rules and Regulations.

1.3.2 A Worker Sent on Secondment To Another Company in the Group of Companies

In labour law, the Corporate group responsible for the indemnity of a wrongfully dismissed worker. This is not the sole responsibility of a company in that group. Who is then a worker in such a group? Who is the employer? Is it the person who initially employed of the employer to whom the worker is sent on secondment? The Labour Code of Cameroon which is the authoritative source in both substantive and procedural matters is very silent as the position of workers in company group. The court of Appeal Littoral in *Cami Toyota et CFAO Technologies c/ Jaime Duran Ngossei*[182] sheds some light on this. The fact of the case is that the respondent who was resident in Cameroon was employed by Cami Toyota in Cameroon and sent to work in Spain. This

---

sexual harassment against him resulted in loss of increments for 12 months. See also in this regard Fredman, S., and Morris, G., [1992] P.L. 485, in Ewing, K.D., Remedies for Breach of Contract of Employment, *CLJ*, 52(3), November 1993, p 405.

182 Cour d'Appel du Littoral/Arret No. 90/s du 28 Mai 2008 (unreported)

contract was signed by the Minister of Labour & Social Security for a period of two years renewable thereby respecting the provisions of section 27 of the Labour Code. He was sent on secondment to CFAO Technologies as director of Telecom services. After the suppression of this position, he was served a latter of termination on 22nd August 2003 which took effect on 31st August 2003. Up till January 2005, he was not given any allowance to travel back to his habitual residence as is required by section 94(4) of the Labour Code, reason for which he lodged a complaint at the Labour Inspectorate Wouri. However, in the meantime, Jaime Duran Ngossei had returned to Cameroon and was working with another company. Although the complaint at the labour inspectorate was against CFAO, Cami Toyota intervened without being surmoned by the Labour Inspector. Cami Toyota proposed to pay the partial sum that Jaime Duran was requesting from CFAO. Jaime Duran then lodged complaint at High Court Wouri after a partial non-conciliation between the parties The High Court awarded him damages of 61,993,456.

The High Court made CFAO and Cami Toyota Jointly and severally liable the said amount above without however giving any breakdown as to how the amount of damages was arrived at. The defendants (CFAO and Cami Toyota) appealed against this decision at the Court of Appeal Littoral. The appeal was granted since the decision of the High Court was neither reasoned nor properly motivated.

The Court of Appeal after re-examination of the substance of the case, ruled in favour of the respondent, granting him the initial amount of 61,993,456frs that he had requested at the high Court. The Court of Appeal gave a break-down of the damages according to the various heads as follows:

broken down as follows-

- right of benefit in salary =	42.787.288
- school fees of children =	5.387.746
- Water bills =	122.120
- electricity bills =	1.534.542
- security guard =	3.449.760.
Total	61.993,456frs

Two questions come to mind: Who is the employer in a corporate group of companies? Was the decision of the Court of Appeal Littoral correct?

M.A.Mouthieu *epse* Njandeu made the following observations[183]. Concerning the first question, there are two possibilities of determining the employee of a corporate group of companies.

i. When there is a *de facto* employer gaining directly from the work by the employee, that employee could be termed a worker of that company. In this regard, the Court of Appeal was right because of Cami Toyota's intervention without being summoned show the link between the actual employer and the benefiting employer. It has been observed that in corporate group, it is difficult to identify the employer on the basis of payment of salary as sometimes the payment vouchers may emanate from any of the members of the group whereas the order for payments make come directly from the parent company. It becomes necessary in such a situation to differentiate between the employer with whom the employee has a contract and one who benefits from the employee's services.

ii. The status of an employee in a corporate group may also arise from the fact that the companies share the same assets. In The case under review, Jaime Duran The employee/respondent was recruited by Cami Toyota but was transferred to CFAO technologies without any new contract between CFAO and the employee, implying therefore that they are companies of the same group. The respondent worked for CFAO Technologies under the contract he signed with Cami Toyota. He was therefore a worker in a group of companies in which CFAo was a subsidiary of Cami Toyota. That is why the Court of Appeal did not hesitate to make Cami Toyota jointly and severally liable for the damages, even though Cami Toyota had argued that at the time of the termination The respondent was no longer their employee.

2. Regarding the correctness of the decision of the court of Appeal, the conditions required by section 94(1)[184] of the Labour code were not met because the respondent was born in Nkongsamba, signed a contract of employment the Douala, he leaves and work in Douala.

183 Njandeu, M.M.A," *Travailleur dans un Groupe de Societes*" in *Les Grandes Decision du Travail et de la Securite Sociale, JusPrint*, 2016, 130-137.

184 Section 94(1) of the Labour Code 1992 provides that "where, because of the employer, performance of employment contract requires or has required a worker to move from his usual residence, the employer shall be responsible for the traveling expenses of the worker, his spouse and minor children normally residing with him, as well as for the transport of their luggage.

> He was no longer in Spain and for that reason was not entitled to the section 94(1) Labour Code 1992 compensation since he was already in Cameroon. The defendants failed to raise this point during the session at the Labour Inspectorate. The transportation cost is therefore unjustified.

The Court of Appeal ought to have proceeded to reinstate the respondent-employee in his right as a worker of another subsidiary in the group.

CHAPTER 2

THE NATURE OF EMPLOYMENT CONTRACTS & EMPLOYMENT RELATIONSHIP

A contract of employment is the foundation upon which all labour relations are predicated. The strength of the employment relationship depends on the nature of the contract. Anderman[185] has observed that a proper understanding of the characteristics of the contract of employment is a virtual pre-condition to an understanding of labour law as a subject, pointing therefore to the central position of employment contracts to labour law.

Employment may either be the product of consensus between the employer and the individual employee, collective bargaining agreements brokered by trade unions or terms implied by statutes or usage. Although the content of the contract itself is residual as it regulates situations left unregulated by statutes[186] and collective bargaining process, Anderman[187] has observed that the contracts of employment besides being prominent and pervasive, attests to the veracity of the kind of relationship contemplated by the parties.

When a worker's contractual obligations are breached by the employer, proper redress can only be offered by a justice system in which judges dispense judgments based on just laws and impartiality.[188] This kind of justice system has in labour matters been preserved by sections 131-155 (in case of individual dispute) and sections 157-164(in case of collective disputes). The Labour Code is unique as it contains the substantive law on labour relations as

---

185 Amderman, S.D. *Labour law: Management Decision and Worker's Rights*, 3rd Edition, London: Butterworth, 1998, p.31.

186 *Ibid* at p. 31.

187 *Ibid.*

188 As ordained by article 37(2) of the 1996 Constitution of Cameroon as revised, "....Magistrates of the bench shall, in the discharge of their duties, be governed only by the law and their conscience."

well as the procedure for the settlement of labour disputes.[189] Quite apart from the fact that both affect the nature of the employment relations, the process for the resolution of disputes is relevant to any employment relationship.

Both at common law and under section 23 of the 1992 Code, employments must result from agreements where in return for a remuneration, a worker surrenders his labour to the employer.. To achieve this, there ought to be a valid offer of the job to the public not just to a selected few. The worker must accept the offer of employment after going through the required interview, the acceptance could be oral, written, or by conduct through the assumption of duty. This must be followed by pay which as consideration for a worker's services must not be lower than the minimum wage fixed by the law. The contract must be entered into with the intention to create legal relationship between the employer and employee and must not be shrouded with illegality. The parties to the contract of employment must have capacity to contract. Despite the laissez-faire and the sanctity of contracts which bred individualism, Lord Jessel recognises that for men to be accorded the utmost liberty in contracting, they must be of full age and competent understanding. In Cameroon, the Labour Code 1992 provides in section 86 that children under the age of 14 may not be employed except with the approval of the Ministry of Labour, although children of this age can enter into contracts for necessaries.

2.1 Definition and Nature of Employment

According to section 23(1) of the Labour Code 1992, a contract of employment within the Cameroonian legal framework is an engagement which by the agreement of the parties, a worker undertakes to put his services under the authority and management of an employer against remuneration. This definition was adopted *in toto* by Bawak JCA in *Centre Africain de Recherche et de Formation Phytosanitaire (CARFOP). v. Kan Elroy Moses Payne*[190] as the basis of the conclusion that there was a contract of service between CARFOP and the respondent who was seconded to it from the Ministry of Finance.

---

189 Disputes involve disagreements over issues capable of resolution by negotiation, mediation or third part adjudication. The differences inherent in a dispute can usually be examined objectively, and a third party can take a view to assess the correctness of one side or the other. See generally *ADR and Commercial Disputes*, Russel Caller (eds), London, Sweet & Maxwell, 2002, p.2.

190 Appeal No. BCA/7.L/98 (2001) (unreported). 1 CCLR 18-29 at p. 23 para 35-40.

2.1.1 Choice of Contract

Contracts of employment according to section 25 (1) of the Labour Code 1992 may be divided into two based on the tenure of the employment; viz; employment of specified or unspecified duration. Contracts of indefinite (unspecified) duration according to section 25 (1) (b) are contracts where termination is not fixed in advance. Although this specie of employment is of an indefinite duration, the contracts may be terminated at any time by either party, subject however to prior written notice of the party terminating.[191]

A contract of specified duration is, on the other hand, defined in section 25 (1) (a) of the Labour Code 1992 as one in which the duration is specified in advance by both parties to the contract. It is not subject to notice since the contract ends at the time specified or on the occurrence of a specified event or the completion of an agreed task or work. These employments which are for periods not exceeding two years are renewable once. However, at the end of the renewal period, if a working relationship ensues, the contract can be transformed into a contract of unspecified duration as provided for in section 25 (3). However, an extension of a contract of specified duration more than once automatically converts the contract into a permanent employment. Since generally, workers are oblivious of this fact, they continue to work as if they were under a contract of specified duration. Where the worker involved is not of Cameroonian nationality, such renewal will be possible only after endorsement by the Minister in charge of Labour.[192]

Do employees under the contracts of specified duration enjoy the rights and privileges that flow to employees under the unspecified duration? Such workers may have all the privileges only so long as they have the appropriate length of service, except where the worker is employed on temporary basis, for example, to replace a worker on leave or if they are recruited to carry out exclusively seasonal jobs generated by the cyclical or climatic nature of their employment activities.

Contracts of employment may be specified but non-renewable. The termination of such contracts may depend on the intention of the parties, an event so stated in the contract[193] or the performance of a specified activity[194] for example, the setting up of a laboratory.

---

191 As required by section 34 of the Labour Code 1992.

192 Section 25(2) of the Labour Code 1992.

193 Labour Code 1992, section 25 (1) (a) paragraph 1 of Labour Code 1992.

194 *Ibid* section 25 (1) (a) paragraph 2.

According to Section 25(4) of the Labour Code 1992, contracts of employment do not include i). seasonal job contracts which are contracts resulting from the climatic nature of a company's activity[195]. All of such contracts can only be for periods of 6 months non-renewable as per Art 6(4) of Decree No. 93/577/P of July 1993[196]. ii).Occasional jobs[197] which are contracts created by the unexpected growth of company activities resulting from urgent work to prevent accidents, organising emergency measures, repairing company equipment, facilities or buildings that are dangerous for workers. All of such contracts can only be for periods of between one to fifteen days renewable once – s. 6 (3) although iii) temporary jobs[198] which are contracts to replace suspended or absent workers in order to complete a piece of work within specified time limit requiring additional workers. All of such contracts can only be for periods of 3 months renewable once per year 6(2) of Law No 93/577/P of 19th July 1993.

Article 7(1) of Law No 93/577/P of 19th July 1993 converts all such seasonal job contracts into contracts of unspecified duration if they exceed the legally authorised period without termination.

Common law recognises that there could be part time employees (casual workers) who are not servants as conceptualised above. Although the amount of work given is not an indication of the status of employment, persons working on part time basis may never the less be employees if the element of control and the mutual obligation to work and provide work are present.

Although labour regulations between employees and employers under section 25 (4) are not binding on temporary or seasonal workers, section 26(5) does nevertheless recognise that a contract of employment exists between these classes of workers and a temporary job contractor who engages them.[199] Section 39(3) of the Labour Code 1992 and the decision in the *Akamangwa Martin Case* combined provide that it is a question of fact whether an individual is a worker once he has declared his status as a worker. The fact that the temporary job contractors pay the salary, medical bills and social insurance benefits of such seasonal workers does not make

195 *Ibid* section 25 (4) (c).

196 See also *Lay Private Education v. Ebede Patrick Agi*. Suit No. CASWP/L.14/2000. (unreported)

197 *Ibid* section 25 (4) (b).

198 *Ibid* section 25 (4) (a).

199 A temporary job contractor according to section 26 (2) of the Labour Code shall mean any individual or corporate body whose sole activity consists in temporarily providing users with workers whom they recruit and pay.

them their employees. However, they are workers of the 'users' who employ them.[200]

Common law recognises that there could be part time employees (casual workers) who are not servants as conceptualised above. Although the amount of work given is not an indication of the status of employment, persons working on part time basis may never the less be employees if the element of control and the mutual obligation to work and provide work[201] are present.

2.1.2 Sub-contractors

The independent contractor is one who renders a contract for service which is different from employment contracts (contract of services). In this regard he is not a worker of the establishment for which he renders such services. he has his own tools, workers, and Social insurance.

The Cameroonian Labour Code in section 48 recognises the existence of subcontractors in employment relationships. Subcontractors are required[202] to permanently furnish information of their status as subcontractors including their full names, address and the address of the contractor even if the work is done outside the business premise of the contractor. In this regard, it defines it as 'a person who enters into a written contract with a contractor to carry out a specified piece of work or supply specified services for an agreed price. In this regard, the subcontractor recruits all employees. However, in case of insolvency, the independent contractor shall assume all the sub-contractor's obligations if the work was done at the contractor's workshop, or other business premise.[203] If the work is otherwise done at any other place, the contractor shall be responsible only for the payment of the worker's wages.[204] This gives an aggrieved worker power to sue the contractor directly in case of breach. This is only possible if the subcontractor has not registered with the trade and personal credit register as a business and so holds no business licence.

---

200 *Mersey Docks & Habour v. Coggins & Griffith Liverpool Ltd* [1947] A.C.1 the labour board lent the defendant company a crane plus an operator. The contract specified that he defendant would be the employer but the harbour board retained the ultimate right to employ, dismiss and pay wages. It was held that the harbour board was still the employer despite the terms of the contract.

201 *O'kelly v. Trust House Forte* [1983] 1RLR 254 contrast with *Market Investigations v. Minister of Social Security* [1969] 2 QB 173.

202 Section 50 of the Labour Code

203 Section 49(1) of the Labour Code

204 Section 49(2) of the Labour Code

Section 50 requires all such sub-contractors to display in a notice at his work shop or other business premises that he is a sub-contractor, giving his full name and address of the independent contractor who entrusted him with the work and the sub-contractor must also include working hours. This notice becomes important if the work is carried out in the workshops or any other business premises of the contractor.

2.2 Nature and Content of Employment Contracts

Both at common law and under section 23 of the 1992 Code, employments must result from agreements. To achieve this, there ought to be an offer of the job to the public not just to a selected few, although in cases of personal services, for example, a valet, a cook, the employer can go directly to them.

The worker must accept the offer of employment after going through the required interview, the acceptance could be oral, written, or by conduct through the assumption of duty. This must be followed by pay which as consideration[205] for a worker's services must not be lower than the minimum wage fixed by the law.[206] Autonomy based theorists[207] are of the view that if there were no payments for the promises made, individuals would be deprived of the freedom to place themselves under a moral or legal obligation to fulfil their employment contract.[208] The contract must be entered into with the intention to create legal relationship between the employer and employee and must not be shrouded with illegality.

The parties to the contract of employment must have capacity to contract. Despite the laissez-faire and the sanctity of contracts which bred individualism, Lord Jessel[209] recognises that for men to be accorded the utmost liberty in contracting, they must be of full age and competent understanding.

---

205 This is the wage given to the employee in return for the work done which could be either monthly, weekly or as the parties agree.

206 Prime Ministerial Decision No. 95/099 of 1st February 1995 fixing minimum wage at 23000frs as revised to 28.216frs per month by Decret No. 2008/2115 PM du 24 Juin 2008.and revied to 36270 by Decree No. 2014/253 of 7th July 2014 revaluig the Guaranteed inter-Occupational Minimum wages

207 Fried, C., "Contracts as Promise," p. 7 in Trebilcock, M.J. (ed), Trebilcock, M.J. (ed) *The Limits to Freedoms of Contract,. op. cit.* at p. 164.

208 Fried, C., "Contracts as Promise," p. 7-8 in Trebilcock, M.J. (ed), Trebilcock, M.J. (ed) *The Limits to Freedoms of Contract,. op. cit.* at p. 164-165.

209 See generally Lord Jessel in *Printing& Numerical Registering Company. v. Sampson* (1875) LR 19 Eq 462 at 465

In Cameroon, the Labour Code 1992 provides in section 86 that children under the age of 14 may not be employed except with the approval of the Ministry of Labour,[210] although children of this age can enter into contracts for necessaries.[211]

2.3 Formation of Employment Contracts

This section in the main shall dwell on the creation and form employment contracts.

2.3.1 Compulsory Conditions of a Contract of Employment

These are requirements which all contracts of employment must fulfil.

2.3.1.i Basic Conditions

Section 23 (2) of the Code provides that contracts of employments are a product of free negotiations between the parties with the parties in *consensus ad idem*. That is why the labour code in section 2 has proscribed all forms of forced and compulsory labour. As pointed out in the preceeding chapter, all elements of a valid contract of employment are present. The Lȧbour Code 1992 provides in section 86 that children under the age of 14 may not be employed except with the approval of the Ministry of Labour after taking into consideration local exigencies - s. 86 (1) LC. However, labour contracts allow a minor of 14 to enter into valid contracts for apprenticeship with the support of their parent or guardian. As per S. 86 (2) (a), Minors below 18 cannot be employed to work in a ship. The minister has been given discretion to specify other categories of works that minors may not be employed in - s. 86 (2) (4). The parties must have intended to create a valid legal contractual relationship and must not be shrouded with illegalities.

---

210 The employment of children for night job is also proscribed by section 83(2) of the Labour Code 1992. Recently, Cameroon signed the ILO Convention No. 182 on the Worst Form of Child Labour this is defined in article 3 (d) of the convention as work which by its nature can harm the health, safety and morals of the child. Article 35 of the UN Convention on the Rights of a Child 1993 imposes a duty on state parties to take appropriate measures to prevent sale and trafficking in children for any purpose or form. In flagrant disrespect of these laws even after the crisis children are still employed without the ministerial fiat. Although contracts involving foreigners must be in writing, and receive fiat from the minister of Labour, children from neighbouring Nigeria continue to work under 'masters' without fulfilling such statutory conditions in the guise that the children will be 'settled' after serving for a number of years.

211 Cheshire, Fifoot, Furmston's, *Law of Contract*, Butterworth, London, 1986, p.410-427.

2.3.1.ii Negotiation and Form of Contracts of Employment

Section 23 (2) of the Code provides that contracts of employments are a product of free negotiations between the parties with the parties in *consensus ad idem*.[212] This concept[213], which was profoundly influenced by the economic philosophy of laissez faire, is premised on the idea that the freedom to negotiate employment promotes economic self-interest, as the parties would bargain to obtain the maximum social wealth of the society. The doctrine of freedom and sanctity of contracts of employments were no longer based on religion and social status of the worker but on decisions of two free and voluntarily consenting minds. To this extent, once the employer and employee have entered into such employment contracts, each must abide by it unless relieved by the other. However, with the changing times, the sanctity of the individualist theory[214] could no longer hold in the face of changing social, political or economic circumstances. The laissez-faire idealism was supplanted by social security, which suggests status rather than the contracts[215] so that there is a compulsion to protect the contractual parties against economic and social exploitation in the guise of liberty to contract.

It can be gleaned from the foregone that section 23(2) of the Labour Code 1992 is a thorough breed of the above classical theoretical idealism. The big question here is whether in the post-economic recession period of Cameroon where there are still many desperate and psychologically beaten men /women chasing too few jobs, true *consensus ad idem* where the wills of men of majority age and full faculties meet as propagated by Sir Jessel and

212 According to Napier, this liberal approach to employment contracts may produce an illusion of equality between employer and employee. Although equal rights on paper may comfort the employee, one can correctly question the textbook assertion that employer and the employee have the same rights. See generally on this Napier, R.W., in Voize-Valayre, "The French Law of Dismissals," *23 New York University Journal of International Law and Politics*, 1991, p. 520.

213 According to Atiyah, judges of the 18th century believed that classical contracts take root from theories of natural law which provide that man have inalienable rights to own property (in this case his labour) and so has authority to make his own arrangements to sell his labour through proper employment contracts with no interference from government. This in a bid to enable contracting parties realize their wills irrespective of the justice or fairness these ideals of laissez-faire will mean to an imprudent and weaker employee. See generally Atiyah, P.S., *Introduction to the Law of Contract*, Clarendon Law Series, 5th edition, p. 8. Also as per Lord Cairns in *Cundy v. Lindsay* (1878) 3Cas 459 at p. 459, for there to be a valid contract there must be consensus of mind.

214 Led by Sir Frederick Pollock greatly influenced by Savigny. See Generally Anson's, *Principles of English Law of Contract*, in Cheshire, Fifoot, Furmston's, *Law of Contract*, London: Butterworths,1986, p.18.

215 Cheshire, Fifoot, Furmston's, *Law of Contract*, London: Butterworths, 1986, p.19.

Lord Cairns can exist?[216] The answer is in the negative because true consensus ad idem where the parties realise their wills (intentions) because of free negotiations and laissez-faire comes only from parties with equal bargaining power who are strong enough to stand on their feet in the job place.[217] This theoretical and idealist position of equality clearly does not exist in Cameroon where, as earlier observed, has an army of unemployed chasing very few employment. The situation in Cameroon is similar to that vividly captured by Lord Denning's dictum in *Lloyds Bank v Bundy*[218] thus:

> "....gathering all together, I would suggest that in all these instances there runs a single thread. They rest on inequality of bargaining power. By virtue of it, English law gives relief to one who, without independent advice, enters into a contract on terms which are very unfair or transfers property for a consideration which is grossly inadequate, when his bargaining power is grievously impaired by reason of his own needs or desires, or by his own ignorance or infirmity, coupled with undue influences or pressure brought to bear on him by others."[219]

The position adopted by the common law arising from the assumption of the equality of the parties has resulted in situations where the law does not concern itself with the question of the reasonableness of the terms of employment. With the advent of covid-19, financial melt down,etc and few job that are available, the power differential between employers and employees is so wide that employers are looked upon as thin gods since they are the providers of employment the only means by which workers can survive. It became obvious that it was not possible for the worker from his inferior position to talk of true consensus in terms of the laissez-faire philosophy. This situation invariably compounded the weakness of the worker. The powerful employer has an inexhaustible supply of potential employees he could treat them with disdain and complete disrespect of the contract terms.

Although section 23 of the Code assumes that employments are freely negotiated, few employments are in practice a product of such negotiations.

---

216 *Ibid dem.*

217 *Ibid dem.*

218 [1975] Q.B. 326.

219 *Ibid* at p.339.

The recruitment by the government[220] of Cameroon specifically into the Ministry Higher Education is a case in point. Once an applicant has gone through an interview and offered employment as an assistant lecturer, the terms of employment which have not been negotiated neither individually nor collectively are imposed on the 'new recruit' who must sign the standard form contract as presented by the state. Contracts of this nature which are shrouded in secrecy are accordingly not the result of the parties agreement and cannot result in secured employment. Ewing[221] posits that, the content and the substance of contracts have been enriched by new implied terms such as an embryonic duty on the part of the employer to disclose information about the terms of the contract.[222]

This potential for weakness of the contract of employment is further compounded by the fact that section 29(1) of the Code allows the employer to unilaterally draw up the internal regulations governing employment. The internal regulation so drawn becomes binding as prescribed under section 29(3) of the Code after it has received the fiat of the labour inspector as well as proof that it has been relied upon previously as was held by Mokwe J in the Buea High Court case of *Eboa Moukery. v. S.G.B.C.*[223] It is my contention that in a proper system where unions operate freely and collective bargaining is tolerated, such work rules ought to have been drawn up by the employer and the trade unions after the collective bargaining process. The fact that the labour inspector has to visa the work rule is not enough guarantee that the work rule will contribute to strengthening the employment. The labour inspector is a government employee who is likely to act in the interest of an employer, which is a para-public entity. The labour inspector is unlikely to act against the interest of his employer for fear of losing his/her position. Besides, problems of integrity may undermine his ability to make a fair decision.

Although in some common law jurisdictions like Britain collective agreements prima facie do not have contractual force,[224] section 18 (1) (e)

---

220 Although employment into the higher education for purposes of teaching is outside the contemplation of private sector employment as conceptualised here.

221 Ewing, K.D., "Remedies for Breach of the Contract of Employment," *Cambridge Law Journal*, *52*(3), November 1993, p.406.

222 See for example *Scally v. South East Thames* R.H.A [1987] ICR 700.

223 Suit No. HCF/L.20/1998-1999 (unreported). Yanou *op. cit.* at p. 32, citing in authority Enonchong *Memorial College v. Edward. J. Ngale* Suit No. CASWP/L.8/1987(unreported) is however of the opinion that a worker cannot be prevented from relying on the work rule simply because it has never been acted on previously.

224 Rideout, R.W., *Principles of Labour Law*, London: Sweet & Maxwell, p.31.

of the Labour Code 1992 makes collectively bargained agreements part and parcel of the terms of the employment of a worker in Cameroon. This provision gives statutory recognition to a trade union's capacity to enter into collective agreements with the employer on the workers' behalf. This, notwithstanding, trade unions in practice are rarely involved in the collective bargaining[225] process in companies or enterprises. Indeed, in Cameroon,[226] until early 2010 when the Minister of Labour and Social Security signed two collective agreements for the private sector banking and hydrocarbons corporations, there were virtually no such agreements in the country. Even these agreements are objectionable because the minister should not be involved with them. Government participation definitely brings pressure on the trade unions as well as gives the collective bargaining process a tripartite quality, distorting its original bilateral character (trade unions and employers). It clearly turns the collective bargaining process into a regulatory transaction that negatively affects the security of the service of the workers on the obvious basis that the negotiations may not be free in the circumstances of government interference.

In addition, although it is correct to assume as Atiyah[227] rightly points out that employment contracts are relational and for this reason different from simple classical contracts, this does not however mean that everything about them has to be negotiated and agreed upon. Since the employer may amend some aspects of the employee's obligations without his/her agreement, this gives an upper hand to the employer who may jump at the opportunity to negatively amend the contract against the interest of the employee. A combination of this common law position and section 42 (2) of the Labour Code 1992 weakens employment by giving the employer the discretion to sack a worker under the pretext of 'economic reason' should the worker reject changes made by the employer.

This feature of Cameroon's labour law shows that it evolved out of a capitalist system that accommodates the interest of those who hold power in the country. This philosophy insists on allowing employer/entrepreneur the liberty to manage the enterprise to maximise profit. This philosophical foundation makes the employer/entrepreneur to develop monopolistic and

225 Collective bargaining is an internationally recognized right of the ILO as per its Convention No. 98 on the Right to Organise and Collective Bargaining Convention, 1949 ratified by Cameroon in 1962.

226 Trade Union Rights and Industrial Relation in French Speaking Africa: "The Impact of Structural Adjustment," *Trade Union and Labour Series*, No. 1, September, 1995, p.8.

227 Atiyah, *op. cit.* at p. 51-52. See also *Cresswell v. Board of Inland Revenue* [1984] 1All E.R 713.

clientelist tendencies creating a situation of 'take it or leave it' contracts of service. It is opined that, the freedom to negotiate under section 23 (2) of the Labour Code 1992 is a mirage with grave consequences on the security of employment in the country.

2.3.1.iii Form of Employment Contracts

By section 24(3) of the 1992 Labour Code, the contract of employment need not be in any particular form.[228] These notwithstanding, section 27 LC requires all contracts of employment of specified duration of more than 3 months or that which requires the employee to live abroad to be mandatorily be in writing and a copy sent to the Minister of Labour.

All contracts of employment with a foreigner must be in writing and must be endorsed by the minister of employment for it to be valid. - section 27(1) & (2). Should the minister reject it the contract becomes null and void - Section 27(3) LC. Such endorsement is done pursuant to an application to the minister and if within 2 months of application the minister does not give a decision, the contract shall be deemed to be endorsed - section 27(4) LC

Also, those involving an apprentice,[229] must be in writing. Any form of evidence may be adduced as proof of an unwritten contract. It seems obvious that the fact that contracts of employment are not required to be in any form creates insecurity of service since contracts of employment are relational in nature spanning many years. For its terms to be definitive without leaving anything to chance, it is imperative that the contracts of employment just like contracts involving an interest in land, ought to be in writing if it has to be enforceable. This is so because employment contracts come with enormous rights and obligations on both contractual parties.

The employment contract terms, which are in a flux or where the parties depend on bits and pieces of evidence drawn from work rule, particulars of contracts, collective bargaining agreements, code of practice, statute and common law, and others, the contractual parties will not know with certainty the terms of the contract since it is not contained in a comprehensive

228 According to Uvieghara *op. cit.* at p. 21 contracts of employment need be in writing because of the enormous responsibility that flow to both contracting parties so it must be proved and not left to chance. In case of any grievances especially wrongful termination which ends up in a law suit, no evidence of the contract terms or its particulars being pleaded by especially the employee exist, making it disastrous for his/her case.

229 Section 46 Labour Code 1992.

document. In Britain, for example, even if the contracts are oral, the employer must issue within two months of contract a statement of initial employment particulars as required by section 1 of the Employment Rights Act, 1996.[230]

The employers take advantage of this since they will not have an obligation to make payments to the social insurance funds on behalf of the workers. The absence of a written contract makes the workers pawns in the hands of their employers who may throw them out of their employment. After all, the measure of damage even if unfair dismissal is established, will be inconsequential.

The fact that contracts of employment in Cameroon can be in any form and can be evidenced by any means continue to be a serious draw back to employment as espoused above. This situation has been compounded by the fact that a 'modern' and 'new' law like the Labour code failed to take into consideration the digital age. It is true that the words of section 24(3)[231] carry 'any form of evidence may be adduced in proof of its existence" which necessarily include all new information technology means. The revolutionary transformation in technology and the transformation in manner of doings in every sphere of life cannot leave the employment sector indifferent. The lack of a specific mention of it being mandatorily reduced into a hard form including new technologies leaves much to be desired noting the fact that modern employment contracts are electronic. Based on the code as it is, when do such contracts become effective under Cameroonian law?

The out break of covid-19 and other forms of communicable disease like the ebola and the automation of work and telecommuting are also affecting and are changing the notion of work place, as what a work place is has to be addressed in tandem with new realities which demand new work skills. Work is performed not necessarily in the business premises (factories) of the employer as it then was. It now includes private houses, *etc* of the employee. As opined by Parli[232] the digital revolution also made physical location of work performance less important but with serious effect on employment relations as the worker may be exposed to work for long hours with effect on his health and family life, although it becomes beneficial to the employer who will be able

230 See generally, Painter. R.W., Holmes. A.,& Migdal. S., *Cases and Materials on Employment law*, 3rd Edition, Hampshire: Blackstone Press Ltd, 2000, 79-82.

231 "Subject to the provisions of section 27, the existence of the contract may be recorded in whatever manner the contracting parties find convenient. Any form of evidence may be adduced in proof of its existence."

232 Parli, K, "Impacts of digitalization on employment relations and the need for more democracy at work" *Industrial law Journal* 2021, p. 6.

to not only have access to the employer's life which the Industrial Revolution had syphoned but will now be able to a large extent effectively control the activities of the employee. The employer will be able to have active employees committed to achieving the greater objectives of the employers.

From the employee's perspective, they may be able to enjoy autonomy and the flexibility will give them better balance between their work time, their personal life including family life.

a. Non-Compulsory Conditions

Some employments may require that before employment, the worker undergo vocational training which comprises according to section 10 of Law No. 2018/010 of 10th July 2018 (governing Vocational Training in Cameroon) initial vocational training, continuing vocational training and apprenticeship implanted in centres established by natural or corporate bodies with the sole aim of imparting skills and competences required to practice a trade and gain access to a job - section 1 (2) 2018 Law. Sometimes, the employer may want to appraise a particular worker before employment contract is signed. In this regard, a probationary hiring contract may be entered into - section 28 (1) LC. Such must be in writing and must not exceed 6 months including renewals, safe in the case of managerial staff whose probationary period may be extended to 8 months – s. 28(2) LC. According to s. 28 (3), the time for recruitment, traveling, training and probation shall not be included in the maximum duration of the trial period and in case of repatriation of any such displaced worker, the cost of such shall be borne by the employer irrespective of the reason for such repatriation[233]. If the worker is kept beyond this period, and no new contract is made, the parties shall be deemed to have entered a final contract which takes effect from the trial period - section 28(5). LC. Where the employer is not satisfied with the output of the worker, he has the right to terminate the probationary hire.

b. Employee/worker Participation in the Management of the Company

Workers (labour) are viewed as factors of production from an economic perspective without regard to the human rights implications

---

[233] Section 28(4) L C 1992.

that are inherent in the labour (worker). Factory owners do not see the need to include employees as major stakeholders in the management of the company that is necessary in modern employment democracy. It cannot be gainsaid that workers are not commodities to be hired and fired at the whimps and caprices of the employer, neither are they "outsiders" in employment democracy whose relevance become necessary only in the maintenance of industrial peace and stability. In modern economies, workers are art and parcel of the an enterprise and for that reason merit to seat in not only the board of directors as a worker director[234] for the proper and better management of the company. Such directors are not only loyal to the companies whose board they seat in but are also diligent and trust worthy since they particularly have an interest to see that they companies stay afloat lest they lose their jobs.

In some jurisdictions, such workers are compelled to be shareholders.

The labour code has no such requirement for employees to seat on the board or to be shareholders which becomes very relevant in safeguarding their employment especially when the company is going through financial difficulty. Perhaps it is because of this major drawback of non-recognition in the Labour Code 1992 of employees as major stakeholders and game changers especially in the face of economic difficulties that has led to the folding up of large companies in recent times especially in the face of crises. The case of workers of Cameroon Development Corporation through the Fako Worker's Union (FAWU) is very indicative[235]. Although the workers acted through the trade union, the agreed to mandatorily save 15% of salary, which would increase the cash flow of CDC. The workers by this agreement raised the sum of 3.5billion XAF that kept CDC afloat and saved it from liquidation, salvaging them from redundancies that would have followed had the corporation been liquidated. This is an apt example of involvement of workers directly as major stakeholders.

---

234 They could be loosely defined as workers who are appointed or elected to seat in the Board of directors as a representative of the workforce.

235 Letter from Vewessee to the Provincial Delegate of Labour and Social Insurance, Buea dated 13th May, 1992. See also Report of the Divisional Inspector of Labour, on Mass Meetings with the workers of the CDC Estates/Services in connection with the economic crisis, in file MESP/SWP/BU.134/Vol. IV, CDC General Correspondence in Konings, P. "Plantation labour and Economic Crisis in Cameroon," *op. cit.* at p.532. See also Letter from FAWU president to General Manager of CDC on Imminent privatisation of CDC, CCTU/FAWU/3/V.5/2366 of 9th March 2000, p.2

2.4 Execution of Contracts of Employment

This section explains powers and the different obligations of the parties in a contract of employment.

2.4.1 The Obligations of the Parties

Employment contracts create obligations with incidents on security of service requiring not only a review of such rights[236] and incidents flowing there from but also a detail analysis to ascertain their effect on security of service.

2.4.2 Employer's Power and Obligations to the Employee

2.4.2.1 The Powers of The Employer

2.4.2.1.i Managerial and Supervisory Powers: These are clearly depicted in section 1 and 23 LC gives the employer power to manage and control of the employee. In this regard, he has the right to organise the employment and supervision of the workplace. He is in charge of assignment of tasks, promotion of staff amongst others.

2.4.2.1.ii Regulatory Powers: The employer has the power to formulate rules in the form of internal rules and regulations of the company. According to section 29 (1), these are rules which relates exclusively to the technical organisation of work, disciplinary standards, safety and hygiene. S. 29 (1) gives the employer powers to unilaterally draw up such rules and notify the staff representative (if any). The internal regulation so drawn becomes binding as prescribed under section 29(3) of the Code after it has received the fiat of the labour inspector as well as proof that it has been relied upon previously as was held by Mokwe J in the Buea High Court case of *Eboa Moukery. v. S.G.B.C.*[237]

---

[236] Hart, in his 'Will' or 'Choice' Theory of Rights, hold that it is not correct for one to claim a right in law simply because the law confers to home such a benefit. To him, such a benefit accrues only when such a person has the right to choose whether to waive an obligation imposed and where there is breach or threatened breach of the right, to leave it unenforced or to choice to enforce it by suing for damages, applying for an injunction, etc, and after the duty to pay compensation. Hart, H.L.A., 'Definition and Theory in Jurisprudence,' (1954) 70 *Law Quarterly Review* 37, at p. 47, in Elegido, J.M., *Jurisprudence*, Lagos: Spectrum law Publishers, 1994, p. 163.

[237] Suit No. HCF/L.20/98-1999 (Unreported)

2.4.2.1.iii Disciplinary Powers: The right of control as contained in the definition of a worker, gives right to the employer to discipline an erring worker. Jani JCA in the North West Court of Appeal decision in *Assurance des Provinces Reunis. v. Tiogum David*[238] after elaborating on the meaning of control, extended the control test to include the power of the employer to discipline his employee where the latter is in breach. He specifically spelt out that one will be a worker amongst others if the master has rights 'of suspension or dismissal.'

Such disciplinary powers include financial sanctions as contained in section 30 (2) which spells out the penalty as being suspension from work with loss of benefits. This is effective only if the procedures contained in section 30(3) (a-c) LC are followed. No employer has the powers to impose fines on workers as a form of workplace discipline - section 30(1) LC.

As noted above the employer has the right to dismiss without notice as a form of professional sanction. This is resorted to if the worker is engaged in a gross misconduct - section 38. But the judge will adjudge proportionality of the sanction and if the proportion of the sanction is less than the misconduct then the dismissal will be deemed wrongful - see the supreme court decision of *Brasseries du Cameroun v. Messe Nzesse Gaspard*[239]. Where a worker was dismissed for consuming two bottles of beers with his visitors during working hours.

2.4.2.2 The Employer's Obligations to the Employee

Sections 1 and 23 of the Labour Code place an obligation on the employer to remunerate anybody who has accepted to place his/ser services under the employer's management and control. This therefore implies into all such employment contracts the obligation not only to remunerate but also to provide work. With the recognition and protection of various rights of the employee by the ILO through the several conventions and other related human rights conventions, the government and employers are obliged to provide labour and social security rights to the employees. This is grounded in article 23 of the Universal Declaration of Human Rights 1948[240] which is the foundation of Ben-Israel's labour justice model. In this model, she contends

[238] (1998) I CCLR Part 4, 62 (Unreported).
[239] Arrete No. 87/ S du 14 Mars 1987.
[240] And Article 6 of ICESCR 1966.

that human rights as contained in the aforementioned two statutes are basic to employment relation, which is an exchange relationship of a special type. She argues further that the social justice for the worker will be achieved under this model only when the dignity of the worker is assured through clearly defined work conditions which must not only be just and favourable but must also reflect the market value and dignity of the worker as well. According to this view, the worker's dignity can only be guaranteed when these rights are scrupulously protected.

2.4.2.2.1 The Obligation to Provide Work

An employer's most basic obligation is to provide work for his/her employee. For purposes of security of tenure, the right to work remains important for the employee. The old English saying that 'practice makes perfect,' is very correct in employment contracts since it is only through work that a worker can improve on the quality of his work. Thus approached, where no work is given, a worker becomes dormant and loses his/her skill in the particular fields he/she was trained in. With time, the quality of his/her work will fall, attracting minimum salary, instead of the high salary he/she would have commanded had their skills been honed through constant practice.

Where a worker's remuneration depends on the amount of work done, refusal to offer work to such a worker could be interpreted as refusal of an opportunity to earn a salary under section 63 of the Labour Code. Where payment is based on commission, there is an implied common law obligation to give work to the servant in spite of the decision of Asquith J in *Collier v. Sunday Referee Publishing Co. Ltd*[241] that contracts of employment do not oblige a master to give a servant work so long as the servant has been paid.

The refusal to offer work even where the worker is paid may amount to constructive dismissal as demonstrated in *Breach v. Epslon Industries Limited.*[242] Here, Breach had been employed as the defendant's chief engineer.

---

241 [1940] 2KB 647. See also Painter, R.W., Holmes, A, & Migdal, S., *Cases and Materials on Employment Law*, Hampshire: Blackstone Press Limited, 3rd Edition, p.136. However, in the case of *Breach. v. Epsylon Industries Ltd* [1976] IRLR 180, Philips J. held quoting Stirling L.J. in *Turner v. Sawdon & Co* [1901] 2KB 653 that there are exception to the general rule where it can be shown that the nature of employment and the circumstances of the case are such that an obligation to provide work on the part of the master arises.

242 [1976] IRLR 180.

The contract for which he was employed was transferred to an overseas office leaving Breach with no work to do. It was held that failure to provide him with work amounted to a constructive dismissal.[243] The rationale behind this view was justified on the basis that once employed, some workers use their work to advertise themselves. Hence, denying them that opportunity is refusal of an opportunity to advertise their skill.[244] Where the job gives a worker an opportunity to advertise his/her skill, not providing the worker with work to do leave such a worker with no possibility for capacity building and the potential to grow in the career including, low job satisfaction and frustration with adverse effect on his psychology and human dignity. The effect on his security of service is only obvious.

In addition, refusal to give work could be seen as a denial and deprivation of equal and fair opportunity for the worker to become skilled in his art. This will negatively affect the worker's proficiency in a highly competitive labour market where employers seek only the finest brains and skills to maximise production and improve on the profitability of the employer.

Ancillary to this is the obligation to be given work within the statutorily required time, which is forty hours per week for all public and private non-agricultural businesses - Under section 80(1) of the Labour Code 1992 and forty-eight hours for agricultural workers which must not exceed two thousand four hundred hours per year under section 80(2) of the Code. S. 2 of Decree No. 95/677/PM of 18th December 1995 has provided equivalent working hours for of 40 hours for night watch men and fire brigade who work for 56hours; 40hours for health personnel and petrol and laundry service who work for 48hours. In order that a worker is not unduly exploited and for purposes of ascertaining over time and remuneration accordingly, the terms and hours of work are negotiated before employment. The weekly work hours does not take into account over time for which extra money has been paid for. - See the case of *Enongene Williams v. University of Buea*[245]. The rate of payment for overtime is calculated as follows: 20% of salary for first 8 hours,

---

243 See however the decision Industrial tribunal's decision in *Turner v. Sawdon & Co* [1990] KB 653, where it seems lays the principle that employers are under no obligation to provide their employees with work to do. Notwithstanding, Phillips J in the *Breach Case* held that if that were so, then there was a misdirection of the law because there was the need to look at the background to the contract to see how it can be construed, and whether a term ought not to be implied that in the circumstances of the case there is an obligation to provide work suitable for the work with such rank and skills.

244 Epie, N.M, *Rights and Duties of Employers and Employees under the Cameroon Labour Code*, Unpublished LL.B dissertation, 2008.

245 1999, CFIK (unreported)

30% of salary for the next 8 hours; 40% of salary for the rest up to 20 hours per week; 40% of salary for Sunday's hours 50% of salary for night hours and holidays. For a worker without a contract of employment it becomes difficult to ascertain if the employee has the normal working hours. This is important in ascertaining the hour which the work is to be executed, since it will amount to night work if the work is done between ten p.m and six a.m pursuant to section 81 of the Labour Code 1992, warranting additional pay except the night shift is a consequence of the nature of the job. The employer has the right to recover lost hours which the worker did not work for the statutory 40hours but he must inform the competent labour inspector of his intention.

Section 82 (2) of the Labour Code 1992[246] prohibits women and children from night work except where the woman holds an executive position or the work to be done by the woman is not manual. The relevance of this to security of employment is that even after the crisis with the difficulty in finding jobs, violation are scarcely reported as it may cause them to lose their badly needed jobs.[247] This is so notwithstanding the fact that the Code in sections 168 (1) and 168 (8) punishes employers with a fine of from two hundred thousand francs to one million five hundred thousand francs. In case of recidivism, the punishment is imprisonment for from six days to six months in accordance with section 170 (1) of the Code.

2.4.2.2.2 Safety at Work

Both the Common Law and the Labour Code protect the worker against industrial accidents and occupational diseases. Under both regimes, there is a duty to provide not just a safe work place but also a safe and suitable work system. In deed an employer is supposed to take reasonable care not to subject his employees to unnecessary risk in the course of employment[248].

---

246 And ILO Convention No. 89 on Night Work (Women) Convention (revised), 1948 was ratified by Cameroon in 1970.

247 Such protective legislation may in a way hold back a woman from gaining independence and economic and social power.

248 The likelihood of injury and other factors must be taking into consideration in deciding whether some precaution should be taken against foreseeable risk, to weigh on the one hand the magnitude of the risk, the likelihood of an accident happening and the possible seriousness of the consequences. – see The House of Lords decision in *Morris v. W. Hartlepool S.N* [1956] 1 All. E.R. 385. In this regard, as pointed by Whincup, the more likely the injury the more the employer is required to guard against such. Secondly, the employer is supposed to take reasonable care of the potential seriousness of the damage and whether the damage was obvious

This duty is established only if there is the existence of an employer/employee relationship. The duty has been construed to include the organisation of work, safe plant[249] and safe work environment. Since labour is resident in a human being as well as his/her skill and proficiency which is her/his human capital, his/her safety is a primary consideration and his/her job security is dependent on it. There is therefore a real link between safety at work[250] and security of service. It was demonstrated in *Mofa Ngoe David v. Plantation du Haut Penja*[251] that an employer may be tempted to terminate the services of an injured worker who because of his industrial accident or occupational disease became uncompetitive.[252]

The employer's liability to the worker is two-fold. The first relates to the personal liability caused directly by the master's lack of care or the vicarious liability imputed on him through the lack of care of another servant acting in the course of lawful employment.[253] Both liabilities were extended by Lord Wright in *Wilson & Clyde Coal Co Ltd v. English*[254] to a fourfold duty requiring

---

249 Where the plant or any of its parts are potentially dangerous they must be fenced. The employer's obligation does not end with the provision of these work tools as an employer has an obligation to warn and insist on the usage of the protective devices throughout the execution of their functions. In Cameroon, even after the economic crises, this has remained purely theoretical as workers in the informal sector especially in small and medium size enterprises are not provided with such safety devices by employer. Buying such devices is waste of money which could have been ploughed into the business to generate more profits, oblivious of the fact that a worker whose right is guaranteed will be more performant than other wise. An employer rarely regards a worker as a factor of production worthy of protection like the other production implements.

250 Which started as employer's liability in tort if the worker suffered from injuries, it was considered that he had voluntarily consented under doctrine of common employment, although the master was duty bound not expose the servant to risks if he knew of the danger. Per Lord Abinger in *Priestley v. Fowler* (1837) 3 M. & W.1 In Cameroon, this doctrine of Common employment was abolished by Ordinance No. 59/100 of 31st December 1959. It provided that any term in an employment purporting to exclude the liability of the employment or his insurance company for injuries sustained by his worker through the default of a fellow servant is void and against public policy.

251 Suit No.HCF/L.001/2004-2005 (unreported).

252 See also *TRAPP Groupement d'Entreprise v. Che Guza Cletus* Appeal No. BCA/L.2/98,

253 A position explained by Lord Hershell in *Smith v. Baker & Sons* [1831] A.C. 325 as including the duty of taking reasonable care to provide proper appliances and to maintain them in a proper condition.

254 [1938] A.C 57. See also Pearce LJ in *Wilson v. Tyneside Findow Cleaning Co.* [1958] 2. All. E.R. 265. Who pointed out that although one may divide up the duty of a master into three main headings for convenience of definition, or arguments; all three are ultimately only manifestations of the same duty of the master to take reasonable care so as to carry out his operations as no to subject those employed by him to unnecessary risk.

the responsibility to[255]; i) select competent fellow servants[256]; ii) provide safe machinery and appliances[257]; iii) proper work system[258]; iv) a safe work place.[259] The Court of Appeal of the South West had recognised the above in the case of *CDC v. Akem Ben Bella*,[260] where CDC was held liable for failing to provide appropriate work tools for its workers. Viscount Simmonds in the House of Lords case of *Davie v. Newton Merton Board Mill*[261] obligates the employers to warn against danger inherent in the employment, the work tools and system.[262] Where this is done but the employee remains adamant, the

---

255 The defendants in this case are a mining company. The plaintiff is a workman suffered injuries that led to his death at his work place whilst repairing an airway –a main haulage road. The haulage plant was put in motion crushing him as he was unable to escape. His family brought an action for damages. But the employers claimed that his negligence caused his death as he should have told the person in charge of the machine or taken an alternative route. The house of Lords held that the employers had a non-delegable duty to create a safe work system. Even where the employer gives that duty to another person, they still remain accountable for workplace safety.

256 *Rudd's Case* [1933] 1 KB 566 which makes the employer vicariously liable should the co-worker cause injury to another employee in the course of employment. This may occur where a co-worker lacks necessary skills thereby exposing co-workers to danger. This may also occur in case of dangerous personality of co-worker (e.g bully, reckless joker, games) – *Smith v. Crossley Brothers* [1951] 95 Sol. Jo 655. Whether the employer fulfils this obligation depends on the employer's knowledge of the employee.. see for example *Coddington v. International Harvester Co. of Gt Britain* [1969] KIR 146.

257 See Also *Reid v. Rush & Tomkins Group PLC* [1989] IRLR 265' *Bradford v. Robinson* Rental [1967] 1 ALL ER 267 employee suffered from frost bite as a result of driver for long hours in winter without necessary safety gear; *Sloan v. Almond* [1992] access to a 22feet high vertical ladder with no protective hoop; *Riddick v. Weir Housing Corp* [1970] industrial accident of dermatitis as a result of handling cement and brick in a building site;

258 An experienced workman is expected to know the risk inherent in the job he is supposed to do (see for example *Baker v. Clarke* [1992] where an electrical was injured because he failed to lock the wheels of a mobile scaffolding and the employer was not held liable, although the employer is supposed to maintain a safe work environment

259 *Ibid* at p. 80. See *Latimer v. A.E.C* [1953]. This duty includes and requires the employer to assess the way the work is to be done, precautions to be taken, supervision, warnings and notices of such, protective gears. The employers obligation may be limited to the provision of such material if the risk was obvious or foreseeable - *Qualcast (Wolverhampton) Ltd v. Haynes* [1959] AC 743. In addition, this obligation extends to protection of the employee against acts of violence if there is a foreseeable risk given the nature of the work - *Charlton v. The Forest Painting Ink Co.* [1978] IRLR 559. See in general - Painter *et al, Cases and Material On Employment law*, Hampshire: Blackstone Press Limited, p 842.

260 *Supra* where Bawak JCA highlighted the extent of this common law obligation adopted in Cameroon as ' reasonable care to provide proper appliances and to maintain them in proper condition and to carry on his operation as not to subject those employed to unnecessary risk'. See in particular Yanou *op. cit.* at p. 49.

261 Per Viscount Simmonds in the House of Lords Case of *Davie v. Newton Merton Board Mills* [1959] A.C 604.

262 As per Lawton LJ in *White v. Holbrook Precision Castings Ltd* [1985] 1RLR 215 at p. 218; ' ....generally speaking, if a job has risks to health and safety which are not common knowledge but which an employer knows or ought to know and against which he cannot guard by taking

employer may exceptionally in that instance plead the defence of *volenti non fit injuria*[263] as was held in *Imperial Chemical Industries v. Shatwell.*[264]

As pointed out by Whincup[265] the employer must ensure that the employee knows of the existence of the danger by making a full and frank disclosure of this[266]. In addition, such an employer must ensure that the employee knows the precautions to take against such danger and that such precautions are available and the employees are put on notice of the available precautions.

Section 95 (1) of the Labour Code 1992 incorporates the common law duties articulated in the *Wilson's Case* above, which requires that safety at work must conform to the ILO standards. The Cameroonian position is fixed by Ministerial Order No. 139/MTPS/1MI of 26th November 1984. Although the National Occupational Health and Safety Commission was put in place to determine the occupational health and safety conditions of employees, suffice it to say much is still left to be done.[267]

Although popular opinion thinks otherwise, where workers suffers from occupational[268] or industrial accidents[269] they are supposed to be compensated by the National Social Insurance Fund[270] regardless of whether they are registered with (NSIF) or not. Section 17(6) of Law No. 77/11 of 13th July 1977 places responsibility on the NSIF to take charge of all such accidents and to claim re-imbursements from the employers who have not registered their employees. It is in the alternative possible for the employee to recover damages covering compensation for injury sustained from an employer who failed to

---

precautions, then he should tell anyone to whom he is offering a job what those risks are if, on the information then available to him, knowledge of those risks would be likely to affect the decision of a sensible level-headed prospective employee about accepting the offer.'

263 See however the decision of Scott L.J. in *Bowater v. Rowley Regis Corporation* [1944] K.B. 476. Where he doubted whether the maxim can often apply in circumstances of an injury to a servant by the negligence of his master.

264 [1965] A.C. 656. Here,

265 Whincup. M.H., *Modern Employment Law: A Guide to Job Security and Safety*, Oxford: Butterworth Heinemann, 8th edition, 1995, 266-265.

266 *Stokes v. G.K.N* [1986]

267 The breach of statutory duties by the employer is different completely from other common law duties. As was held in *Dairies v. Health & Safety Executive* [2002] although the statutes may impose strict liability on the employer, the burden is on the employer to show that it is not reasonably practicable to comply with the safety regulations.

268 Any disease emanating from the performance of certain employment as per section 3 of Law No. 77/11 of 13th Jul 1977. This must first be in the list of occupational diseases adopted by the Ministry of Labour.

269 Defined in section 2 of Decree No 78/549 of 28th December 1978 governing industrial accidents and occupational diseases as all accidents resulting from work or during work, or travel to work and from principal or secondary residence which gives a certain character of permanence.

270 Created in 1973 by Ordinance No. 73-17 of 22nd May 1973.

register its employee.[271] Employers are aware of this non-implementation of section 17 above. A lot of them do not register their employees, thus depriving the workers of their wages and causing them hardship when they suffer from occupational or industrial accidents or finally retire. A case in point is *Mafany Godlove Namme v. Mbonge Rural Council.*[272] Here, the employee asked the court to redress the injustice he had suffered as a result of non-registration and non-payment of his insurance dues to the NSIF in spite of the fact that the defendants had retained 2.8% of his monthly salary for seventeen years. This caused the plaintiff to lose his retirement pension, delivery allowance for four children and also family allowance. The High Court judge held that, having failed to contribute, the defendants are bound to step into the shoes of the NSIF and pay the plaintiff his dues. Therefore, the plaintiff was paid for all the accrued benefits he had requested amounting to eight million FCFA.[273]

2.4.2.2.2.a Vicarious Liability of Employers

This obligation opens up responsibility on the employer to be liable for injuries in the course of employment caused to the employee by employer and other co-workers[274]. This liability has been conceptualised in s. 173 of the Labour Code. The four fold obligation on safety at work as expounded by Lord Wright in *Wilson & Clyde Coal Co Ltd v. English*[275] requires not only

---

271 This is in addition to the fact that the worker can press for criminal prosecution of the employee

272 Suit No. HCF/L.001/2003-2004. NSIF could not pay CDC's pensioners during the periods between 1998-2003 because of non – respect of payments by the corporation of quotas of social insurance contributions which the corporation had already deducted from these employees. These caused serious hardship to old retirees would had dutifully contributed but which because of the corporation's bad faith jeopardised their social security labour justice and hence security of tenure, which involves payment of dues even after retirement.

273 Instead of dealing with the issue on one to one basis, there ought to be heavy penalty for non-payment and non-registration of a worker with the NSIF by the employer.

274 The defense of common employment or fellow servant rule where an employee was injured or contracted a disease as a result of the unsafe practice of a fellow employee, the employer could escape responsibility for that employee's actions and there could not be any claim against the employer and there will be no reason claiming from the fellow employee who would in any case be a man of straw. This was based on the fictitious implied term in the contract of service to the effect that the servant agreed to run the risks naturally inherent to his employment one of which was harm by a fellow co-employee. See the case of Priestly v.Fowler (1837) 3 M & W 1. where it was first applied. Where Lord abinger refused the workman's claim on grounds that it will act as an encouragement to the worker to omit that he has the duty to exercise diligence and caution against the misconduct of his co-worker. This defense abolished in Cameroon by ordinance No. 59/100 of 31st December 1959

275 [1938] A.C 57. See also Pearce LJ in *Wilson v. Tyneside Findow Cleaning Co.* [1958] 2. All. E.R. 265. Who pointed out that although one may divide up the duty of a master into three main headings

for the employer to provide safe work environment and plant, he need to also ensure that the employee is not exposed to or suffer from harm as a result of the fault of a fellow co-worker. In the above case, the fault might have been as result of poor supervisory control for which he knew or ought to have known that the employee was dangerous[276]. It has been argued that there is no need to differentiate between vicarious liability and the employer's primary liability but this differentiation becomes important if the injury caused to the employee is outside the course of employment, the employer is not vicariously liable although he will be in breach of his primary obligation to provide competent staff.

Vicarious liability is the liability imputed on the employer as result of the injuries suffered by employees caused by fellow co-workers in the course of employment.[277] The injured worker has the right to either sue the employer instead of the erring employee and/or the employee. As explained by Lord Brougham in *Duncan v. Findlater*[278]:

> ...... I take to be this: I am liable for what is done for me and under orders by the man I employ, for I may turn him off from that employ when I please; and the reason that I am liable is this, that by employing him I set the whole thing in motion; and what he does; being done for my benefit and under my direction, I am responsible for the consequences of doing it.[279]

for convenience of definition, or arguments; all three are ultimately only manifestations of the same duty of the master to take reasonable care so as to carry out his operations as no to subject those employed by him to unnecessary risk.

276 Whincup, M.H., *Modern Employment: A Guide To Job Security And Safety; Op. cit.* at p268, see Lord Scarman in *Rose v. Plenty* [1976] 1 All E.R. 97, at page 103 where he explained the situation as 'the employer putting things in motion'.

277 This doctrine could be traced back to the case of *Priestley v. Fowler* (1873) 3 M & W 1, where it was assumed that am employee impliedly accepted the risks incidental to employment including negligence of other fellow employees. This was based on the assumption that there would be heavy financial burden on the employer if the number of compensation to such victims was large. As pointed by Jones, "the unholy trinity of common employment, *volenti non fit injuria* and contributory negligence prevented virtually any employees. The concept of an employer's personal, non-delegable duty for the safety of his workers was developed specially to avoid the common employment defense." Jones, M.A., *Torts*, Blackstone Press Limited, 1995, p.173

278 (1839) 6 CL & F 894

279 *Ibid* at 909-910. Similarly in *CDC v. Akem Benbella* (1997) 1 CCLR 313-319, Bawak JCA held that" in law, one reason it may be important whether B is a Servant or an independent contractor is that a master is vicariously liable for torts committed by his servant while acting in the course of employment."

This doctrine has roots in the maxim that - he who acts through another acts for himself. Mindful of this, the master is responsible for acts of his servants especially as he had the responsibility of choosing his servants[280] acts under his control and who has the responsibility of exercising that function with skill and care. Lord Reid in the case of *Staveley Iron & Chemical Co. Ltd v. Jones*[281] averred that the employer is liable based on the maxim of *respondent superior*. The liability of the employer is joint and several. This gives room for the injured to choose who to sue and enables the party with stronger financial strength to bear the financial burden. In some jurisdiction this is seen as part of the financial risk of the company and also as cost of production.[282]

In the case of safety at work as explained above, the employer is liable for his acts of omission or commission which the injured employee has to so prove[283]. But in the case of vicarious liability, the employee has to show proof of negligence on the part of the co-worker in the course of employment not necessarily due to any negligent acts or fault of the employer. The employer is liable even if there was nothing he could do to avoid such accident. The burden is on the injured employee to adduce evidence as to the vicarious liability of the employer. For such an employer to be held liable, it must be shown that:

i. There must be a legal wrong (tort, contract or crime) committed by the employee. In this regard the person who commits the injury must be an employee with the meaning and context expounded in chapter one above.
ii. The employee's wrongful act must be in the course of employment otherwise the employee alone will be liable. As pointed out by Salmond:[284]

"...... the master is responsible for acts actually authorised by him; for liability would exist in this case, even if the relation between the parties was merely one of agency and not one of service at all. But a master, as opposed to an employer of an independent contractor,

---

280 See Bramwell LJ in *Swanson v. North-Eastern Railway Co* (1878)11 Ex D 341 at p348.

281 [1956] AC 627, at p 643

282 That is why in Britain, for example Insurance against liability for personal injury to employee is compulsory under the Employer's Liability (Compulsory Insurance) Act 1969

283 In cases where the employee sues for negligence in employment, the employee must establish that duty of care exists, breach of which led to the injuries suffered - See *Donoghue v. Stevenson* [1932] AC562; Lord Wilberforce in *Anns v. Merton LBC* [1977] 2 All ER 492 and Lord Bridge in *Caparo Industries v. Dickman* [1990] 1 All ER 568

284 Salmond On *Torts*, 18th edition p. 437-438.

is liable for acts which he has not authorised, provided they are so connected with acts which he has authorised that they may rightly be regarded as modes-though improper modes-of doing them.....on the other hand, if the authorised and wrongful act of the servant is not so connected with the authorised act as to be a mode of doing it, but is an independent act, the master is not responsible; for in such a case the servant is not acting in the course of his employment, but has gone outside of it".

It is clear that the employer vicariously liable for what he expressly, impliedly or apparently asked the employee to do. He will be still be liable even if the employee does what he was employed to do in a disobedient, dishonest or careless manner. The employer will therefore be vicariously liable in tort for careless or negligent acts of his employees in the course of business as was seen for example in the case of *Kay v. I.T.W*[285] where a store man whose job involved driving a fork lift truck and small vans moved a five ton lorry that was in his way. There was no emergency and the store man made no attempt to find the driver of the lorry. It was held by the Court of Appeal that the store man acted in the course of employment since he wanted to remove the obstructing lorry in order to do his own job. The employer will also be liable for breach of contracts by his employee in the course of employment.[286] Also the employer can be held vicariously liable for the crimes of his employee in the course of employment. However, though the employer will not be sentenced for the crime committed he will be liable to pay compensation for any injury resulting therefrom.[287] Vicarious liability does not free the employee from any legal action as such a workman may be dismissed from his function if his action violates the terms of his employment. He may also have to indemnify the employer especially if he did not have authority to act or in particularly blameworthy cases.

Sometimes a workman may be sent to work for another employer and an injury is caused to another in the course of employment. The question usually arise as to who of the two is vicariously liable for the injury. In the Privy Council

---

285 [1967] 3 All E.R. 22

286 See the case of *Photo Productions and Securicor* [1980] 1 All E.R. 556 where the a company which contracted to supply a night patrol service would have been liable but for the exclusion clauses for the damage done by its patrol man who not appreciating his job requirements set ablaze the factory.

287 In *Nahhas v. Pier House* [1984] 270 EG. 328 the employer was liable to compensate the residents of the property when a resident porter with whom keys were entrusted and was job it was to care for the property stole the property of the resident.

decision of *Donavan v. Laing, Wharton & Doan Construction Syndicate*[288] it was held that the employer who has control over the activities of the employee is responsible. But the decision in the case of *Mersey Docks & Harbour Board v. Coggins & Griffiths (Liverpool) ltd*[289] it was held that although the temporary employee had control over the crane driver with regards to what they wanted him to do but not how the work was to be done. The burden of proof was therefore on the permanent employers to proof that the temporary employer had control over the employee - crane driver as to how to do the work. On that basis, the crane driver remained the permanent employer's employee.[290] If however the injury is caused by the execution of authorised orders given by the temporary employer, the temporary employer may in such circumstance be vicariously liable.

2.4.2.2.2.b The Doctrine of Contributory Negligence

At law, there is no recovery of damages for one whose negligence proximately contributed to his injury.[291] This position also applies in employment law.[292] This position is justified in that the worker could have avoided harm through his/her own care by taking necessary precaution and protection. In addition it will seem improper to provide total recovery to someone who is blameworthy in causing the injury. Contributory negligence was a total defence with no account being taken of any fault on the part of the employer, as per Lord Campbell CJ in *Butterfield v. Forrester*[293] the want of ordinary care in avoiding an injury disentitles the party inured from suing. Because it is inequitos to place the burden entirely on the employee when both the employee and the employer were negligent in their actions. The comparative contributory negligence now gives the court some allowance to apportion damages to both the employer and employee commensurate to the level of their contribution to the injury.

---

288 [1893] 1 QB 629

289 [1947] AC 1

290 Per lord Uthwatt "the workman may remain the employee of his general employer, but at the same time, the result of the arrangements may be that there is vested in the hirer a power of control over the workman's activities sufficient to attach to the hirer responsibility for the workman's acts and defaults and to exempt the general employer from that responsibility".

291 Cole, R.B., "Negligence – assumption of risk-duplication of scope of duty or contributory Negligence" *Natural Resources Journal*, Vol 7, 1967 at p. 657.

292 Sugarman, S.D. "Assumption of risk," *Valparaiso Law Review*, Vol 31(3), 1997, 1t p.852.

293 (1855) 5 T & B 855.

2.4.2.2.2.c Assumption of Risk

Where workers were injured in the course of their employment or contracted diseases in the course of their employment, their claims was defeated in the basis that that they assumed all risk incidental to their employment. In this regard, a worker who confronted a known danger was held necessarily to have chosen to do so as per Cockburn LJ in *Woodley v. Metropolitan District co*[294], "a man who enters on a necessarily dangerous employment with his eyes open takes it with its accompanying risks". This Common Law Position was adopted in Cameroon by Moutchia JCA in *China International Water & Ano v. Ndinwa Wilfred*[295] where he held that' contracting to work with dynamites is accepting all the risk that go with it....[296]. This decision therefore presupposes that the employer owes no duty to the worker. It is assumed that the employer has the responsibility to inform fully the worker of all the dangers inherent in his employment to enable such a worker make informed consent to the employment.

2.4.2.3 Duty to Provide Social Insurance

All employers have an obligation to register their employees with the NSIF 8 days after employment. The employer must declare all professional risks and occupational diseases and assist the worker in the submissions for NSIF benefit such as family allowance, industrial accidents, old age, and deaths. The employer must make NSIF contributions for all workers to the tune of 8.4% of the emplyee's basic salary for old age, invalidity and death pensions, increased with 4.2% as employer's contribution for same and 1.75% to 5% for industrial and professional risks.

2.4.2.4 The Obligation to Provide Rest

In order to protect the worker from wanton exploitation by an employer, Section 88 (1) of the Labour Code, 1992[297], prescribes compulsory weekly rests which shall consist of at least 24 consecutive hours each week. The

---

294 (1877) 2 Ex D.384.

295 (2005) 1 CCLR 111.

296 *Ibid* at page 122

297 See also article 24 of the Universal Declaration of Human Rights 1948, ILO Convention No. 14, On Weekly Rest (Industry) Convention, 1921, ratified by Cameroon in 1960.

provision also makes Sunday a non-working day which cannot be replaced by a compensatory allowance[298]. Where the employee is a woman or a child, they shall be entitled to a daily rest period of not less than twelve consecutive hours.[299]

Paid annual leave accrues to workers who have worked for a period of one year[300] to a leave of eighteen working days calculated at the rate of one and a half working days for each month of actual service except the parties agree otherwise.[301] Ancillary to this is a right to a maximum of ten days a year for an unpaid leave of absence to attend to family issues affecting his nuclei family.[302]

According to section 84(1) of the Labour Code, a female employee whose pregnancy has been attested by a medical officer is protected from dismissal on account of the pregnancy. The fact that she may without notice terminate the contract without paying the necessary compensation required by section 36 of the Code,[303] clearly shows that the provision was intended to strengthen the security of service of employment involving women.

Furthermore, since a worker is not a slave, where there is a certificate of ill health as defined by sections 1(1) and (2) of Decree No. 78/549 of 28th December 1978,[304] their contracts of employment can be suspended by a six months sick leave. This is a provision that also strengthens the security of service, which may be extended if the worker can no longer assume his/her function.

---

298 See *Ndode Ajang Mbo Elvis v. Muyuka Agro-industrial firm* MINTSS/PDTSS/SWP/BU-28/C/607, where a worker sued for work done on Sunday amongst others and it was held by the labour inspector that the plaintiff be compensated for work done on Sunday. Yanou questions whether the strict and inflexible tenor of section 88 are not amendable by the contracting parties. He concludes that it will be absurd if parties are not given the opportunity to act otherwise mindful of the peculiarities of certain employments. After all, it is a contract and all contracts are private negotiations tailored to suit the contracting parties needs, Yanou *op. cit.* at p.46. Tabe is of the opinion that since leave is given for the worker to rest in order to be better performant and so payment in lieu of leave is prohibited according to section 92(2) Labour Code 1992. Tabe *op. cit.* at p.173. In addition it is opined that tis section raises a lot of dust as it gives preference to Christian workers to the detriment of their non-Christan counterparts.

299 Section 82(1) Labour Code 1992.

300 This could however be for periods above a year but not over two years if so bargained for during the contract negotiations.

301 Section 89(1) Labour Code 1992. These are calculated according to modalities specified in section 89(3) of the Labour Code 1992. However as prescribed by section 90 (3), depending on the seniority of the worker, the leave period shall be increased to two working days instead of one and a half. For persons under the age of 18 the leave shall accrue at the rate of two and a half days as per section 90(1) of the Code. For mothers the period will be for two working days for each child she has who is below the age of six.

302 As defined in Yanou *op. cit.* at p. 48.

303 She will not be liable to pay the employer.

304 The decree Governing Industrial Accidents and occupational Diseases.

2.4.2.5 The Obligation to Pay Wages

The right to consideration for work done by a worker is fundamental under sections1(2) and 23(1)[305] of the Code. The duty to pay wages is an essential feature of employment. It may be observed that by article 7 of ICESCR 1966, the wage earned must be capable of supporting the worker and his family otherwise this may lead to debt bondage[306] forcing the worker to become a bonded labourer.[307]

Although wage must be paid in money (legal tender)[308] at regular intervals not exceeding one month, a worker may request for half month's pay at the end of fifteen (worked) days pursuant to section 68(1) of the Code. Pay whether

---

305 Section 61 (1) of the labour Code defines remuneration (wage) as earnings however calculated capable of being evaluated in terms of money and fixed by mutual agreement, regulations or collective agreements paid as consideration for work done. See also the Supreme Court Decision in *Affaire SCTA* Bulletin *D'arrêts* p.175 of 2nd May 1967 which defines wages as consideration for work done. This definition is extended in Britain in section 27 Employment Rights Act 1996 to include any fee, bonus commission holiday pay or any emolument referable to his employment, sick pay, statutory maternity leave, sums payable on suspension on maternity grounds, pension, allowance or gratuity, expenses incurred by a worker in the course of employment and sums payable as a result of re-instatement order or re-engagement. This clarity and certainty of the benefits which accrue to a worker stemming from their employment strengthens security of service as a worker knows in advance with certainty (even if only constructive) the entitles due in any given situation. Section 27 of the Employment Act 1996 is more far reaching than section 67 which does not expressly see all these other payments as wages.

306 See for example the Supreme Court of India Decision in *Bandua Mukti Morcha v. Union of Bank of India & Others, Supreme Court Reports (1984)*, Vol 2. p.67, in Weissbrodt, D., *op. cit.* at p. 15

307 To avert this especially in developing countries, ILO Convention No. 131 concerning the Minimum Wage Fixing, with special Reference to Developing Countries 1970 and also convention No. 135 to give wage-earners the necessary social protection in terms of minimum permissible levels of wages, Convention 99 and its recommendation No. 89 applicable to agriculture all require that the minimum wage should not be fixed at a lower rate than one which ensure the subsistence of the worker and his/her family, Weissbrodt, D., *op. cit.* at p. 16. Notwithstanding these, the take home pay of workers in Cameroon ought at least to be not less than 36270FCFA this cannot sustain a worker in major towns where the cost of living keep rising. With these low incomes the dignity, mental and physical integrity of the worker cannot be assured. In a Cameroonian setting, a worker (especially A man) who cannot adequately provide for his family is no worker (man). This impacts on their output and may result in his /her inefficiency and eventual dismissal.

308 Section 67 Labour Code 1992 also makes any other mode of payment unlawful to the extent that any other contrary mode of payment is null and void. This is similar to section 1(1) of the Labour Act (Cap 198 of the Laws of the Federation of Nigeria, 1990, that where wages are paid for otherwise than by legal tender the contract is not only illegal but null and void and the servant will then recover the wages as a *quantum meruit* although the contracting parties may agree to payment by Cheque or postal order if it is not prohibited by statute and if expressly agreed by writing by the worker. Uvieghara *op. cit.* at p. 118. This notwithstanding, Many of those employed as domestic servants who usually do not have contracts and who are not paid wages or if at all it is in kind where the master/mistress promise to send the servant to learn a trade after rendering services for the former for an indefinite period. In some instances, these servants are 'settled"

for a full or half month interval shall be evidenced by a pay voucher made out in the prescribed form.[309] A worker is entitled to his/her wages only when as noted in *Pamol Plantation Ltd v. William Kimbeng*,[310] it has become accrued.[311]

The obligation to remunerate the worker also covers all fringe benefits, which a worker is entitled to, including severance pay, which accrues to a worker who has worked for at least two consecutive years.[312] Under section 36(1) of the Code, employers are obliged to pay bonuses and allowances which a worker would have received for the period of notice which was not observed by the employer in the event of termination without notice.[313]

Where a worker is owed wages, prompt action must be taken to redress his/her situation by lodging a complaint with the Labour Inspector otherwise they will be time barred if they exceed three years[314] as per section 74(1) of the Labour Code. This does not strengthen security of employment as the worker may only realise after the three year period that they had some financial dues pending. This is because not all employers give documents to employees informing them of their due wages.

A worker is not supposed to suffer from unauthorised deductions from his salary except there is an error in computation. Any short fall in wages is an authorised deduction, especially if the worker has already earned the wage. Although this is prohibited by section 75 of the Code, it is still common in Cameroon today where it is difficult to say with certainty the exact wage one earns at the end of the month as the salary varies.

In order to meet up with, for example, high taxes, employers push the cost of the taxes on to the workers. Without any formal negotiations they cut off salaries, which even though regarded by some as insignificant, at the end of the day the entrepreneur comes out with a treasure.[315]

---

the servant to start of his own trade. It is this promise to settle or learn a trade that keeps the servants bonded to the employers since they cannot leave for fear of losing the promise of a future entitlement based on uncertainty and the goodwill of their master. This is a typical example of bonded labour and therefore contemporary form of slavery, bad for security of service. See generally on this Weisbrodt, D., *Abolishing Slavery and its Contemporary Form*, United Nations, 2002. P. 15

309 The payments is due not more than eight days after the end of month under section 68 (2) of the Code.

310 (2001) 2 CCLR 127-251

311 As was held By Ngange J, in *Mbide Carles kude v. GEACAM* Suit No. HCF/L.021/ 2000-2001 (unreported).

312 Also under Section 37 of the Labour Code 1992 a contract of unspecified duration is terminated by the employer.

313 These payments are made according to modalities spelt out in Ministerial Circular No 016/MTPS/SG/LJ of 26th May 1993 which took effect as from 1 July 1997.

314 *Catholic Education Secretary v. Ndip Aaron Oben* Suit No. CASWP/L.12/2001-2002 (unreported).

315 Although civil servants are not within the contemplation of book, in practice their salaries are not fix as the amount received by them vary with no explanations given as to the deductions. This attitude extends even to pensioners.

The requirement for the provision of payslips enhances the security of service in employment. Forbang J., in the case of *Barro Gregory v. National Employment Fund,*[316] has held that in cases of disputes the payslip helps the courts to ascertain which components of a worker's wages his employer has dropped. Since from the above decision the use of payslips tends to increase the damages to be paid, it is more likely that employments in which payslips are paid are potentially more secured.

Generally, workers employed for the same type of work ought to receive like payments.[317] In Cameroon, pay must meet the requirement of Prime Ministerial which fixes the minimum salary scale to be 36270 francs CFA per month. This amount is too small to meet up with the basic needs of food, shelter and health of the worker and dependents, especially with the current high cost of living. Weissbrodt[318] observes that a worker must not earn a salary that will make him/her extremely desperate as it will not allow him/her the opportunity to a decent living for himself/herself and dependents, thereby offending his/her dignity which the work was supposed to protect. With the ever-rising food prices as well as those of most basic needs, it is opined that this salary scale cannot afford a worker a decent living but will instead convert such workers into perpetual debtors, in contravention of ILO Convention No.131.[319]

Veweesee[320] has observed that the watering down of employment and wage protection measures in the Labour Code, 1992, raises questions as to the seriousness of the government of Cameroon in dealing with the labour and

---

316 Suit No HCF/L.022/2005-2006 (unreported).

317 See article 23(2) of the Universal Declaration Of Human Rights 1948 the ILO Convention No. 100 on Equal Remuneration 1951, which Cameroon ratified in 1970, Article of African Charter on Human and peoples' Rights and Section 61(2) of the Labour Code 1992. section 62(2) requires that wages applicable to occupational categories shall only be determined by collective bargaining agreements between the enterprise, the workers representatives and a labour inspector. The body in charge of fixing the salary scale is the *Salaire Minimum Inter-Professionnel Guarantee (SMIG)* it is difficult to ascertain whether the salary scales are based according to zones, regions or hourly.

318 Weisbrodt, D.. *Abolishing Slavery and its Contemporary Form*, United Nations, 2002. p. 15.

319 On Minimum Wage fixing with special reference to Developing Countries 1970 ratified by Cameroon in 1973. The state by ratifying this makes a firm obligation to protect workers from 'slave-like salaries which this far it has failed to do as is seen in corporations undergoing privatisation especially CDC. Yanou and Fonyam observe that the unilateral change of salary rate based on flat rate in disrespect of the skill, proficiency and longevity coupled with the suspension of certain fringe benefits and medical facilities by the new owners of Tole Tea estate that led to the strikes and unrest in that enterprise. Furthermore quoting the United Nations Commissioner For Human Rights they drew an analogy that where a person's choice and control absent in the activities they are engaged in that person is in same footing as a contemporary slave. *op. cit.* at p. 28

320 Vewesseee, C.P.N., "The New Labour Code A French Inspired Instrument For the Exploitation of Cameroonian Workers," Unpubished article, p. 4.

the biting crises. The Minimum wage rate of 36270 confirms arguments put forward by some trade unionists like Vewesssee, that not only have workers been reduced to modern day slavery, but also that the Code itself is a giant step backwards to early 1920s colonial type economy in which wages were so low that a building contractor would rather employ porters to carry cement because it was far cheaper than investing in wheel-barrows. This, of course, has negative impact on the security of employment as conceived in write-up.

2.4.2.6 The Obligation to Provide a Certificate

Section 44(1) of the Labour Code places an obligation on the employer to issue a departing worker with a certificate of employment immediately on termination. The certificate must carry only the dates of his arrival and departure and the types and dates of the various posts he/she has held. The importance probably is to attest to the fact that the employer had actually employed the employee for the stated period. Where this is not respected,[321] the violating employer will be liable under section 167(1) of the Code to the payment of a fine of between 100.000 – 1.000.000francs CFA. It is ironic that this benefits the state and not the employee as the fines are paid into the state treasury. Such payments will increase cost of business for the employer and may influence him to give the certificate when he terminates. It seems that the requirement of the provision of certificate of termination weakens security of service as some employers could casually dismiss a worker and simply give them the required certificate. The fact that section 44(1) does not make it an obligation on the employer to state the reasons for termination of the contract of service, further buttresses this opinion. On the other hand, deliberate refusal to give this certificate to a departing worker who has found another job may cause the worker to lose the new found job for want of the certificate. If section 44 of the Labour Code 1992 is a commandment and not a suggestion, and therefore a fundamental right of the employee as held by Justice Ngassa in the *Ndongo Case*[322] above, then the worker must not only be redressed but the reasons for termination must be

[321] Infact Ngassa J in *Ndongo Fred Ebanja v. The Chamber of Agriculture* (2008) 1 CCLR makes this a fundamental right of a worker which is a commandment and not a discretion of the employer.

[322] *Ndongo Fred Ebanja v. the Chamber of Agriculture* Suit No. HCF/l.42/2003-2004, CCLR Part 12, 62 at p. 63 paragraph 20-25. In fact she stressed that employers tend to treat the issuing of this certificate to an employee as if it is optional and they have a discretion as whether to deliver the certificate or not, which is a very incorrect line of reasoning and interpretation of section 44 of the Labour Code 1992.

clearly indicated if his security of service has to be strengthened.[323] This in a way will deter callous employers from dismissing their employees and issuing them with such certificates.

2.5 The Obligations of an Employee

Since employment relations emanate from contracts, including the statutorily mandated terms, parties have responsibilities the respect of which tends to strengthen the security of service in employments. The extent to which this can be assessed depends on the obligations imposed on the employees.

2.5.1 The Obligation of Obedience

The duty to respect reasonable orders of the employer is an obligation emanating from section 1(1) and 23(2) of the Code. This is similar to the common law duty, which obliges the worker to discharge his employment responsibilities under the control of the employer. The fact that under this duty the employee is expected to adhere only to orders connected to the job he was employed to do strengthens the security of service because a dismissal for the disrespect of reasonable orders not linked to the worker's employment is invalid. The effect of this principle on the security of service was illustrated in *Laws v. London Chronicle*.[324] The brief facts of the case are that the managing director at a business meeting said to the plaintiff, 'you stay where you are.' She did not do so but walked out of the room. Although she had been a good employee up until then, she was summarily dismissed. On appeal, it was held that the worker's conduct did not go to the root of the contract of employment to justify her dismissal. Her dismissal was void and she was re-instated in her position as an advert clerk in the company.

The duty of cooperation and adaptability is an enlarged duty of obedience, requiring the worker not to be deliberately non-cooperative. It places an obligation on the employee to perform the contract of service in a manner, which will not frustrate it.[325] Since the whole idea of running an enterprise is to make profit,[326] in order to make the workers more professional, proactive

---

323 Yanou *op. cit.* at p. 51-52.

324 [1959] All ER 311.

325 Per Buckley LJ in *Secretary of State for employment v. ASLEF No.2* [1972] Q.B.455. Lord Denning MR sees it as a specific prohibition of wilful disruption by the employee.

326 Watkins LJ in *Wood v. WM Car Services (Peterborough) LTD* [1982] ICR 693, held that 'employers

and productive, employers have obligations to train the employee if change in the enterprise requires it. Employees owe a duty to adapt themselves after such training to new methods and techniques. This duty is connected to security of service in a fast moving world of this computer age. Only employees who adapt to new methods and techniques in their particular fields will be able to escape job insecurity, especially in times of redundancies.[327]

2.5.2 The Duty of Faithful Service

Employment relationships are grounded in trust and confidence. It follows that employees must be dutiful and faithful to their masters. Indeed, section 31(1) of the Code, which encapsulates this duty requires that workers should use all their time[328] for the master's business. During the duration of their employment, they have to look after their master's interest and not their own, in this regard, Workers may use their leisure time to engage in their own business so long as it does not hurt the business of their employer by, for example, compromising trade secrets[329] or setting up rival competing business.[330]

---

must not, in my opinion, be put in a position where through the wrongful refusal of their employees to adapt to change, they are prevented from introducing improved business methods in furtherance of seeking success for the enterprise.'

327 See generally, Anderman *op. cit.* at p. 38-39.

328 That is all his gainful activity.

329 This is also breach of confidence emanating not only from contract, but is a criminal offence under section of the Penal Code. See also Goulding J. in *Faccenda Chicken v. Fowler* [1983] 1RLR 61 at p. 65-66 and 731-732 where he explained the employees duty in this way ".... Because of its trivial character of its easy accessibility from public sources of information, cannot be regarded by reasonable persons or by the law as confidential at all. The servant is at liberty to impart it during his service or afterwards to anyone he pleases even his master's competitor.
Secondly, there is information which the servant must treat as confidential (either because he is expressly told it is confidential, or because from its character it obviously is so) but which once learned necessarily remains in the servant's head and becomes part of his own skill and knowledge applied in the course of his master's business. So long as the employment continues, he cannot otherwise use or disclose such information without infidelity and therefore breach of contract. But when he is no longer in the same service, the law allows him to use his full skill and knowledge for his own benefit in competition with his former mater; and.... There seems to be no established distinction between the use of such information where its possessor trades as a principal, and where he enters the employment of a new master, even though latter case involves disclosure and not mere personal use of the information. If an employer wants to protect information of this kind, he can do so by an express stipulation restraining the servant from competing with him (within reasonable limits of time and space) after the termination of his employment. There are some trade secrets ..... though they may necessarily, have been learned by head and even though the servant may have left the service, they cannot lawfully be used for anyone's benefit but the masters.' This is so even if there is no express contract term to that effect.

330 *Hivac Ltd v. Park Royal Scientific Instruments Ltd* [1949] 1 Ch. 169. Hivac was a manufacturer of midget valves for hearing aids. Two of their workers worked for a rival firm and encouraged

Although an employee is not supposed to use the employer's services or property to make secret profit as it goes against the principle of good faith[331], which require the worker to be honest, the duty of faithful service further requires the worker not to collect bribe. This is not only a criminal offence but also contributes greatly to the reduction in the profits made by the employer. The relevance to security of service is that where a worker collects bribes, whether openly or in secret, he/she compromises his/her security of service as the employer will be justified in firing him/her.

2.5.2.a Employees as Inventors

There is no gainsaying that an invention[332] belongs to the commissioner, inventor or employer of an employee purposefully employed to invent. To this extent, section 11(2) of Annex 1 of the Bangui Agreement,1999, emphasises that all inventions made by the worker during the tenure of the employment contract are regarded as the property of the employer[333] irrespective of whether the worker was employed for the task that resulted in the invention. Such

---

others to do same and so an injunction was sought to restrain the respondents from employing the workers of the plaintiffs, which was granted.

331 Although this important common law principle has not been incorporated into the Labour Code, it would seem that where an employee in Cameroon for example makes secret profits in the form of tips, even if justified, he must inform his master in order not to jeopardise their security of service. Such moneys at common law are held in constructive trust for the benefit of the employer and the employee is liable to pay the said amount back to the employer. See for example the case of *Boston Deep Sea Fishing v. Ansell* (1888) 39 Ch D 339.

332 According to Black's Law Dictionary, in patent law, an invention is contrivance and production of something that hitherto did not exist, by the exercise of independent investigation or experiment. It is anything that is created or devised. Black, H.C, *Black's Law Dictionary*, Minnesota: West Publishing Co, 2009, 901. Though an invention is not expressly defined in Bangui Accord 1999 as revised (the law that regulates intellectual property rights in Cameroon), it could be inferred from the definition of patents that an invention is any technological advancement that is new (one that has not been anticipated by a prior art - Art. 3 Annex1 Bangui Agreement 1999 see also *Windsurfing International Inc v. Tabur Marine (Great Britain) Ltd* [1959]RPC 59 CA); resulting from an inventive step having regard to the prior art (art. 4 Annex1B.A 1999. see also *Hickman v. Andrews* [1983] RPC 147 CA); it can be applied in any kind of industry (Art 5 Annex1 B.A 1999, see also *Chiron v. Murex Diagnostics* [1996] FRS 153). For it to qualify for patent it must not fall within the category excluded for patentability by any statute (see art.6 Annex1 B.A 1999). See in same light World Trade Organisation Agreement on Trade-Related Aspects of Intellectual Property Rights (TRIPS). Inventions are different from discoveries in that the latter denotes the bringing into knowledge and use of something although it existed, was before unknown.

333 See Art. 10 Bangui Agreement, Annex 1, 1999, in same vein see also the French position in decision of the *Cour de Cassation (French Civil Supreme Court)* where the court held that the invention belongs to the inventor except for the restrictive legal exceptions - Cass.com., 25 April 2006. Section 7 Patent Act 1977 (Britain) which is to same effect.

a worker is entitled to compensation only if the invention is of 'exceptional importance'[334]. The reasoning behind this is that the data and time used for the invention comes from his/her employment.[335] The issue of claims and compensation of employee-inventor is becoming contentious mindful of the technological revolution and especially as freedom of contracts send green signals that if well drafted, employees may have strong claims to their inventions. On the other hand, free market economies see labour as one of the production implements owned by the factory owner requiring that all the products of labour rightfully belong to the owner of the business. Encouraged by this economic assumption, the rise of corporate capitalism has led to the declaration by Lord Simonds in *Patchett v. Sterling*[336] that "it is an implied term in the contract of service of any workman that what he produces by the strength of his arm or the skill of his hand or the exercise of his inventive faculty shall become the property of the employer"[337]. This has been buttressed by the fact that the conceptualisation of a worker as contained in section 1(2) of the Labour Code 1992 read together with section 23(1) of same gives the employer very wide powers and seemingly all rights to invention, granted that the employee is not only a production implement but a servant of the employer who is rightfully paid his dues in the remuneration he receives during employment.

From the above perspective, whether or not there is a written contract, at common law, a duty of fidelity[338], trust[339] and good faith is implied into an employment relationship. This position finds support in section 31 (1) of the Labour Code 1992 that imposes devotion to service on the employee in all gainful activity he undertakes even after working hours, safe the contract provides otherwise. This line of thought is buttressed by article 11 (2) of

334 Section 11(3) Annex1 of the Bangui Agreement, 1999.

335 This and based on the principle that the entrepreneur (employer) owns the factors of production, the proceeds there from should rightfully go to him. To further support this philosophy is the fact that the employee's contract is that of service (and fidelity, confidentiality and good faith).

336 (1955) 72 R.P.C. 50.

337 Ought such rights not be extended to the employee considering John Locke's theory of appropriation that ",... yet every man has a property in his own person: this nobody has any right to but himself. The labour of his body, and the work of his hands, we may say, are properly his. Whatsoever then he hath mixed his labour with, and joined to it something that is his own, and thereby makes it his property." John Locke, *Second Treatise of Government*, Cambridge: Hackett Publishing Company, Inc, 1690, p. 19.

338 Section 31(2) Labour Code 1992, provides that "....it may be stipulated by agreement between the parties that in the event of a breach of contract, the worker shall not engage, on his own account or on account of another person, in any activity liable to compete with the employer ....."

339 *Pepper v. Webb* [1969] 1 W.L.R.514.

Bangui Accord 1999[340] which provides that all employee inventions are that of the employer if made during gainful employment whether or not she/he was employed to invent, so long as the invention was as a result of the use of data or any means from his employment. Such an employee has no claim to it safe for just and reasonable compensation according to the invention. Where, however, his employment contract requires the inventor to exercise an inventive activity, she/he has no claims except the invention is of 'very exceptional importance'. The latter engagements must be created pursuant to a contract expressly specifying that the employee is hired to invent.

Even if the worker invents at home it goes against the duty of good faith of the employee for the employee to keep the invention as he/she has firm obligations under section 31 of the Code and sections 11(1) of the Bangui Accord 1999.[341] There is exception in case the employer expressly renounces his/her claims over the invention as required under section 11(5). If the employee keeps the invention, it will infringe on the no conflict of duty rule where the personal interest of the employee to invent may conflict with the interest[342] of the employer to further his business and make profit.[343] It would seem that the British position is more protective of employee inventors as was seen in *Harris Patent*[344] because as per Falconer J;

> an invention cannot mean any invention whatsoever; it is governed by qualification that it has to be an invention that might reasonably be expected to result from the carrying out of the employee's duties or in the alternative, that which is specifically referring to an invention which was the aim or object to which the employee's efforts in carrying out his duties were directed.[345]

---

340 A statute signed in February 1977 in Bangui the capital of Central African Republic to regulate intellectual property in the signatory member states. Cameroon being a signatory, this is the text that regulates intellectual property rights in Cameroon safe for copyrights. Mindful therefore of Art. 45 of the revised 1996 Constitution of Cameroon, this law takes precedence in Cameroon over any other law in this regard.

341 See generally Sama-Lang, I D.N., "Employee Inventors in Cameroon: Any Claims to Invention?" *Journal of Applied Social Sciences (Ub-Jass)* Volume X, Number 1, 2017, 37-47.

342 Per Lord Cranworth LC in *Aberdeen Railway Co v. Blaikie Bros* (1854) 1 Macq 461 at 471, HL, ' It is a rule of universal application, that no one, having (fiduciary) duties to discharge, shall be allowed to enter into engagements in which he has, or can have, a personal interest conflicting, or which possibly may conflict, with the interest of those whom he is bound to protect.'

343 See for example *British Syphon v. Homewood* [1956] R.P.C.225 and *Harris Patent* [1955] R.P.C 19,

344 (1985) R.P.C 19.

345 Cornish,W.R., *Materials on Intellectual Property*, Oxford: ESC Publishing LTD,1990, p. 122.

The nature of sections 11(1) and (2) to give the employer stronger rights and as such, the employer may not pay the worker proportionate to his invention or may coerce the employee into renouncing his /her rights over the invention. The conceptualisation of a worker as a servant has paved way for the misuse of employer's rights who may greedily want it all.

The conceptualisation of employee/employer relationship as servant and master has led to imbalance of power between the two[346] necessitating the need for balance to be struck between an employer's interest in managing his business as he sees fit and the employee's interest in not being unfairly and improperly exploited. This unfairness on the employee prompted Phillips to aver that '......imbalance of bargaining power between employer and employee have led so clearly to injustice in the distribution of the fruits of inventions made by an employee while in his employer's service'[347]. Employees may wish to preserve some autonomy and ownership rights over their creations especially if they wish to go independent by creating a rival business[348]. From this perspective, therefore, and as contained in section 11(1)-(2) Bangui Agreement, Annex 1, 1999, there is a pressing need for the employees to enter into pre-invention contracts to adequately protect their interests, lest they be left with crumbs while their masters reap the juicy bits of their labour.

2.5.2.b Employees and Contracts in Restraint of Trade

These are express terms in the contract of employment restricting the freedom of the employee on the termination of employment from engaging in a competing business or working for a competitor for a specified period of not more than one year and such prohibition shall not apply outside a radius of 50km as required by section 31(3) Labour Code 1992. This is so provided such a clause is inserted to protect a genuine proprietary interest of the employer for example, confidential information, trace connection and clients and it is reasonable in extent, the express restraint will be valid and enforceable. Such

346 Otto-khan Freund explains that it is between bearer of power and one who is not a bearer of power. Otto-Khan Freund, *Labour and the Law*, London: Stevens, 1977, p. 17. According to Napier, this liberal approach to employment contracts may produce an illusion of equality between employer and employee. Although equal rights on paper may comfort the employee, one can correctly question the textbook assertion that employer and the employee have the same rights. See generally on this Napier,R.W., in Voize-Valayre, "The French Law of Dismissals," *23 New York University Journal of International Law and Politics*, 1991, p. 520.

347 Phillips,'Employee Inventions and the New Patent Act' (1978) 7 ILJ 30

348 A fact permissible under section 31(3) Labour Code 1992.

a restraint must have been drafted so that it is not wider than is reasonably necessary to achieve desired intention. As well in the *Nordenfelt v. Maxim Nordenfelt Guns & Ammunition Co Ltd*[349] contracts in restraint of trade are void and unenforceable as being against the public policy except such a clause is reasonable. In determining whether it is reasonable, heed is paid to the employer's business, the spatial and temporal scope.

The worker's duty of fidelity extends beyond the termination of the contract of employment, especially where there is a contract in restraint of trade, which must not be contrary to the requirement of section 31(3)[350] of the Labour Code. The obligation of faithful service continues after the termination of contract as required by section 31(2) of the Labour Code 1992, as upon termination of the contract of employment the ex-employee can set up his business[351] so long as it does not infringe on the restraint of trade clause. Since the employment contract determines what a worker can do, it is imperative for clarity of rights that these contracts be written and should adequately and readily determines the terms, which delimit the employees' responsibilities and avoid future conflicts of rights. Though the employer may introduce appropriate terms in the contract of employment to protect his secret, it must not prevent competition from the former employee.[352]

2.5.3 The Duty of Care and Skill

Section 31(1) of the Code requires that the servant should personally do the work and not delegate the same to others. This is an employee's most basic and most important duty as it goes to the foundation of contracts of service for if a worker does not personally do the work but delegates the same, he becomes something else, namely an independent contractor.[353] The standard of care required is an objective one which takes into consideration the skill

349 [1894] AC 535

350 According to this section, such prohibition shall not apply outside a radius of 50km from the work place and its duration shall not exceed one year. This works out well for a worker who might have gained his reputation and would want to exploit the good will of that reputation to his personal advantage rather than staying in the shadows of his employer for ever.

351 *Ibid dem.*

352 Lord Atkinson in *Herbert Morris Ltd v. Saxelby* [1916] 1 AC 688 at p. 702

353 See for example the decision in *Ready Mixed Concrete (South East) LTD v. Minister of Pension* [1968] 2 Q.B. 497, where it was held that one of the characteristics was inability to assign performance to another. But in Britain, in *MacFarlane v. Glasgow City Council* where two gymnastic coaches were entitled to have their classes taken by a substitute chosen from an approved list and paid by the Council, it was held that limited delegation is permissible.

he/she professes to have. A worker who executes his tasks according to the skills he possess, exercising in course due care, is most likely to enjoy security of service employment as he will not be exposed to redundancy in case of economic hardship. Such a worker will also be eligible for promotion and other benefits that go with it. For example, increase in salary or the award of a labour medal. Conversely, a worker who works negligently or shows signs of incompetence jeopardizes employment as he can be easily terminated in the event of economic difficulty of the firm or even when he /she is found wanting of the skill he claims to possess.

Where a worker steals from his employer in order to unjustly enrich self, it is not only a breach of faithful service but also such would have acted in bad faith and with lack of care for the employers' business on which his security of service is hinged. A case in point is *Omog Etien v. CAMAIR*[354] where the plaintiff, an employee of the defendant, defrauded the latter causing them great loss. The High Court did not hesitate to hold that the dismissal of the plaintiff was justified as such an employee cannot be said to have exercised due care and diligence.

2.6 Incidents of Execution of Contracts of Employment

Section 32 of the Labour Code 1992 has provided an exhaustive list that may lead to the suspension of the contract of employment. During such periods, the employee shall not work and shall not be paid even though there is a subsisting employment contract. This may occur when;

i. There is a suspension of the employment as a result of the employer's military service
ii. Suspension as a result of the employee's military service
iii. The non-occupational illness of the employee. Such may include accidents not necessarily industrial or occupational incidental to employment, surgery, ordinary illness. The illness must be dully certified by a medical practitioner approved by the employer or one who works in an establishment recognised by the state. If so certified, the employee's contract shall be suspended for six months until a replacement if found. The employee must notify the employer attaching the medical certificate explaining the nature of the illness and probable duration. During such suspension and

[354] HCF/ L.53/2000/2001.

the cases of suspension for military service, the employer must pay the worker if the contract is one of unspecified duration, the compensation will either be equal to the compensation in lieu of notice when the period of absence is equal to or exceeds the period of notice, or the remuneration to which the worker would have been entitled during his absence when the period of absence is shorter than the notice period provided in section 34 of the Labour Code. During this period, the employer cannot dismiss the worker.

iv. Where the worker is under disciplinary sanction as provided for in section30 of the labour Code, such a worker shall loose only their benefits. This shall take effect only upon notification in writing of such a suspension and the reasons clearly stated. The employer must notify the appropriate Inspector of Labour within 48 hours.

v. Section 32 (f) and 91 read together gives room for the suspension of the contract of employment for the worker's education. The worker has the right to further education since it hone's their skill and improve on their professional competitiveness and career upgrading and other openings. This has been further guaranteed the law No. 2018/010/11th July 2018[355]. Such courses are usually for short periods of not more than 18 working days as per section 91(2) and shall be deemed to be a period of actual service for the calculation of the worker's paid leave, family allowances and length of service in the enterprise. The arrangements for such short courses are either collectively bargained or by statute.

vi. By mutual consent, during the exercise of political or administrative duties following an election or appointment;

vii. During the period in preventive detention or police custody[356]

viii. During the absence of a worker who has to follow the spouse who has been transferred. Such suspension is for a two years period renewable by mutual agreement between the two parties.

ix. Where there is interruptions of the workplace due to *force majeure*, economic difficulties or accidents.

---

[355] Governing Vocational Training in Cameroon

[356] See Chapter five

CHAPTER 3

VOCATIONAL TRAINING AND EMPLOYMENT RELATIONSHIP

The right to work is a fundamental right preserved by Section 6 (2) of the International Covenant on Economic, Social and Cultural Rights 1966. This right enjoin State Parties to the covenant to in protecting the right to work and in order to achieve the full realization of this right include technical and vocational guidance and training programs, policies and techniques to achieve steady economic, social and cultural development and full and productive employment under conditions safeguarding fundamental political and economic freedoms to the individual. The ILO Recommendations on Human Resources Development: Education, Training and Lifelong Learning[357] require Member States to "ensure that vocational education and training systems are developed and strengthened to provide appropriate opportunities for the development and certification of skills relevant to the labour market."

A worker may be required to undergo vocational training which comprises according to section 10 of Law No. 2018/010 of 10th July 2018[358] initial vocational training, continuing vocational training and apprenticeship implanted in centres established by natural or corporate bodies with the sole aim of imparting skills and competences required to practice a trade and gain access to a job-section. These vocational training comes on the heels of recognition that firms that invest in vocational training reaped more benefits than firms which did not. In results from a research carried out in Germany,[359] though the financial returns to firms vary as a result of vocational/ apprenticeship training, some recoup their investment during such

357 R.195, Human Resources Development, Recommendation 2004.

358 Governing Vocational Training in Cameroon

359 Euler, D., *Germany's dual vocational training system: a model for other countries?* Bertelsmann Stiftung, 2013; Haasler, S.R. The German system of vocational education and training: Challenges of gender, academisation and integration of low-achieving youth. *SAGE Journals*, 2020; Spees, A-C., Could Germany's vocational Education and training system be a model for the US?, WENR, 2018.

apprenticeship training, others see their investment within the apprenticeship period, while others see their investment pay-off only after accounting for reduced turn-over, recruitment, and initial training cost. It further indicated that although the cost of training is initially high, subsequently, the apprentice contributions exceed wages and supervisory costs. These vocational training become even more necessary at a time when professionalization in a bid to kill youth unemployment crisis has been at the fore of education reform in the country.[360] Mindful of these gains, and on the prompting of the Minister of Employment, the concerted efforts of the Minister of Higher Education, Secondary Education and Agriculture and Rural development led to an overhauling of the frameworks for apprenticeship training which is now regulated by the 2018/010 of 11th July 2018 on Vocational training. This law and the Labour Code 1992 remain the basic laws on such employment relationship.

3.1 Overview of the 2018 Law on Vocational Training

This is the basic regulation on vocational training in Cameroon. Which is intended for initial vocational training, continuing vocational training and apprenticeship under the supervision of the State and approved private partners. As provided for in section 5 of this Law, the intention is to promote and develop:

- A vocational training system that enables individuals to achieve professional and personal fulfilment and to integrate the society, particularly in the labour market, while making them fair and willing to show professional flexibility and remain in the labour market;
- A vocational training system that promotes corporate competitiveness;
- Equal training opportunities for all;
- Gender equality, as well as elimination of inequities inhibiting persons with disabilities in vocational training;
- Permeability of training types and fields within vocational training, as well as between vocational training and other sectors of the educational system; transparency in the vocational training system.

In furtherance of these ideals and based on the principles of the State, employer and worker tripartism, decentralisation, secularism, public-private

[360] D. Maingari, "La professionnalisation de l'enseignement au Cameroun: Des sources aux fins", *Recherche et Formation*, No. 25, 1997, pp. 97-112.

partnership, social equity and dual training, the State shall prepare, implement and monitor public vocational training in the promising sector by supporting research and putting in place structures for such developments. All these shall be done on the basis of the needs of the socio-professional sector. In order to properly realise this, the State has come out with managerial and supervisory control guidelines in addition to administrative and criminal sanctions in case of violations.

3.2 Supervision and Finance

According to section 15(1) of the 2018 Law, the technical and supervisory control over the running of these vocational training centres rests with the State. In conformity with this provision, the State lays down vocational training standards[361] and nomenclature,[362] supervises the assessment at the end of training,[363] and approves professional qualifications. In this capacity, the State has both pedagogic and administrative control over these training as it verifies compliance with standards set by the government, the facility, the type of training and training methods used. In order to ensure proper implementation of this, the State created the National Council for Career Guidance and Vocational Training whose organisation and functioning shall be fixed by regulation.[364]

In a bid to ensure the quality that is received in such facilities, the instructors are accredited by the State which in addition shall set up instructor training and curriculum. This shall be done with the assistance of socio-professional partner[365] that also help in the development, validation and implementation of vocational training and career guidance policy and strategies.

These vocational training are financed by the State and other stakeholders[366]. More precisely, it is out of public funding by the State or its institution gotten from budgetary allocations and special grants; support from

[361] See Section 35.

[362] See Section 36.

[363] See Section 37.

[364] Section 42 of the 2018 Law

[365] According to section 45 (2) of the 2018 Law, such socio-professional groups include; association of vocational training entity promoters, as well as professional information and career guidance association; Local and regional authorities; public and private corporations; professional organization; consular chambers; trade chambers; non-governmental organisations; universities and specialized academic institutions and social partners.

[366] Section 19 of the 2018 Law.

local and regional authorities; State subsidies and special tax incentive[367]. The private funding could also be gotten from resources of the training institution usually derived from fees and other income generating activities and other resources provided by the law.[368] This could be in the form of sundry support from technical aid gotten from international stakeholders if meaning is given to section 40.

3.2.1 Management, Control and Monitoring

Vocational training needs monitoring and evaluation to ensure that the standards of every vocational training does not fall[369]. In this regard, the vocational training and all its components shall be subject to regular periodic internal and external assessment by the Ministry of Employment and vocational training together with the relevant government department[370]. For coherence in the training, section 47 clearly:

- "Lay down the rules governing the organisation and functioning of public vocational training entities, taking into account their respective specificities;
- Specify the terms and conditions for the creation, opening and functioning of private vocational training entities and supervise them;
- Make available to the public information on training opportunities as well as information on the qualification requirements in the various sectors of the national economy;
- Periodically update the vocational training map, in conjunction with local and regional authorities and socio-economic partners;
- Ensure the relevance, quality and constant adaptation of vocational training to national economic, social and cultural realities, as well as the international context;
- Lay down common rules applicable to the development of training curriculums, obtainment, recognition, equivalence, categorisation and approval of vocational training diplomas and qualifications;

---

367 Section 16 of the 2018 Law.

368 Section 49 of the 2018 Law.

369 Section 7 (1) of the 2018 Law is very clear on this as it requires that the state to prepare, implement and monitor public vocational training and career guidance policies in partnership with local, regional authorities, professional organisations, enterprises and other relevant national stakeholders.

370 Section 48 of the 2018 Law.

- Exercise permanent control over the pedagogic activities of vocational training entities, in particular the quality of the vocational training, examinations and qualification procedures as well as compliance with apprenticeship contract."

To ensure efficacy and quality of the institutions for proper training, section 14 is very clear in providing that no training institution[371] shall operate without the prior approval of the minister in charge of employment and vocational training. These training facilities shall be operated on the basis of state priorities in accordance with:

- "Direct training towards meeting the needs of the labour market and economy;
- Rationalise and optimise vocational training management, access, equity, quality, organisation and financing; and
- Establish financing mechanisms with the support of the private sector and technical and financial partners."[372]

According to section 31 of the 2018 law, Career information Centres and Guidance entities shall be put up by the state which may be public or private with the objective of providing families, persons seeking training and enterprises with accessible, comprehensive and diversified information relevant to their particular fields/ trades, training opportunities vocational integration, required skills to enable them make informed choices.[373]

3.2.2 Penal and Administrative Sanctions

To ensure compliance with the rules laid down for the proper functioning of the vocational training centres, any breach in the implementation of the laws shall lead to total or partial closure of the training centre either permanently or temporarily or a permanent ban on any suspected official or staff involved according to the severity of the offence.[374] However where there is a serious operational breach by a private vocational training centre, such a centre will be placed in receivership to safe guard the interest of the trainees.

---

[371] Such institutions which may either be set up by natural or corporate persons which may either be public or private, according to laid down procedures.

[372] Section 12 of the 2018 Law.

[373] Sections 28 and 29 of the 2018 Law.

[374] Section 50(1) - 2018 Law.

In case of criminal activities, any promoter of such centre involved in criminal activities shall be punished according to the provisions of the Code. Such Promoters will also be punished according to the penalty in section 321 of the penal Code if they open a training facility without prior authorisation or they operate such a facility which had permanently closed, or they close such a training facility in the middle of training without prior authorisation of the competent supervisory authority. The penalties provided for in Section 318 above shall be doubled, and the court may in addition impose the forfeitures as described in Section 30 (6)of the Code.[375]

In addition to this sanctions, at Common Law, although the change of status cannot anyway terminate an apprenticeship contract[376], should the firm, etc, in which the apprentice was carrying out training is dissolved without more, the promoters will be liable to the apprentice for breach of contract warranting damages.[377] The "apprenticeship supervisor'/ 'master' is vicariously liable for the activities of his/her apprentice.[378]

3.3 Vocational Training

According to section 6 of the 2018 Law, vocational training[379] consists *in imparting knowledge, skills and competences with a view to ensuring a qualified labour force, and based on the qualitative and quantitative needs of employers and workers.* According to S. 8 of same, these training that will match the vocational training system to the expressed needs of the socio-professional sectors in a bid to curb the training mismatch is engaged in three levels; initial vocational training, continuing vocational training and apprenticeship[380]. The vocational training is invaluable as it increases the capital of the labour especially when seen from the arguments that a worker's career is his property-[381] capital, since it makes them more competitive and enhances job mobility (local and international) as their skills become even more relevant

---

375 This provision covers the prohibition on keeping a school, on teaching in any educational establishment, and in general on holding any post connected with education or care of children.

376 *Batty v.Monks* (1865) 12 L.T. 832

377 *Titmus v. Rose & Watts* [1940] 1 All. E.R. 599

378 *Hancke v. Hooper* (1835) 7 C. & P. 81. See in general Atiyah, *Vicarious Liability*, p. 72

379 See generally Chankseliani, M., Keep, E., &Wilde, W., *People and Policy: Comparative Study of Apprenticeship across eight national contexts*, University of Oxford, 2017.

380 Section 9 - 2018 Law.

381 Kazuo Sugeno & Yasuo Suwa, "Technological Innovation and Social Protection: 'Career is Property' as a concept of Labour Market Policies", *Kluwer Law International*, the Hague, The Netherlands, 1998, p. 99 *et seq.*

to the stakeholders. Although these lofty programs are welcomed relief in the turbulent and worrisome situations of the labour market in Cameroon, safety measures should have been put in place to ensure that it should not become a matter of labour accumulation by the different vocational training stakeholders.[382] It has been argued[383] that some of these stakeholders may want to develop only workers' firm specific skills which will make the worker not to be as productive as he would have been since form specific skill are complementary. The more general skills possessed by a worker, the more productive the worker will be after adding up with more complementary firm-specific skills. According to the Organisation for Economic Cooperation and Development offers a second chance to those who have not benefited greatly from general schooling as according to them ‘ vocational education and training (VET) is a valuable alternative to academic schooling. It prepares young people for the labour market with a view to responding to employer's skills needs. The practical training component of VET should be work based, ideally in the form of apprenticeships matching young people with employers at an early stage. Such programmes may be particularly attractive and beneficial for youth tired of school.[384]

3.3.1 Initial Vocational Training

Though this concept is not defined in this statute, one could inferred its definition from section 19 of same to mean; a training for persons with no skills or qualification in the field/ industry, comprising two parts; one being theoretical devoted to general knowledge and the other -professional devoted to skills acquisition derived from practical trainings, field placements in industries, additional training and professional practice intended for skills development in the work environment. The sole aim here being acquisition of skills, knowledge and know-how for the carrying out of professional activity.[385] According to section 17(2), this will enable the trainee to in particular acquire four fold capacity:

---

382 Who Have been identified in section 9 of the 2018 Law to include-Local and regional authorities, private vocational training promoters or guidance, entities, trainees and socio-professional partners.

383 Lerman, R., "Do firms benefit from apprenticeship investments?", IZA World of Labour 2014

384 Organisation for Economic Cooperation and Development, *Society at a Glance*, 2016b in Chankseliani, M., Keep, E., &Wilde, W., People and Policy: Comparative Study of Apprenticeship across eight national contexts, University of Oxford, 2017 p. 17

385 Section 17(1) 2018 Law.

- "The specific qualifications enabling him/her to carry out a professional activity competently and safely;
- the basic general knowledge he/she requires to access and remain in the world of work and for social integration;
- the economic, ecological, social and cultural knowledge and skills enabling him/her contribute to sustainable development;
- the capacity and readiness for lifelong learning, critical judgement and decision making."

Where persons are not eligible for direct entry into the specific initial training program, the State shall ensure that preliminary courses are available to enable the prospective trainee meet up with entry requirements.[386]

3.2.2 Continuing Vocational Training

This can be gleaned from section 20 of the 2018 law to mean a continuing vocational training aimed at further training[387] or retraining[388] of professionals in a public or private training facility, with the aim of fostering professional integration, re-integration and mobility on the one hand and upgrading of the worker's competences in tandem with technological and trade developments.

These continuing training programs are refresher courses for workers. Where a worker benefits from such programs, he/she shall continue to works for the employer for the specified period based on the vocational training.[389] This is in line with sections 32 and 91 of the Cameroon Labour Code 1992 which provides for an unpaid leave of studies to the worker, and that the contract of employment of the worker can only be suspended at such periods of education.

3.3.3 Apprenticeship

According to International Labour Organisation Convention 138 on the minimum age of employment, 1973[390], the minimum age for engaging into a

---

386 Section 18(2) 2018 Law.

387 Defined in section 6 of the 2018 Law as, additional training enabling competence upgrade or capacity building in a given branch of activity.

388 Defined in section 6 of the 2018 Law to mean, training aimed at building partly forgotten or lost practical skills and knowledge needed for a job or profession.

389 Section 21 of the 2018 law.

390 Ratified by Cameroon on 13th August 2001.

contract of employment is 14, although heed must be paid to local reality. In line with this, section 86 (1) of the Labour Code 1992 provides that;

"No child shall be employed in an enterprise even as an apprentice before the age of 14(fourteen) years, except as otherwise authorised by order of the Minister in charge of Labour, taking account of jobs which the children[391] may be asked to do". According to section 6 of the 2018 Law on Vocational training, Apprenticeship[392] is a 'long-duration dual training method, a good part which takes place in an enterprise, but is also supplemented in a training establishment, aimed at on the job transfer from a skilled person, referred to as the 'apprenticeship supervisor' to a person referred to as the 'apprentice'[393], of a recognised initial professional skill, enabling the latter to practice a trade'. As observed by Keep *et al*[394] apprenticeship carries with it connotations of training, leading to meaningful and reasonably well-rewarded work in what were traditionally seen as the 'skilled trades'. Technically, such a contract of apprentice does not give rise to the relationship of employee and employee as the principal elements of contract of employment as elaborated above do not attach to such a relationship. This notwithstanding, under general contract law, a minor (who in this case may involve children below the age of 14) can enter into a binding contract for nesseccaries[395]. In this regard, such contracts of apprenticeship may be seen as both contracts for neccesaries and beneficial contracts of service and so binding to the minor who may be even below the statutory 14 years, although section 23(1) is categoric that no 14 year old can engage in any such apprenticeship relationship and even though such beneficial contract of services may carry all the characteristics of an apprenticeship contract.

---

391 Art. 1 of the United Nations Charter of the rights of a child defines children anyone below the age of 18. However, see generally Boma, A,L., "The age of majority in Cameroon: A critical Review," *Annales de la Faculte des Sciences Jurisdique et Politiques, Universite de Dschang*, Tome 7, 2003,155-164 at pp159&160.

392 It is a model of learning for an agreed duration that formally combines work-based training (periods of practical work experience at a workplace) with institution-based education (periods of theoretical/ practical education followed in a school, college, or training center) and that is regulated by a contract/agreement between apprentice and their employer, provides remuneration for the apprentice, and leads to a nationally recognized qualification/certificate upon successful completion. Chankseliani, M., Keep, E., & Wilde, W., *People and Policy: Comparative Study of Apprenticeship across eight national contexts*, University of Oxford, 2017, P. 19

393 Trainee in an enterprise or workshop within the context of a long-term process. - section 6 of the 2018 Law.

394 Keep, E., & James, S., *Rethinking Apprenticeship*, Institute for Public Policy Research, 2011, p. 55.

395 Necessaries here being things which a human needs to live a healthy life. These go beyond bare neccesaity and they depend on ones socio-economic standing.

For there to be a legally enforceable relationship, section 6 of the 2018 Law requires a written[396] 'contract whereby the manager of an industrial, commercial or agricultural establishment or a craftsman undertakes to provide or ensure, under his/her responsibility, methodical and comprehensive vocational training to a person, and whereby the latter undertakes in return to follow the instructions he/she will receive and carry out his/her assignment for apprenticeship purposes'. This is in line with section 45 of the Labour Code 1992 which by section 46 of same makes all apprenticeship contract not in writing void.

From the wordings of section 6 above, it can be gleaned that the apprentice supervisor who must not be less than 21[397] has the obligation to carry out a methodic and comprehensive training, the apprentice is in turn required to submit to the teachings and must obey instructions and perform all assigned tasks.

The form, effect of this apprenticeship contracts are supposed to be elaborated in a decree after consultation with the National Labour Advisory Board. – Section 47. To supplement the 2018 decree which did not cover certain aspects regarding duration of the apprenticeship, Decree No. 69/ FD/ 287 of 20th July 1969 governing apprenticeship provides that such a contract cannot go beyond 4 (four) years at the end of which the apprentice is entitled to a certificate. The apprentices supervisor can recruit the apprentice at the end of the training period. However, in absence of complete training the contract will be seen as one of unspecified duration. Death of either party can also terminate the contract.

It should be noted that although the training of apprentice in Cameroon is regulated by law as expoused above and no individual whether natural or corporate is eligible to run such vocational educational training centre without fiat from the state, there are still a lot of unregulated informal training apprenticeship relationships[398] in trades like hair dressing, iron bending,

---

[396] As required by section 22, it must be written between the apprenticeship supervisor and the apprentice or their legal representative.

[397] Section 23(2) 2018 Law on Vocational training and who must not have been convicted for crimes against public morals or any grounds leading to imprisonment.

[398] This refers to the system by which a young apprentice acquires the skills for a trade or craft in a micro or small enterprise learning and working side by side with an experienced practitioner. The Apprentice and master crafts person conclude a training agreement that is embedded in local norms and traditions of a society. Apprentices learn technical skills and are inducted into a business culture and network which makes it easier for them to find a job or start business when finishing their apprenticeship. See ILO Department of Skills and Employability https://www.ilo.org>skills>

trading, carpentry, tailoring, motor mechanics which are still very functional though unregulated with each of such entities having their own subjective and specific training methods, duration of training and the amount of fees paid. The age of the 'apprentice' is usually not an issue in such entities as minors below the age who upon the completion of primary education are unable to continue with formal or formal vocational training are engaged in such informal training. As observed in such informal training, there are issues of quality of training and shows risk of exploitation and incidents of child labour. The apprenticeship being too long or risk incomplete transmission of skills especially if the apprentice leaves before completing.[399]

3.3.4 Dual and Distance Training

This is a type of training that involves "workplace situations and learning and training activities within an institution," with the aim of helping the trainee develop a business plan, enhance and update knowledge use of different equipment, familiarise the trainees with the socio-professional environment, help the trainee obtain a recognised qualification while facilitating their entry into the job market create and environment conducive for self –employment. Such institution which is run under the direct involvement of the state[400] must impart professional skills and knowledge; promote the development of entrepreneurship, business acumen, a sense of responsibility and autonomy; provide the trainees with requisite information, advice and resources for executing the work assigned them.

---

399 Just like elsewhere in Africa, informal apprenticeship has evolved from a system largely focused on skills transmission within clans system to a few paying training of the "learner boy" outside the clan or family circle which may end in "settlement ' of the 'learner boy' by the master to whom the 'learner boy' continue to depend on for guidance in the field of trade. See generally *Upgrading Informal Apprenticeship, A resource guide for Africa*, International Labour Organisation, Skills and employability Department, 2012

400 Section 25 of the 2018 Law.

CHAPTER 4

SOCIAL WELFARE AND SOCIAL INSURANCE IN EMPLOYMENT RELATIONSHIPS

Since the Philadelphia Declaration of 1919, the social welfare[401] and social security[402] of workers has been at the core of employment relations. The Philadelphia Declaration did not only mandate the ILO to free the world from fear, and poverty but in so doing, to cater for the social security of workers by ensuring the provision of basic income and medical care to all. This declaration opened the runway for positive law on social security and social welfare model that made it both an obligation and a core human right as seen in the gamut of laws and recommendations. This did not only guarantee decent work[403] but assured worker's dignity during employment in the form of paid leave, maternity, medical care, sick pay, schooling for minor children, and social insurance, and after employment in the form of pension and unemployment dues.

Indeed, social security/social welfare has been a major driver for a peaceful work place which is reflective in the larger society. It cannot therefore be gain said that this has become a core obligation on State Parties of the different conventions on social welfare and social security which has evolved a system that recognises, respects, protects and fulfills these rights. Social protection has become a productive factor as it preserves and enhances the health and quality of workers.[404] The right to social protection of a worker has evolved into a core human right which guarantees a secure, healthy and decent standard of living necessary for the worker to be productive.

---

401 These are programs to assist workers with food, accommodation, education for children transportation, utility, recreation.

402 Defined as measures providing protection to workers against contingencies such as unemployment, old age, maternity. Typically in Cameroon Labour relations, it will cover areas of protection of workers against life hazards which includes maternity and death; Professional risks and protection against layoffs, dismissals and old age pensions.

403 Part 11, chapter 1 A Social security as human right and duty of the state.

404 ILO, *Social Protection as a productive factor*, GB294/ESP/4, Geneva, November 2005.

It is because of the relevance of this social security and welfare of the worker that this chapter bothers about the rights of female workers during and after pregnancy, sick and leave claims, industrial and occupational diseases and indemnity for technical lay off pension benefits.

4.1 The Social Benefits and Protection of Workers

In Cameroon the social protection of workers is done under two umbrellas; a scheme for civil servants (which is not the subject matter of this book) and Protection under the National Social Insurance fund for workers in the private sector who are regulated by the Code and other government workers who are not covered by the Civil Service Code. This section shall bother specifically on the situation of women as workers and the protection of workers and dependents in case of ill.

4.1.1 The Protection of Working Women

The Labour Code 1992 which is the substantive and procedural positive law on employment in Cameroon is not indifferent to the protection of the rights of women in employment as it has dedicated an entire chapter of the Labour code to demonstrate relations of such protection in employment relations. This is over and above the protection given to all workers irrespective of gender.

The labour code is paternalistic in its protection of women as it prohibits in s. 81 (2) all women from night work[405] safe those holding executive positions[406] and those not involved in form of manual work.[407] Furthermore, the inspector of labour within the limits of his competence has power to order the examination of women by a certified medical practitioner in order to ascertain if the work given is within her physical strength. A woman may *sua motto* request for such a physical examination which in such a case becomes automatic. Should the result indicate that the work is beyond her physical strength, she must be transferred to a more suitable work by the employer. However, where this is not possible, the contract must be terminated forthwith without notice and without either party being held liable for breach of respect for the duration of required notice[408].

405 Section 81 of the Labour Code defines night work as work done between 10 p.m. and 6 a.m.
406 Section 82(3) (a) Labour Code 1992.
407 Section 82(3) (b) Labour Code 1992.
408 Section 87(2) Labour Code 1992.

4.1.1.a Maternity Protection

The protection of pregnant women first came up in 1956 law in the French Cameroon. This was subsequently followed by the 1967 law (Law No 67-LF-7 of 12th June 1967and its decree of implementation in 1970 by Decree No. 007-MTLS-DPS of 14th April 1970 and its amendments of 1995 and 1996) and the Labour Code 1992.

The regime for maternity protection which is our bother here like the whole of this book is on private sector employment. Under this sector, pregnancy and maternity protection is dependent on whether the woman or spouse is employed in this sector. Where this is the case, the National Social Insurance Fund is charged with the cash maternity, medical and pre-natal benefits of the woman. The government health facilities provide free medical care to the pregnant woman and her children. Section 84(5) of the Labour Code is actually in line with this as such a pregnant employed woman is entitled to a daily allowance payable by the National Social Insurance Fund that is equal to the amount of the wages actually received at the time of suspension of her contract.

In this regard, Section 83 of the Labour Code 1992 has expressly charged the National Commission on Industrial Hygiene and Safety[409] with the types of jobs which women in general and pregnant women in particular cannot perform. More specifically, Section 84(1) Labour Code 1992 provides that once her pregnancy has been medically certified, she may terminate her contract of employment irrespective of the notice period and she will not be liable to pay compensation as required in section 36 of same. Her employer cannot terminate her contract of employment because of the pregnancy.

Once a pregnancy has been duly certified, the woman is entitled to 14 weeks of maternity leave which may begin four weeks before the due date of confinement, which may be extended by six weeks in cases where there is a certified illness resulting from the confinement or pregnancy. The employer again does not have the powers to terminate the employment contract[410]. If however the pregnant woman's confinement occurs before her due date, section 84(3) makes provision for her extension of the maternity leave so that she benefits from the full fourteen weeks of rest. Where the confinement occurs after the due date, leave will be extended to the due date without any

[409] Section 120 Labour Code 1992.

[410] Section 84 (2) Labour Code 1992.

prejudice to the post-natal leave. She is also entitled to any benefits in kind during this period even if she suspends her contract of employment.

For a woman to benefit from the cash maternity and medical bills, she must have been in covered employment for at least six consecutive months at the time of childbirth. If she is covered, She is entitled to pre-natal grants if she undergoes two medical examinations during pregnancy. A lump-sum of nine times the monthly family allowance is paid in two installments, one after each pre-natal examination. The monthly family allowance is 2,800frs. After birth of her child, the covered pregnant woman or the wife of an insured man is entitled to payments. Such maternity benefit are 100 percent of the insured's last monthly earnings paid for four weeks before and ten weeks after the expected date of childbirth which may be extended to up to six weeks after childbirth if there are complications resulting from pregnancy. A lumpsum of twelve times the monthly family allowance is paid for each living and viable child at the rate of 2,800frs per month. Generally, an employed pregnant woman is reimbursed for childbirth medical expenses of up to 1,400CFA and200 frs for each prenatal and pediatric examination until the newborn reaches the age of six months.

4.1.2 Family Allowance

Family allowance is paid to employed private sector workers. The employer contributes 7% of monthly covered payroll in case of domestics; 5.65% for agricultural workers and 3.7% for private sector teachers. The calculations are based on the minimum legal wage of 36.270frs and the maximum legal earnings of 750,000frs. This family allowance is paid to workers for children younger than six right up to the age of 2 if a full time student or if disabled; 14-18years for children who are apprentices. The children must provide proof of school attendance and the parent must have been working for between 18days or 120hrs a month or receiving an old age or survivor pension. This benefit is paid quarterly.

4.1.3 Sundry Benefits

These are social and other health benefits that accrues to a worker during their employment.

Where for example a worker works outside his normal residence according to section 66(1) of the Labour Code and has been given accommodation in that regard, the employee, spouse and children shall be entitled to medical care within limits specified by the Minister of Labour after consulting the National Commission for Industrial Hygiene and Safety.

In addition where a worker has been transferred out of his domicile, section 66(3) of same imposes a duty on the employer to ensure regular supply of food stuffs for the any worker and his family if the worker cannot access such. Such food supply are however paid for at a rate determined by the Order of the Minister of Labour after consulting the National Labour Advisory Board, although these are not payable when the wages are not yet due.

4.2 Benefits and Protection of Workers Against Professional Risks, Sickness and Health of Workers and Dependents

Under the employer's liability, it is his responsibility to cater for the health and safety of his workers, which is his production implement. Section 95(1) of the Labour Code 1992 makes it incumbent on the Minister in charge of Labour in consultation with the National Commission on Hygiene and Safety to determine the safety conditions at work place.[411]

Section 98 (1) of the Labour Code makes it a duty on all factories on the employer to provide medical and health services to all its workers. The health and safety services are charged with the responsibility of supervising hygiene conditions at work, risks of contagion and health and safety of workers and their spouses. - Section 98(2).

According to section100(1) of the Labour Code 1992 in tandem with Article 11(1) of Order No. 039/MTPS/IMT of 26th November 1984[412] in a bid to ensure the health, hygiene and safety of all workers, all must undergo medical examination prior to their employment and shall be subjected to such medical supervision throughout their career-art 100(2) of the Labour Code and article 11(2) of Arrete No. 039/MTPS/IMT of 26th November 1984. An employer must ensure that a worker who is engaged to do work which constitutes serious risk must undergo post-occupational periodic test for an adequate period of time as per Article 12 of Order No. 039/MTPS/IMT of 26th November 1984.

Where the worker is sick and hospitailsed, it is the duty of the employer to take charge of their board as per section 101(2). And where they cannot

---

411 Section 108 Labour Code gives posers to the labour inspector to enter, any such work place for purposes of inspection and report to their administrative superior the extent to which these legal obligations are respected by the employer.

412 Regulating General Modalities of Hygiene and Safety at Workplace.

be properly attended to, the employer must arrange for their removal and transfer to the nearest medical unit. Where the employer does not have appropriate means of transportation of the sick worker, it is obligatory for the employer to notify the nearest administrative unit who shall cause the transportation of the worker. In case the worker cannot be moved, the notified authority shall make arrangement for the worker to receive treatment on the spot. The financial costs of all these are borne by the employer.[413]

4.2.1 Professional Risks

A worker in the course of employment may be exposed to types of accidents. Such accidents may arise due to the danger inherent in the job, machines, negligence of the workman or other workmen in the course of duty. Compensation becomes relevant only when the workman suffers from personal injury or a process which may either be an industrial accidents or an occupational disease[414]. This therefore does not extend to loss of property.

4.2.1.a Industrial Accidents

Industrial accident is a sudden, fortuitous and unexpected personal injury of the workman in the course of employment. As per Lord Macnaughten in *Fenton v. Thorley Co Ltd*[415] it means "an unlooked for mishap or an untoward event which is not expected or designed[416]. According to section 2 of Law no. 77/11 of 1st July 1977 as amended and supplemented by Law No. 80/05 of 14th July 1980, An industrial accident ia an accident in which a worker is involved regardless of its cause. Such may include accidents resulting from work or during work, during travel to and from the worker's principal residence or

413 See section 102 Labour code 1992.

414 In English Common law, Such compensation extends to trauma such as nervous shock or other psychological illness - *Yates v. South Kirkby,etc Colleries Ltd* [1910] 2 KB 538

415 [1904] UKHL 460, [1903] WN 149

416 *Ibid* at 448. See also Lord Loreburn in *Clover, Clayton & Co Ltd v. Hughes* [1910] AC 242, 246 where he averred that" No doubt the ordinary accident is associated with something external; the bursting of a boiler, or explosion in a mine, for example. But it may be merely from the man's own miscalculation, such as tripping and falling. Or it may be due both to internal and external conditions, as if a seaman were to faint in the rigging and tumble into the sea. I think it may also be something going wrong within the human frame itself, such as the straining of a muscle or the breaking of a blood vessel."

secondary residence which gives a certain character of permanence. What is of relevance here is that three things must be fulfilled before the workman is entitled to any compensation; it must be :

i. Personal injury on a living body distinguished from a process which leads to occupational disease. It does not extend to artificial parts attachments such as limbs, teeth, etc;
ii. Resulting from an accident which must be sudden and unlooked for mishap which may however be one of several occurrences but which one is capable of identifying as the accident as the lack of identifying act may be seen as a process and not an accident. In this regard in the *Akem Benbella Case*[417], the bone fracture immediately the Akem Ben Bella was struck made it an industrial accident.
iii. The accident must arise in the course of employment. This does not necessarily mean in the employer's factory. As per Lord Shaw in *Thom v. Sinclair*[418] 'If the condition of his employment oblige a workman to work in a particular building or position which exposes him and on the occasion of the accident to the injury...., then, although the accident is not consequent on has no causal relation to the work on which the workman is employed, such accident arises out of his employment, as incident, not to the character of the work, but to the dangers and risks of the particular building or position in which by the conditions of his employment he is obliged to work."[419] There must be a causal link between the accident and the employment. Under the 1977 Law as revised extends this to accidents to and from work (to permanent place of residence and *vice-versa*).

4.1.2.b Occupational Diseases

According to section 3 of Law No 77/11 of 13th May 1977 as Amended and Supplemented by Law No. 80-05 of 14th July 1980, Is any disease resulting

417 See in the same light *China Water & Anor v. Ndinwa Winifred* (2005) 1 CCLR, 11, where the respondent suffered from deafness immediately after there was a blast at the construction site where he was working. See also *Chou John v. CDC* HCF/L.29/2002-2003. (Unreported),where the worker suffered from severe laceration from a tapping knife.

418 [1917] AC 127.

419 *Ibid* 144-145. It extends therefore to the nature of employment, its conditions, its obligations and its incidents (*R v. Industrial Injuries Commissioner* [1966] 2 QB 31).

from the performance of certain professional activities and must feature in the list drawn up by the Minister of Labour and Social security in consultation with the National Occupational Health and safety Commission. As provided in Article 3(2) of the above law provides the list of occupational diseases is not exhaustive as new diseases may be included by the Minister of Labour and Social Security after Consultation with The National Occupational Health and safety Commission.

The occupational disease is distinguished from industrial accident in that the former is a process in the course of employment that gradually incapacitates the worker. Per Lord Porter in *Roberts v. Dorothea State Quarries Co ltd*[420]' the difference between injury by accident and disease had always been recognized and some one incident or definite and distinct series of incidents had recognised'. The series of incidents must have occurred over a length of time making so that one cannot tell the exact time the disease was contracted making it a process and not an accident. A case in Point is *TRAPP Groupement d'Entreprise v. Che Guza Cletus*[421] where a worker whose work involved blasting of stones at a quarry suffered from deafness as result of excessive and continuous noise at his job. It was held to be occupational disease.

For there to be an occupational disease, certain requirement must be fulfilled:

i. It must fall within the disease classified by the Minister of Labour and Social Security in consultation with the National Commission on Industrial Health and Safety.

ii. The disease must have been due to a process not an injury associated with the particular occupation or any number of occupation in the course of employment. In this regard, *Evouna Hypolite v. Boulangerie Moderne*[422] who sued for compensation for occupational disease-hernia which he claimed to have been contracted as a result of his work was dismissed on grounds that based on the nature of his job he could not have contracted the said disease in the course of that employment. Although however, it might have been as a result of strenuous work from another employment. That is why the medical examination before employment becomes very relevant to determine with

---

420 [1948] WN 246

421 Appeal No. BCA/L.2/98 (unreported).

422 Appeal no. 164 of 29th June 1971.

certainty where the disease might have emanated. Since certain diseases might be aggravated by the nature of the employee's work, the routine medical examination becomes even more relevant.

4.2.2 Workman's Compensation for Industrial Accidents and Occupational Diseases

The first law on accidents at work was Order No 59-00 of 31 December 1944 on work injury and occupational disease in French Cameroon. Law No. 77-11 of 27 July 1977 on work injury compensation which was implemented in 1978 by Decree No. 78-547 of 28th December 1978 and its 1980 amendment. Where the case of industrial accident or occupational disease is founded, the liability to pay compensation is on the employer of the injured worker without the requirement of any fault or blameworthiness of the employer. That is why the definition of a worker is imperative in employment relations. Such a worker who has suffere from partial or temporal disability is not supposed to be laid off but ought to be transferred to another service of the employer in addition to the compensation that is due. The employer has only three days to report such diseases when diagnosed and such accidents to the National Social Insurance Fund as per section 17(2) of the 1977 Law as revised. The workman has three years within which to make his claims for compensation from the national Social Insurance fund - Section 17(3) 1977 Law. Otherwise the worker loses the right to compensation be the Fund - *Chenze Tonga James v. NSIF*[423] where the complainant worker of CDC sustained personal injury in the course of employment in 1981, The fact of which was reported to the employer who did not inform the National Social Insurance Fund until 1988 and he was held to have been time barred.

This compensation is not available to self-employed only to private sector employments where the employer in such cases must make payments of 1.75%, 2.5%-5% of gross monthly payroll depending on the assessed degree of risk. For the worker to benefit although there is no required longevity of service before being entitled, the said worker must however been assessed with a work injury or occupational disease.

423 Unreported.

According to section 37 of the 1977 law as revised, no compensation is due if the accident is as a result of a criminal activity or intentional fault of the worker.

4.2.2.a Compensation for Temporal Incapacity

This is a situation where a worker is unable to work due to injury obtained or occupational disease in the course of employment but will eventually recover and return to work. According to section 27 of the 1977 Law as revised, if a certified medical officer confirms that an employee suffers from less 20% incapacity such a worker will be said to have suffered from temporal or partial incapacity. The worker is entitled to an allowance equal to four times their annual basic salary corresponding to the percentage of incapacity. See for example the case of *Ebong Joseph Akong v. FOURGEROLLE*[424] where the worker who was in charge of construction in SONARA sustained injury while lifting a large stone and sustained 15% temporal incapacity after the medical doctor's assessment. His compensation as shown above on his salary of 150.000frs was 15/100x150.000/1 x 4 =90.000frs.

Such an injured worker is also entitled to a constant attendant supplement if the injured insured requires the constant attendance of others to perform daily functions.

4.2.2.b Compensation for Partial Permanent Incapacity

Partial Incapacity is said to occur when the capacity of the worker is reduced permanently the earning capacity below the level of his capacity before the accident or injury. This occurs if there is a loss of a member or injury to parts of the body for example injured spine. According to article 26 of the 1977 Law as revised, in the case of partial disability for assessed degree of disability of at least 20% but less than 100%, a percentage of the full permanent disability pension is paid based on the assessed degree of disability of less than 20%, a lump sum of the partial disability pension is paid. In this regard, if a workman sustains injury which results to partial permanent disability that has been duly certified, the worker shall be entitled to a period payment obtained by multiplying the yearly payment for permanent incapacity by the percentage of disablement.

424 Unreported.

4.2.2.c Compensation in Case of Permanent Disability - Disability Pension

Disability pension is also payable where the workers being disabled can no longer work. Permanent disability is when a worker has 100% disability as certified by a medical officer rendering them incapable of performing any work because he/she is disabled for life. the disability must therefore affect his/her capacity to earn a salary. The worker's permanent injury must cause him permanent incapacity. That is why such a worker is immediately put on pension. In case of such permanent disability, i.e 100% disability, such a worker is entitled to 85% of the insured's average monthly earnings in the three months before the disability began is paid - section 23 of the 1977 Law as revised - see the case of *Nkem Patrick v. NSIF*[425]. According to section 25 of same, if the disabled worker in order to perform the ordinary acts of life resorts to the aid of a third party, his said periodic payment is increased by an amount equal to the salary for category 1.

For such benefits to avail him, he must be younger than the age of retirement, has an assessed loss of earning capacity of at least 66.66% and have at least five years of coverage and at least six months of contributions in the last twelve calendar months before the disability began. If the disability is not related to work, then no contribution is required. The disability pension ceases at the age of retirement and is replaced by the old age pension.

4.2.2.d Compensation in Case of Death

In case of the death of the employee, Section 29 oblige that their dependents and surviving spouse are entitled to periodic benefits payable by the National Social Insurance Fund.

In case of death, 85% of the deceased's average monthly earnings in the last three month is paid to the eligible survivors who are the widow(er), orphans younger than 14, 18 if an apprentice, 21 if a full time student or if disabled and dependent parents. In this regard, according to section 30 of the 1977 Law as revised, the following are dependents :

- Surviving spouse-section – section 30(a)
- Divorced or separated spouse who have been awarded alimony - Section 30(b)

---

[425] Unreported.

- Spouses who have remarried and their current spouse has no taxable income-Section 30(c)
- The dependent children of the deceased – section 30(d)
- Parents and grand parents who are dependents of the deceased worker - section 30 (e)

These dependents must however adduce evidence to attest that they depended on the deceased worker either totally or partially and they have suffered pecuniary loss because of their death - section 30(g). The amount of the period payment available to these dependents is the same as that paid to a permanently incapacitated employee as provided for in section 31 of the 1977 decree as revised. They hall therefore be entitled to quarterly periodic payments until they die in case of spouse (unless they remarry) and parents. In case of dependent children, such payments will stop when they attain 21.

Section 29 of the 1977 law as revised also makes provision for the payment of funeral expenses. Such funeral expenses include; the supply of a coffin, transportation of the corpse to place of burial; transportation of the deceased family and luggage from the place of death to the deceased worker's place of residence. The employer is entitled to reimbursement by the National Social Insurance Fund should they cover such funeral expenses.

4.4 Social Welfare Benefit in Case Unemployment

4.4.1 Employee's Severance Pay Benefits

According to section 37 of the Labour Code, all employers must provide severance pay to all their dismissed workers with a contract of unlimited duration and who had worked for at least 2 years and had not committed any serious misconduct. The pay here is based on longevity of service as follow 20% of employee's monthly wage for the first five years of service, 25% for each year of the service from 6th to the 10th year; 30% from the 11th-15th year; 35% from the 16th-20th year and 40% for each year of service exceeding 20 years.[426]

4.3.2 Technical Lay-off

These are terminations of employment contracts by reasons not inherent from the conduct of the employee. This usually occur when the company is

[426] According to Order No 16/MTPS/SG/CJ of May 26th 1993.

undergoing economic stress, technological changes or internal re-organisation when the company for example changes its status - Section 40 (2). The employer must however convene the staff representative and the competent labour inspector to discuss possibilities of reduction of working hours, part-time work, lay-offs, review of different allowances and wage cuts[427]. Should an agreement not be reached and the worker refuses in writing to accept these measures, (s)he shall be laid-off with a pay in lieu of notice in addition to being given a severance pay in case they meet the criteria for enjoyment of severance pay as explained above. The employer must determine an order of dismissal taking into consideration professional proficiency, seniority in the company and the family responsibilities of such a worker.[428] Such a worker will have prior claim with professional proficiency, the employment in the same establishment for a period of two years. - Section 40(10) Labour Code 1992.

4.3.3 Old Age Pension

The employer is supposed to pay 4,2% of the monthly payroll of the worker's earnings. At the age of 60 with at least 20 years coverage and at least 180 months of paid or credited contributions, including at least 60 months in the last 10 years.

The worker may also request for early pension at the age of 50 years with at least 20 years of coverage and at least 180 months of paid or credited contributions including at least 60 months in the last 10 years. (Minimum monthly pension is 50% of the legal monthly minimum wage)

In case of death, his pension (funeral grant and survivor pension) is paid to legitimate survivors who include his spouse and children under 21 if full time student or disabled. If the spouse remarries, the payment of the pension ceases.

4.4 Legal Actions Against Employer in Case of Non Compliance

The employer who fails to take proper action when the worker suffers from work related injuries or diseases is open to sanctions. Section 46 (1) of the 1977 law as revised, punishes any employer who neglects to notify National Social Insurance Fund within the period of three days about the accident or

[427] Section 40(3) of the Labour Code 1992.

[428] Section 40(6) of the Labour Code 1992.

disease with a fine of from 50000frs to 500.000 or six months imprisonment or with both such fine and imprisonment. The same sanction is meted on the employer who fails to register their employee with the National Social Insurance Fund.[429]

4.5 Judicial Procedure in Case Worker is Not Satisfied With Compensation

Where a worker is not satisfied with the amount of compensation received, the worker must report to the Administrative Complaints Commission situated in Yaounde which is in charge of resolving disputes over compensation rates or indemnities paid by the fund to injured workers. The dissatisfied injured worker must first petition the competent Regional commission situated at the headquarters of each region, which is chaired by a Magistrate, with two representatives of the National Social Insurance Fund, A representative of the Ministry of Labour and Social Security. In case the worker is not satisfied, they can go on appeal and finally to the Supreme Court whose decision is binding and final. - See Section 42 of the 1977 Law as revised.

4.6 Privileges and Guarantees of Wage Claims to Workers During Economic Difficulties of Factories

The Labour Code 1992, in its section 70(1), Up to the limit of the percentage of wages not liable to attachment wages are seen as preferred claims having priority over all other general or special preferential claims[430]. These priority position also extends to compensations due a worker in case of breach and to damages arising from wrong termination.[431]

To facilitate the payment of debts of employees have been due to their debtor the Uniform Act Organising Simplified Recovery procedures and

---

429 See Section 46(2) of the 1977 Law as revised.

430 Such preferential claims according to art 180 (3) of the OHADA Uniform Act on Securities such preferential claims include sums owed workers and apprentices for work done or as severance allowances during the last year prior to the debtor's debt, the seizure of his property or the court decision ordering collective proceedings. Mindful of Articles 225(3) And 226 (3) of the OHADA Uniform Act on Securities, such employees are ranked as creditors of super privileged wages and so receive their debts (wages) in priority over and above other creditors. In in the same regard Articles 166 and 167 of the OHADA Uniform act on Collective Proceeding for Clearing of Debts which gives high and priority ranking (2nd and 3rd position) to creditors of highly preferred wages in proportion to the value of the property with regard to the assets as a whole.

431 Section 70(2) Labour Code 1992.

Enforcement Measures in art 171 has made it possible for the creditor to attach the earnings due to the employees's debtor by an employer, although such attachment by the creditor is only possible after an attempt at conciliation[432] by a competent at the place of residence of the debtor. Such wages may only be attached in proportions determined by the state which may be on portions of the wages or even extra earnings after the deduction of taxes and other deductables.[433]

In addition, as per section 72, should a company become bankrupt or go into liquidation, sums which are withheld by the treasury after the cease to make payments to such employers shall be paid as asserts. This become relevant to worker because once such sums are paid in as assets of the employer, the available amount of money to pay the wages of such workers also increase. Section 66 of the Labour Code requires that where a worker is transferred out of their normal place of residence, such a must worker be provided adequate accommodation mindful of their family status. A worker shall continue to reside in the accommodation provided for him and his family before the commencement of bankruptcy or liquidation proceedings. Such a worker in addition is entitled to legal aid without any pre-application.[434]

---

[432] This procedure is spelt out in articles 179-182 of the Uniform Act on Simplified Recovery of Debts and Measures of execution on Attachment and Transfer of Earnings

[433] See Art 177 Uniform Act on Simplified Recovery of Debts and Measures of execution on Attachment and Transfer of Earnings.

[434] Section 73, Labour Code 1992.

CHAPTER 5

RESOLUTION OF EMPLOYMENT DISPUTES

In a bid to meet up with its international obligations, Cameroon has signed and ratified several ILO Conventions and other international treaties to ensure that rights are respected, protected and fulfilled. This is in consonance with article 6 ICECSR 1966 which gives state parties[435] the triple-pronged legal obligations, aimed at promoting security of service. The obligation to respect under article 6 ICESCR 1966 requires state parties to refrain from interfering directly or otherwise with employment through the passing of policies or programmes stifling employment.

State parties also have the obligation to protect, protect and fulfil which enjoins members to ensure that third parties do not interfere with a worker's employment. Despite these triple-pronged human rights obligations which are binding on private enterprises, much is still to be done. This situation results from the fact that some entrepreneurs /employers regard the worker as nothing more than a factor of production whose value is hinged exclusively on what he/she produces. Based on this reasoning, where the worker's capacity to work falls as a result of having contracted an occupational or industrial accident as in the *TRAPP Case*,[436] it makes sense to dismiss him since his skill in the art would have dropped.

A worker's labour, which is resident in his /her human person, is no doubt a factor of production, but not a mere commodity, which once it gets dysfunctional, should be discarded. Radin[437] in her theory of property and personhood has contended that because labour resides in a human being, it is of a special type, which cannot and should not be limited to the market value it

---

435 The right to work, General Comment 18, Committee on Economic, Social and Cultural Rights, 24th November 2005, p. 7-8.

436 In fact in Support of this idea is decision of the International Labour Tribunal in *Case Re Duran* where the tribunal held that where a worker can no longer render services because of complete incapacity he should be terminated. See Yanou *op. cit.* at p. 53.

437 Radin, M.J., 'Property and Personhood, ' 34 Stan. L.R. 1982, p957-959.

commands. When approached from Radin's theoretical perspective, the service that a worker offers during employment should be protected over and above what is being done under sections 38 and 39 of the Labour Code. This is all the more so as the country, by ratifying 44 of the ILO Conventions since 1960 when it became a member of the ILO, ought to enjoy a higher level of security than that prescribed by the Labour Code. Where therefore the right of one of the parties to the contract of employment have been infringed on, the proper procedure is to seek redress as provided for in sections 131 and 157 of the Labour Code 1992.

5.1 Resolution of Labour Disputes

Labour actions, whether individual or collective, are commenced on the basis that there is a dispute between the contracting parties. Section 131 of the Labour Code,1992, defines a labour dispute as an individual dispute arising from a contract of employment between workers and their employers or from a contract of apprenticeship. In the case of a collective dispute, section 157(1) of the Labour Code defines it as including any dispute which is characterised by :

a) the intervention of a group of wage earners, whether or not the said workers are organised in trade unions and
b) the collective nature of the intent at strike shall be deemed to be a collective labour dispute....'[438]

Yanou[439] citing the Supreme Court of Cameroon decision in *Total Fina Elf v. Nounda Martin*,[440] contends that it will be wrong to assume or treat as a collective dispute, workers cases filed individually against an employer, even if all of them are for the same grievance.

Unlike in Nigeria,[441] dispute resolution under the Labour Code does not include disputes between workers inter se in the ordinary course of employment. This ought not to be so since the whole idea of alternative dispute resolution in employment contracts is to maintain peace which is required to boost production and turn-over.

---

438 According to ILO Industrial Relations Survey, 2006, 22.73% of collective disputes stem from job security, 30% on wages, 11.82% on trade unions relations.

439 Yanou, M.A., *op. cit.* at p. 139.

440 Appeal No. 146/S/02-03 of 10th January, 2002.

441 Nigeria, for example, has included this category of relationship in its definition of Labour dispute. In fact, section 47(1) of Trade Dispute Decree No. 7 of 1976, Cap 432 defines a trade dispute as 'a dispute between employers and employees or between employees and employees which is connected with the employment or non-employment or the terms of employment and physical conditions of work of any person.

5.1.1 Individual Labour Disputes

Individual labour disputes may arise from a variety of reasons including the non -payment for work done by the employee, wrongful dismissals, and late payment of wages. When this occurs, section 139 (1) of the Labour Code, 1992, mandatorily requires the disputants (employer or employee) to request for settlement by the competent labour inspector, who does so through conciliation.[442] The competent labour inspector for this purpose is that in the division in which the employee was working before the labour dispute. If one of the disputants is an international organisation which has a convention with the Cameroonian government, the Ministry of Labour will take the place of the labour inspector.[443] The labour inspector may after conciliation issue a statement of conciliation,[444] partial conciliation[445] or non-conciliation.[446] As a rule of practice, the disputants together with the Labour Inspector must sign this statement so as to prevent any of the parties from introducing new claims not discussed during the conciliation process with the Labour Inspector.[447]

As provided in section 139(4) of the Labour Code, these resolutions, however, become enforceable only after the endorsement of the resolution by the court with competent jurisdiction. If a court fails to endorse, or endorses only after a long time, the aggrieved worker will continue to suffer grave injustice and hardship especially if the settlement included payment of money.[448] Statements of conciliation or non-conciliation by default are issued by the labour inspectors where one of the parties fails to appear at the labour

---

442 This is sometimes mistaken for mediation. It could be defined as alternative to dispute resolution where the third party makes proposals for settlement to the disputants and helps them to reach a resolution. In the civil system, this is seen as conciliation while in common law this is sometimes taken for mediation.

443 *CARFOP v. Kan Elroy Moses Payne*. Suit No. BCA/7.L/1998 (unreported).

444 where through his encouragement, the parties agree to the terms of settlement.

445 where the parties accept or reject some of the terms proposed by themselves or the labour inspector. In this wise therefore, the Labour Inspector is supposed to include in his statement of partial conciliation the terms agreed upon and those rejected.

446 The parties do not reach an agreement.

447 Yanou, M.A., *op. cit.* at p. 137.

448 This position of the Code lend credence to the views of a Labour Inspector (Tabe Raymond interviewed on 13/12/2010 in Buea, South West Region) at the Regional Delegation of Labour that the code contemplates their activity as a fire brigade to quell down tempers of the disputants before the commencement of litigation. He contends that though conciliation is advised in labour relations, section 139(4) reduces them to a mere transmission zone, a vehicle to the courts. He added that if the Code had given them the opportunity to assert their authority by making the decisions arrived at binding, the desired effect and intends of conciliation, which is speedy redress, would have been achieved as it would have been faster than what obtains currently.

inspectorate after service. This power is to be applauded because it strengthens security of service in that it prevents unscrupulous employers from frustrating the workers quest for justice,[449] as was held in the case of *Njoko Jean Claude v. Societe SOFIDEX & Njoh Francois Maurice.*[450]

If conciliation is not arrived at, it is important for a worker seeking redress to know which court has jurisdiction to entertain the matter as a wrong procedure will render the whole process invalid as was held in *Joseph Nyambi v. CDC*[451]. From the perspective of territorial jurisdiction, the competent court is the place of employment. Where however the worker has moved, the court in the division of his/her new abode[452] is competent. With regard to subject matter jurisdiction, a worker must file his suit in the Magistrate's Court if the limits of his claim is within ten million FCFA under section 15 (1) (b) of Law No. 2006/015 of 29th December 2006.[453] For claims above ten million francs, the worker must file his/her suit in the competent High Court as laid down in section 18(1) (b) of the same Law.[454]

Where the defendant fails to appear[455], judgment is entered by default for the plaintiff (which in most cases is the worker), after examination of the case as provided for in section 143(2) of the Labour Code. This is commendable

---

449 It is trite law that all parties to a suit be given fair hearing and equal opportunity whether it a court or a quasi-legal body like that operated by the Labour Inspector. Although Mbuagbaw JCA in *Chungong Christopher v Pecten Cameroon Company* Suit No. CASWP/ L.2/1992 at p, 269(unreported) held that the right to fair hearing included the right of the person to be affected to be present all through the proceedings and to hear all the evidence against him, by not hearing from the other party who wilfully and intentionally abstain from the proceedings when an opportunity to hear his side has been given does not necessarily go against one of the twin pillars of natural justice-*audi alteram partem* as was held in the unanimous judgment of the Court Appeal South West delivered by Bawak JCA (as he then was) in *Cameroon Lonestar Fishing v.Cali Guiseppe* Suit No. CASWP/60/1997, 127 at p. 133.

450 This same position will be adopted should one of the parties be present but refuse to sign the settlement as decided in *CDC v Andrew S.N. Nfor* (1997) 1CCLR, 127 at p. 166.

451 SCC No. 14/5 of 17th March 1977. See also *Isaac Guh v.Guardian Royal Assurance* SCC No. 15/5 of 17th March 1977 and Lord Denning in *Macfoy v.United Africa Company LTD* [1961] 3WLR 1405 at p. 1409. Where the learned judge held that 'if an act is bad, then at law it is a nullity.

452 The case of *PAMOL Plantation v. William Kimbeng* (2001) 2CCLR 127-251.

453 On Judicial organization.

454 In this wise, in the case of *SONEL v. Lembe Samuel* (1997) 1CCLR, 289 the North West Court of Appeal held that both the Limbe Court of First Instance and the Court of Appeal South West had erred in admitting that the Limbe Court had Jurisdiction to entertain the respondents claim when it discovered that his claim is above five million (the then limit of that court before the 2006 amendments). The importance of this to the security of service of workers is that the worker's claim will be void even where he/she commenced the claim in the court with competent territorial jurisdiction but the subject matter jurisdiction is wrong.

455 Section 141(2) of the labour Code 1992, requires that the summons shall state the name, occupation of plaintiff, subject matter of petition, place, date and hour of appearance.

for security of service purposes as it forestalls any intention by the absentee defendant (who more often than not is the employer) to frustrate the worker's quest for redress and justice.

In a bid to ensure that justice is affordable and accessible to even the poorest worker, before and after conciliation, labour suits are filed cost free under section 138(1) of the Labour Code. Furthermore, it is noteworthy that labour decisions do not attract taxes following 138(2) Labour Code 1992. This is unlike the situation in other actions where the notorious 5% of the amount claimed must be paid pursuant to Finance Circular No. 00012/MJ/SG/DAG of 13/5/96. This has made it impossible for many litigants to file their actions in court regardless of the degree of injustice done to them. The filing of labour actions cost free and the exemption from the payment of 5% deposit has contributed immensely in strengthening security of service in employments. This province of Cameroonian law is laudable.

Since no judgment is good judgment until it is enforced, once a worker has received a favourable judgment, enforcement is by way of simplified procedure of the Simplified Procedures and Enforcement Measures of the Uniform Act of the OHADA 1998[456].

5.1.2 Collective Disputes

Collective disputes are collective industrial disputes arising in situations where workers have a common industrial problem in their work place. Before any collective dispute goes to the competent court for arbitration, which in this instance is the Court of Appeal of the place of residence or employment of the employee,[457] the dispute must go through conciliation. As was held in the *Total Fina Case*, the collectiveness of the dispute must be ascertained. It is not assumed and it is not justified simply because of the collective interests of the workers. Collective disputes strengthen the security of service since workers who act as a group are more likely to protect their interest better than those who act individually. Besides, collective disputes reduce the time that will be spent on a dispute with the same facts had the complaint been lodged

---

456 Labour judgments and enforcements are subject to the general provisions of the Uniform Act dealing with enforcement measures in Cameroon. This is because a labour judgment is an enforceable right on the basis that it is a court decision, which has been declared enforceable. See Yanou., M.A., *Labour Law Principles and Practice, op. cit.* at 158-159.

457 Section 161(1) of the Labour Code 1992.

severally. Under this procedure, all the disputants after being summoned[458] are supposed to be present either in person or through a representative who, as Pougoue[459] explains, could be a staff representative, trade unionist or an advocate. It can be gleaned from this subsection that a worker at this stage can benefit from professional representation. Unfortunately, the workers especially are oblivious of this protective measure and so miss the opportunity of professional advice and representation, compounding further their situation against powerful employers.

Failure to appear in person or through a representation attracts a sentence of 50.000 to 500.000FCFA.[460] This requirement must be condemned because this criminalisation of a purely civil transaction violates the fundamental rights of the worker.[461] This provision shows that the government is not committed to fostering a decent and sane labour environment. It also weakens security of service since it clearly has potentials to scare workers away from challenging employers through the collective dispute process.

The role of the assessors who according to section 161(1) (a) are members of the arbitral board, are not spelled out in the Code. This explains why in every eight cases out of ten examined by this researcher, the two assessors (worker and employer assessor) do not attend the arbitral sessions. It reduces the intended effect of their contribution to the dispute settlement, as the tribunal will not get their expert advice.

It may be observed that it is only after the attempts to arbitrate have failed that the workers can go on strike or lock-out under section 157 (3) of the Labour Code, 1992. This procedure on strike during collective dispute is a gimmick to diffuse the temper of angry workers committed to forcing their

458 According to section 158(2) of the Labour Code 1992, the conciliation is mandatory even if it is not so provided in the collective agreements of the workers. In other jurisdictions like Nigeria and Britain once there is apprehension of a dispute the competent authorities must try to resolve the dispute out of court. In Cameroon, the Labour Inspector does not go to the disputants but wait for them to lodge a complaint.

459 Pougoue, P-G., Tchokomakoua, V., Kenfack, P-E, Seuna, C. And Tchakoua, J.M., *Code du Travail Camerounais Annote*, Yaounde, Presse Universitaire d'Afrique, 1997,p. 229.

460 As provided under section 158(3) of the Labour Code 1992. As observed by Yanou (*Labour Law, Op. cit.* at p. 139 in concurrence with Ngassa J in *Ndongo Fred Ebanja v. Chamber of Commerce (supra)*, instead of paying the penalty to the state treasury, it would have been better for this amount to be paid to the other party as damages.

461 Section 607 of the Criminal Procedure Code gives the powers to Court of First Instance, the High Court, Military Court, Judicial police, public servants vested with judicial police powers charge with simple offences and collect fixed fines under the supervision of the Legal Department. A labour inspector clearly does not fall within any of this class.

employer to yield to their demands when the issue under dispute is still hot[462]. The procedure does not enhance security of service especially as section 165(1)(b) (i) of the Labour Code, 1992, provides that striking workers may be terminated on grounds of serious misconduct or punished with fines of between 200.000fCFA and 1.000.000FCFA. By implication, such workers may be dismissed summarily without notice, compounding a bad situation as, even if a case of wrongful termination is eventually entered, such workers cannot be re-instated or re-engaged except they are union leaders as provided for in section 130 of the Code.[463] The Labour Code is silent as to the legal action the workers can take should the employer remain adamant to their demands even after the strike action.[464] It is this lacuna in the Code that has left many of the striking workers of the Cameroon Tea Estate in a loss as to where to seek recourse, to occupy the South West Regional Delegation of Labour and Social Security.

5.1.3 An Assessment of Arbitration in the Labour Code

The economic crisis ushered in massive lay-offs of workers in Cameroon, some in flagrant disrespect of provisions in the Labour Code as provided for in sections 34, 38 and 40 especially. This continued even after the crisis leading to many individual and collective disputes. By the nature and complexity of labour relations emanating from the contract of employment, disputes are inevitable, especially where one party seeks to act opportunistically by taking advantage of a change in circumstances, uncertainty in the contract or in the substantive

---

462 It should be noted for example that a collective dispute filed in March 2004 by 703 workers of CTE against the CTE in 2004, it was only in may 2009 that a statement of non-conciliation by default was issued. See reference No. 37/MINTSS/DRTSS/SWR/BIT/BU.28/C of 25th May 2009. Seven years after the complaint to the labour inspector arbitration procedure is still in course at the Court of Appeal South West Region see *Simon Tamanjong & 703 Ors v. The G.M of CTE*, Suit No CASWR/l.14/2009 (unreported). This lengthy procedures which delay justice might have forced the apparently helpless workers to resort to street marches that seriously affected Buea.

463 The highhandedness of some employers who have no regard for the rule of law like the GM of CTE, led to the sacking of Metuge George Ndobe, Tafon Charles and Ngwa Jacob staff representatives of CTE in flagrant disrecpect of the due process. They were however re-instated by the Minister of Labour and Social Security, Prof Nkili by Circular No. CTE-GM/01/054 of 29th January 2004.

464 Yanou is of the opinion that the workers should the attempt at arbitration fail the dispute should be remitted to the competent High Court. See generally Yanou. M.A., *Labour Law: Principles and Practice, op. cit.* at p. 158-161. However, a review of applicable law and caselaw of the Court of Appeal and Supreme Court show that there is no authority given to the High Court to entertain dispute which has been subject to the jurisdiction of the Court of Appeal. Furthermore, a magistrate of a lower scale cannot be competent to hear a matter already adjudged by a magistrate of a superior scale.

law. These disputes are not only a waste of valuable time and financial resources, they end up damaging the confidence, trust and reputation both parties might have acquired, which are central to the employment relationship.

The adversary system has often been thought to be inappropriate to the needs of employment relations as it is often protracted with a lot of procedural manoeuvring, which ends up being too expensive for a worker thereby frustrating his quest for justice. This notwithstanding, it can be argued that the refusal to allow aggrieved parties to approach the courts directly without necessarily going through the alternative dispute resolution is a breach of their fundamental right to access to justice. Whatever benefits the mandatory arbitral system has for security of service is superficial. It fundamentally works against the worker in and out of employment. Its major negative effect on security of service is seen in the fact that under it, it is impossible for a worker to get an injunction to restrain an employer determined to terminate his employment unlawfully. In other common law jurisdictions, this is not the case as was held in *Jones v. Gwent County Council.*[465] Here, after receiving a notice of dismissal, the employee applied and obtained an interim injunction preventing dismissal and a permanent injunction restraining the dismissal.[466]

Furthermore, the choice of the Court of Appeal as the seat of the arbitral board where collective disputes are heard is not good for the worker who is seeking justice. The idea of a courtroom defeats the informality and privacy needed in ADR. ADR strives to reach a settlement away from courtrooms, its technicality and environment which may not be 'comfortable' to ADR.

Based on this, therefore, it is opined that the arbitration scheme contemplated in the Code is a far cry from what arbitration ought to be. It is more an employment tribunal because of the manner it is constituted and because of lack of consensual agreement from which all arbitration take their power. It is submitted that the provisions on arbitration be revised to put it on the same pedestal like arbitration in modern employment relations. This will greatly enhance the type of justice dispensed. Perhaps, the type of alternative contemplated by the Code is not the best for employment relations for the first thing to ascertain in order to dispense proper justice is to shop for the best ADR.

---

465 [1992] 1RLR 521. See also *Irani v. Southampton and South West Hampshire Health Authority* [1985] 1 CR 590.

466 The worker must show that there is a prima facie case, the worker will lose the opportunity for his/her case to be heard, loss of his job would not be readily compensable and the balance of convenience is in favour of the worker. Anderman., S.D.,*Labour Law,op. cit.* at p. 94.

5.2 The Role of a Labour Inspector in Dispute Resolution: A Critique

Conciliation, which in strict legal sense is an independent, impartial and fair service, which tries to negotiate a compromise (rather than win a case) after examining the strength and weaknesses of a case, is a user friendly approach in the determination of disputes.[467] The adoption of this option in Cameroon and putting it under the competence of the labour inspector is to a certain degree[468] commended by this candidate.

However, the question is whether within the context of article 37(2) of the 1996 Constitution of Cameroon as revised, and section 18(1) (c) of the Law on Judicial Organisation 2006, the labour inspector can properly discharge this function? This question assumes greater significance as the labour inspector is required by section 139(1) of the Labour Code to settle the individual disputes amicably and under section 158(2) of the Code to attempt a settlement where a collective agreement fails to do so. This is an onerous quasi-judicial responsibility. This responsibility demands that a labour inspector appreciate the fine legal details and intricacies in the dispute. However, being a trained labour (civil) administrator and not a judicial officer trained in labour justice, the labour inspector lacks the requisite knowledge and experience to discharge the serious responsibility. This affects the quality of service offered by the labour inspector and this impacts negatively on the security of service in private employment.

Besides, in a proper system of conciliation, the conciliator is supposed to be independent, neutral and impartial[469], chosen by the disputants themselves. The labour inspector who is imposed on the disputants by section 139 of the Labour Code, 1992, unlike what obtains in classic arbitration situations, cannot attract the confidence of the disputants like is the case in classic arbitration. This alone plays against the dispute resolution mechanism, since he/she is not their choice of referee, the disputants

---

467 Bowers, J.,& Gill, M., 'Employment Disputes,' in *ADR and Commercial Disputes*, Russel Caller (eds), London: Sweet & Maxwell, 2002, p 57-58.

468 There is controversy in industrial relations whether a labour inspector's function as an administrator is compatible with his role as a conciliator. Their functions in this regard is French inspired as opposed to the countries of the common law jurisdiction which have adopted the system where a labour inspector is prohibited from acting as a conciliator as recommended by the Labour Inspection Recommendation No. 81 of 1947.

469 The central pillars of any Alternative Dispute Resolution mechanism. According to Supreme Court Judgment No.9/CS of 22 November 1973 in Pougoue *et al,op. cit.* at p. 229, he is a privileged witness of the eventual agreement.

are most unlikely to adequately collaborate with him in negotiating a compromise as one party (the worker) may see him/her as taking side with the employer.

In Cameroon, whether correctly assumed or otherwise, a worker's success in career is measured by the administrative positions held and maintained. A labour inspector obtains his qualification after post-graduate studies at *Ecole Nationale d'Administration et Magistrature*. He/she is a civil servant, a labour administrator[470] vying for administrative appointments, which are given only to those who do not only maintain a cordial relationship with their administrative and political superiors but also act according to their dictates. The function of a labour inspector as a conciliator[471] must therefore be seen from this premise. Where a labour inspector has a case involving a government organ, his/her impartiality, fairness and neutrality in arriving a proper settlement, is questionable[472]. This has tremendous negative impact on employment security.

The case of *Simon Tamanjong & 6 others v. Cameroon Tea Estate*[473] illustrates this point. Here, workers of the Cameroon Development Corporation(CDC) who were transferred from Ndu and Djutissa respectively to Tole were terminated on the 17/04/2004 and 26/2/06 respectively. They were paid off in September 2006 without repatriation dues as required by section 94 of the Labour Code. The terminated workers continued to stay in the accommodation at their CTE camps in Tole since their employers had not put the usual lorry to transport them back to Ndu at their disposal. They complained about this to the employers but never received any reply.

After they were driven out of the camps where they do not pay rents, electricity and water, these destitute workers complained to the local labour inspector. The matter went to the arbitration board which awarded the complainants 200.000frs each for their transportation. Rather strangely and contrary to section 94(4) of the Labour Code, the inspector failed to award them their remuneration up to when the transport was to be provided.

---

470 Section 105(1) of the Code defines a labour Inspector as "civil servants of the labour administration corps placed at the head of the Labour and Social insurance Inspectorate or his delegate".

471 According to section 11(2) of the Magistrates' Courts (Southern Cameroon) Law 1955, every administrative officer shall ex officio be a justice of peace for the area of the Southern Cameroon to which he is for the time being appointed as such an officer. In this wise, a Labour Inspector appointed to an area *ipso facto* becomes a justice of peace in the execution of his function as a conciliator. See Wackai JCA in *Ndop v. Yenkong* (1994) CAJ-CLC 56-74.

472 This is so even though section 105(3) of the code guarantees their independence.

473 Suit No. CASWP/L.8/2007 (unreported).

In a subsequent letter written by the workers to the representative of the International Labour Organisation in Yaounde, Cameroon, dated 19th September 2010, the ex-workers complained that not even the Regional Delegate of Labour and Social Security (a labour inspector) could make the employer respect the arbitral award.

Furthermore, after attempting a settlement of the labour dispute as required by section 139(1) for individual dispute and section 158 for collective disputes, the Labour Inspector is required by section 139(4) of the Labour Code and section 159 (1) of the same Code to reduce his/her settlement into total conciliation, partial-conciliation and non-conciliation for collective disputes. He/she is further required by sections 139(6) and 140 to send a copy of the settlement signed by him/her and the disputants, to the President of the competent court for endorsement and enforcement.

This role is a pre-condition to the realisation of the legal redress sought by a worker because the enforcement of whatever settlement arrived at is hinged on whether the labour inspector performs the above fundamental role. Meanwhile, the absence of a time bar for the inspector to forward the settlement to the competent court, leads to the possibility of delays in transmitting the conciliation decisions with negative effects on the security of service. The facts of *Abakem v. Labour Inspector Meme Division*[474] shows clearly that the labour inspector's role could be used against the worker. Here, the Labour inspector refused to issue the dismissed worker partial conciliation to commence his action in court. The worker had to compel him to issue it by a *mandamus*.

According to Yanou,[475] article 37(2) of the 1996 Constitution as revised has made the Supreme Court, the Court of Appeal and tribunals the only courts with authority to exercise judicial power. He argues that, this has taken away the powers of the High Court to check the excesses of the labour inspector. This compelling argument is supported by the unanimous decision of the South West Court of Appeal delivered by Fonkwe JCA in *The Liquidator, National Produce Marketing Board v. Egbe Stephen Batuo.*[476] Here, the court held that the powers of the high court to issue prerogative writs commanding public officers to do their duties have been abrogated by the Law No. 89/019 of

474 Suit No. HCK/L.9/1984 (unreported).

475 *Supra* at p. 3.

476 Suit No CASWP/44/97, CCLR part 8 p. 185 at p. 198. Similarly, the Bamenda Court of Appeal in *Ngwayi & 2 Others v Nyam* Appeal No. BCA/13/89 (unreported)where the appellants who brought an action against the Municipal Administrator Nkambe for destruction if his property. It was held that an action against a municipal authority before any other court but the Supreme Court would be barred for want of jurisdiction.

29/12/89[477] on Judicial Organisation and so any such motion is a 'legal fallacy emanating out of void proceedings.' This is further supported by section 18(1)(c) of the Judicial Organisation Ordinance, 2006 which gives powers to the High Court to issue such orders only in non-administrative functions. Clearly, since the labour inspector's function is administrative, it does not come within the contemplation of this subsection. Before now, if a labour inspector fail to perform his/her function, the only redress for a worker is to go to the Administrative Bench of the Supreme Court. Today, Law No. 2006/016 of 29 December 2006 organising administrative courts has created administrative courts in each region.

[477] Now Law No 2006//015/29/12/2006 on Judicial Organisation.

CHAPTER 6

DETERMINATION OF CONTRACTS OF SERVICE

Although employment contracts strike at the core of labour relations, the manner the worker is treated during the duration of the contract and upon the determination of the contract of employment is primary to employment relationships. Although admittedly the contract of employment is not intended to last forever, contracts of service must be managed in accordance with the terms of the employment.

Their termination whether by operation of law or by acts of the parties, must be done in a manner consistent with the norms of the employment and procedure in force.[478] Proceeding from the assumption that the employer and the employee are free and equal parties to the contract, each ought to have the same rights and powers to terminate the employment contract.[479] According to this thinking, to suggest otherwise will convert the relationship into one of slavery.

The manner in which a worker is treated after the contract ends (either by operation of law or acts of the parties) significantly affects the right with real consequences on labour justice and security. This view is soundly predicated on the applicable international treaties and local statutes.

6.1 Determination of Contract Employment

The determination[480] of a contract of employment in common parlance is the process of bringing a contract of employment to an end.[481] This may

---

478 ILO Recommendation No. 119 (1963) on the termination of employment, which provides that an employer should not dismiss an employee without a valid reason and without the dismissed employee having a right to complain to an independent tribunal. ILO Convention No. 158 on Termination of employment 1982, section 4 imposes an obligation to provide valid grounds for dismissal as well as the right to legal and other redresses in the case of unjustified dismissal.

479 Voize-Valayre, R.W., "The French Law of Unjust Dismissal," 23 *New York University Journal of International Law and Politics*, 1991, p. 520.

480 The Labour Code has neither defined this notion nor the notions of dismissals and terminations.

481 English Law Dictionary, Peter Collins Publishing defines determination as bringing to an end of a contract of employment either by resigning, retiring, being fired or made redundant

occur by dismissal,[482] retirement[483] or termination. The notion in general refers to the act of ending the employment in any of the variety of ways that contracts end. This broad definition also covers contracts of specified duration as defined in section 25(1) (a) of the Code, which end upon the expiry of the stipulated time stated in the contract.[484]

The manner in which a contract is determined does affect the security of employment. Firstly, a wrongfully determined employment severs and puts an end to an employment that would otherwise have remained in existence with its privileges like salary, housing[485], car (or their equivalence in cash), just to name a few. Besides, the manner adopted to determine an employment significantly affects the possibility of the employee getting another employment in future. It is because of the potentials for this devastating consequence that it is necessary to ensure that employments are correctly determined. It has for this reason become necessary to identify and analyse the two major modes by which contracts of employment are determined under the Labour Code in Cameroon. These are termination and dismissal.

6.2 Termination of Employment

While in common parlance termination means bringing to an end or conclusion,[486] the notion in the context of employment law, refers to a situation where the contract of service ends in the manner contemplated by the parties in the contract. This could either be by operation of law or mutual agreement.[487] Termination as technically defined is a function of the idea of

---

[482] Which could be defined as summary determination of a contract of employment without notice and for a just cause.

[483] This is what Uvieghara *op. cit.* at p. 46 describes as determination by performance. It could be regarded as the bringin g of a contract of unspecified duration to its logical end upon the attainment of retiring age. Even though private sector employees go on retirement at the age of 60, public sector employee go on retirement as from between the age of 50-65 years depending on their category and rank in the particular cadre in the civil service. This notwithstanding, some of the workers request for retirement before they are due retirement upon the service of proper notice.

[484] However, if there is a breach of contractual term by either party or frustration or by agreement such a contract can also be determined before its due date.

[485] Arrete No. 018/MTPS/SG/CJ of 26/5/1983 makes it mandatory for employers to pay rents to workers staying more than ten kilometres away from their place of work.

[486] See Websters New Collegiate Dictionary, Merriam-Webster Inc Publisher, p. 1217.

[487] It is the process by which a contract of employment is put to an end in accordance with the predetermined rules regulating employment. Freedman, M.R., *The Contract of Employment*, Oxford: Oxford Clarendon Press, 1976, p.142.

the freedom of contracts of employment. Under this philosophy, each party to the contract of service has the right to terminate it whenever he/she desires, after the service of appropriate notice.[488]

It may be observed that at common law, the employer does not even have to give reasons for termination, much less justify it. It would seem that, this common law conceptualisation of termination which requires that a valid notice be served by the terminating party has been incorporated into section 34(1) of the Labour Code. However, under the Code, the terminating party must set out reasons for termination.

Voize-Valayre[489] has observed that termination was scarcely distinguished from the notion of dismissal,[490] which was a brain child of the socio-political demand of the post industrial society[491] designed to compensate for the vulnerability of employees in a liberal state. However, notwithstanding this observation, termination and dismissal are conceptually different as was held by the Supreme Court of Nigeria in *Irem v. Obubra District Council.*[492] Each affects security of service in the country differently. The Court in the above case noted that dismissal brings disgrace upon the employee which is not the case with termination. Although the court did not say so, equally obvious is the fact that it is a lot more difficult for a dismissed worker to get alternative employment. Indeed, because termination carries with it financial cost for the employer (such as severance pay, leave claims, seniority bonuses, etc), employers are generally reluctant to resort to it lightly. Dismissal on the other hand, only require the employer to pay wages which had become due at the date of dismissal. Its limited financial incidence makes it the option of choice for employers as well as it makes it a serious obstacle for strong employment. To this extent, terminations facilitate and strengthen the security of service unlike dismissal (as is explained in details in subsequent sections) which is a dead end.

---

488 Under section 36 of the Code, an attempt to terminate without notice is wrongful and exposes the guilty party to the payment of compensation.

489 Voize-Valayre, R., "The French Law of Unjust Dismissal," *New York University Journal of International Law and Politics*, 1991, 520.

490 This notion is conceived in this write-up as precipitated termination of contracts of employment for genuine cause.

491 See Camerlynck, G-H., « *Normalisation du Licenciement et Sauvegarde des Pouvoirs du Chef d'Entreprise,* » in Voize-Valyre,R., *op. cit.* at p. 520.

492 [1960]5 FSC 24.

6.2.1 Termination by Agreement

This involves the bringing of a contract of employment to an end on terms agreed on by the parties when the contract is being made. Although by section 38 of the Code, a contract of specified duration cannot be terminated at any time before its expiry, except in cases of gross misconduct. However, based on the philosophy of freedom of contract, in the case of contracts of unspecified duration, the parties may agree to terminate before the due date based on any term they so agree upon. This is thus the foundation of termination in the contract of employment.

6.2.2 Termination by Service of Notice

The termination of employment by notice is the most basic form of termination in labour law. This involves putting an end to the contract of employment by either party through the service of proper notice to terminate. At common law, the period of notice may be specified in the contract itself, subject to the fact that such notice must not be less than the statutory minimum period for notice.[493] It could also be implied by the courts based on what is considered reasonable in the specie of employment and the employee's seniority.[494] Even here, such implied notice must not be below the statutory minimum period for notice.

This common law position has apparently been adopted in section 34(1) of the Labour Code which provides that either party to a contract of employment can end the contract at will upon the service of proper notice. This provision, unlike what obtains under the common law, insists that the party giving notice must 'set out the reason for termination.' If a party fails to serve proper notice, the termination automatically becomes wrongful. There may, however, be an agreement to discharge where the employee waives his rights and accepts compensation in lieu of notice. In such a situation, the non-provision of notice will not be considered fatal.[495]

---

493 According to section 34(1) of the Code, notice starts to run from the date of notification. See especially Ministerial Order No. 15/MTPS/SG/CJ OF 26th May 1993 that provides the different periods of notice contemplated.

494 Case in point is *Hill v. Parson* & Co. Ltd [1972] 1 Ch. 305. Where the courts decided that one month's notice for a senior engineer was inadequate and inappropriate. It held that a reasonable notice in this case could be anything six to twelve months.

495 See also section 11 of ILO Convention No. 158, Termination of Employment Convention.

The provision of section 34 is similar to the position taken on notice in the 1974 Labour Code which was interpreted by the Cameroonian Supreme Court in *Ngo Minyemeck Catherine v. COMACIC.*[496] The court construed the provision as giving either party to the employment contract the liberty to terminate it at will subject to notice.[497]

The outright adoption of 'the subject to notice' in the *COMACIC case* is an exemplification of the *laissez-faire* philosophy without more. This philosophy remains a dangerous ammunition in the hands of an employer with the capacity to affect the security of service negatively. The correct interpretation of section 34 requires the terminating party to not only properly serve a written notice but also to state the reasons for termination which must not be frivolous. This is especially so because the service of appropriate notice puts an end to the contract of service from the date the notice period expires leaving the employee with no other financial claims if he/she was paid for the full period of notice.

Section 34 read together with section 39(3) of the Labour Code requires the party terminating the employment to establish the reasons given for putting the employment to an end. Construed together, the provisions strengthen the security of service in private sector employments immensely. It is for this reason that the Supreme Court in *Jourdan Roger v. Izoung Michel*[498] categorically held that the termination of a houseboy who had worked for six years because his employer had been made General Manager of BICIC was apart from being reckless, wrongful. Relying on this Supreme Court decision, Yanou[499] argues that section 34 has not weakened the security of service in Cameroon. On the contrary, the author observes that on a careful review of the current Code, it is obvious that the right to terminate may not be abusively and negligently used against a worker.

In spite of the above conclusion, the sanction for the non-observance of the stipulated period of notice as contemplated in section 36(1) of the Code, does not foster security of service. The fact that a worker who is so terminated is entitled to compensation corresponding only to the remuneration including any bonuses and allowances which the worker would have received for the

---

496 Appeal No. 25 of 21/3/1974. This is the same position adopted by the Supreme Court of Nigeria by Obaseki JSC in *Ajayi v. Texaco Nigera Ltd* [1991] 4 NWLR 750 where held that once notice has been served, its validity cannot be vitiated by the existence of malice or improper motive since the right to serve a notice is totally independent of the motive that prompted the exercise.

497 Yanou, *op. cit.* at p. 65.

498 Appeal No 25 of 25/4/1978 (unreported).

499 Yanou, M.A, *Labour Law Principles &Practice in Cameroon*, *op. cit.* at p. 65.

period in which the notice was not observed is clearly weak and advantageous to the employer. This compensation regime rather than acting as a deterrent against reckless terminations of employment, is a recipe for employers to terminate workers. Clearly, had the remedy under section 36(1) of the Code been a heavier financial penalty, an employer will weigh the cost of his action on his business before engaging in recklessly terminating the employment of workers.

Although the Labour Code does not specifically prescribe for the payment of monetary compensation in lieu of notice, there is a tendency in labour relations towards the payment of money in lieu of notice. Uvieghara[500] has advanced two reasons for this. He posits that the remedy for wrongful termination is the salary the worker was supposed to receive in the form of liquidated damages and not mere notice. In addition, the author notes that at common law, an employer fulfils his/her common law obligation by paying wages and so is not required to provide the worker with work to do. Although the above reasons are plausible especially as the employee gets money in his/her pocket, Uvieghara ignores the fact that the same is bad for security of service for it clearly encourages an employer to go around the statutory dictates of employment law with impunity.

It is plain that for notice to be valid, it must be written. However, it has been rightly observed[501] that a written notice not brought to the attention of a worker is not proper service of notice as contemplated by section 34 of the Code. Yet, curiously, the same author interprets *Hannah Nganje v. University of Buea*[502] as establishing the principle that the service of a radio message warning a worker to resume duty or face termination is regarded as regular and valid notice. This writer differs with the analysis and interpretation in the *Hannah Nganje Case* because neither under the literary rule of interpretation or the purposive rule would the second limb of section 34(1) of the Labour Code, which makes reference to writing carry such a meaning. 'Writing' in this context cannot be synonymous with 'oral', which radio announcements do. It is equally contended that the construction in *Hannah's Case* is profoundly incorrect since 'writing' as used in section 34 means to inscribe or communicate by letter. This view of construction of section 34 of the Labour Code is in the view of this writer conducive to strengthening the security of service.

500 Uvieghara *op. cit.* at p. 61.
501 Yanou, *op. cit.* at p. 67.
502 Suit No. HCF/L.8/99. (unreported).

This notwithstanding, the fact that modes of communication are now instantaneous, the requirement of writing ought to be revisited to include these new forms of instantaneous communication.

It seems obvious that for the purpose of the worker's security of employment, the period of notice is construed to run from the date of the service and not otherwise. Besides, for similar reasons notice cannot be set-off against any leave of the worker as to do so will conflict with section 34(2) of the Labour Code. It is thus important to know the date and time of notice in order to ascertain with clarity when the notice period starts running.

Some schools of thought[503] contend that the date of notification of the termination is the date the contract was terminated, irrespective of the wrongfulness of the termination. However, this view is suspect because from sections 34(2) and 35 of the Code the date of notification is not the date of termination of the contract but the date from which the period of notice starts running. It is plain from the provision that the date of termination is the date of expiry of the notice period.

The duration of the notice period under section 34(3) of the Code depends on factors of seniority and type of work. Indeed by Ministerial Order No. 015/MTPS/SG/CJ of 26th May 1993, a worker who has been in work for between one month to one year of service is entitled to a period of from between fifteen days to a month's notice before termination. Workers who have been in service for from one to five years are entitled to notice of between one to three months. While workers with more than five years of service, are entitled to notice of between two to four months.

This Ministerial Order must be applauded for being sensitive to the security of service because under it, workers are entitled to be given a day each week with full salary to look for alternative employment.[504] The requirement in section 34 which requires the employer to provide reasons for termination is important as it will justify the dismissal.

Although this Ministerial order and especially section 35(2) of the Code look commendable for giving the worker time off on full salary to look for alternative employment, these provisions are a product of the *laissez-faire* philosophy. The possibility of finding gainful employment even after the economic crisis is grim. Even if one is found, such an employee will have to start from scratch to rebuild, for example, seniority in his new job.

---

503 Anderman, *op. cit.* at 98-99.

504 See section 35 of the Labour Code 1992.

Generally, section 34(1) of the Labour Code requires either party to the employment to give reasons for the termination of the employment. Tabe[505] quoting Anyangwe[506] has argued that, even if the none service of notice does not make the termination wrongful,[507] a failure to give reasons for termination will invariably lead to a finding by the court that the termination was wrongful, necessitating different remedies.

Article 7 of the ILO convention No 158, requires that a worker cannot be terminated before he is given an opportunity to defend himself against allegations made unless the employer cannot reasonably be expected to do so.

In France, under the *Code de Travail* of 1973, the employer is not only obliged to serve notice stating the reasons for the intention to terminate under article 122-14, but also the provision allows the worker the opportunity to be heard on the reasons for his termination by the management of the enterprise in a meeting. It is at this meeting that the employer must state the motives for his termination. According to Voize-Volayre,[508] it is only after this meeting that the employer can confirm the decision to terminate the employee. The author observed that the reason for this procedure is two-fold. Firstly, it guarantees minimal due process to the terminated employee while at the same time allowing the parties to narrow the scope of the issues to be determined in the event of litigation. Voize-Valayre praises this procedure for counter balancing the employee's lack of bargaining power and limited access to information, which ordinarily works against the worker's security of service.

In Britain, under the section 92 of the Employment Rights Act, 1996, upon request made to the employer, the employee is given fourteen days to give a written statement of what he/she thinks might be the reason for the termination. This statement is admissible in any subsequent proceedings with the employer to the extent that if there are inconsistencies between that statement and the reasons for termination advanced by the employer, the employer's case against the employee may be undermined. If the employer unreasonably refuses to give the employee permission to provide a written statement, the employee has the right to complain directly to an industrial

505 Tabe, S.T, "Employers' Breach of contract, redundancy, wrongful dismissal and notice: the case of *TRAPP Groupement d'Entreprise v. Che Guza Cletus*, Appeal No. BCA/2.L/ 98 (unreported)," *Jurisdis Periodique,Revue de Droit et de Science Politique*,No. 44, Octobre-December 2000, p. 39.

506 Anyangwe, C., "Wrongful Dismissal, *The Cameroon Development Corporation v. D.N. Embola*," *Cameroon Law Review*, 2nd Series No.26, 1983, p. 26.

507 See for example the case of *Pamol (Cameroon) v. Musoko J.N.* Civil Appeal No. CASWP/23/76 (unreported).

508 Voize-Valayre, *op. cit.* at p. 529.

tribunal, which may carry out its own findings as to what it thinks are the reasons for termination. Article 7 of ILO Convention No. 158, the French and British procedures clearly strengthens the security of service since they deter arbitrary decisions to terminate workers. It can be argued here that it may be necessary to review section 34 of the Labour Code 1992 to introduce similar elements in the employer/worker relations in Cameroon. It is observed that by virtue of section 45 of the Cameroon Constitution 1996 as revised, all duly ratified treaties take precedence over national laws. In this regard, since Cameroon ratified the ILO convention in 1988, Article 7 ought to be the correct procedure to adopt in Cameroon.

To do so will improve on employment security in Cameroon where once a worker has been duly served a notice, he /she has no other alternative than to attempt to get another employment during the notice period. The situation under sections 34 and 36 of the Code denies a worker a fundamental opportunity to be heard on the true motive for his/her termination at the initial stages of the dispute with his/her employer. By making the service of notice to terminate an irreversible[509] unilateral act which does not need anything else, the Labour Code profoundly weakens the security of service in the country. The French and British practices are for this reason commendable because by allowing workers plead their case before the management, there is a possibility that the management may reverse the decision.[510]

6.2.3 Termination by Performance

Retirement is the most common form by which a contract of unspecified duration comes to its natural end. This occurs when a worker has attained the age of retirement which is 60 years. It is the most desirous mode as the retiree gets all the retirement benefits stipulated in his contract of employment and according to the statutory laws in force.

Sometimes, an employee may want to go on voluntary retirement before the due date upon the service of proper notice under section 34 of the

---

509 Except the parties later by mutual agreement accept to reverse the decision to terminate.

510 Unfortunately, the French and British position cannot be applied directly in Cameroon since they are post 1900 laws (by virtue of section 11 of the Southern Cameroons High Court Laws 1955, all post-1900 statutes of general application are no longer applicable) and the Labour Code is all embracing in the sense that apart from the 1996 Constitution, it is the most authoritative Labour law document in both substantive and procedural matters.

Code. Unfortunately, the employer does have the possibility to exploit the situation to his advantage under the current Labour Code. This is often done by the termination of the worker even before the date stated in the notice. Usually, this is followed by a refusal by the employer to pay the worker his/her rightful due thereby affecting the latter's retirement benefits and by extension their security of service. A case in point is *Elakie Ngolo Emmanuel v. CDC*[511] which illustrates this practice graphically. Here, the plaintiff had applied to go on voluntary retirement on the 30 /11/ 1996 on grounds of tiredness and because 'the General Manager had promised a handsome handshake when he leaves.' The General Manager had promised to pay him severance pay as dictated by a new policy from the Ministry of Labour[512] for retiring workers. He was also promised compensation by way of a salary. In September of 1996, he received a letter terminating his service without the dues, which had been promised him by the General Manager. A colleague who had also gone on retirement that same period had all the benefits that had been promised the plaintiff. When he contested these discrepancies, he was informed that he had been given a contract to compensate him for his terminal benefits.

He sued for wrongful termination on the basis that his date of retirement was not due arguing as well that he was not issued a certificate of service as required by section 44 of the Code. The defendants had delayed in sending the plaintiff's retirement documents to NSIF for the necessary fiat needed by the plaintiff before going on retirement. Where NSIF does not endorse a voluntary retirement of a worker, any termination by the employer is considered wrongful.

It was on these facts that Mokwe J. held that by terminating the plaintiff's appointment, the defendant rendered nugatory the letter of voluntary retirement noting that the fact that the defendants paid the plaintiff four months' salary in lieu of notice meant that the defendant knew that they had wrongfully terminated the plaintiff without notice. After declaring the termination wrongful, the court awarded severance pay, loss of seniority bonus, duty allowance, electricity and housing allowances, leave allowance for 15 months plus his salary from 1/10/97 to 15/12/97 as well as general damages, amounting in total to 58.545.234FCFA (fifty eight million five hundred and forty five thousand two hundred and thirty four francs). This case illustrates

---

511 Suit NoHCF/ L.13/2000-2001 p.60-74 (unreported).

512 Decision No. 016/MTPS/CJ/OT 26/5/93, for retiring workers.

how a determined employer could use mere gimmicks to play around an unsuspecting employee who wants an early retirement.

6.2.4 Terminations by Operation of Law

This refers to the determination of a contract of employment through the automatic effects of law and not by private agreement or the direct intervention of the parties to the contract of employment.[513] A contract of employment can be terminated by operation of law when two things occur, to wit: frustration of the contract of employment or dissolution of a partnership or compulsory liquidation of a company where the company is the employer. Contracts of unspecified duration can be determined by frustration. This has been extended by section 38 of the Code to contracts of specified duration as well. For the latter, the contracts can lawfully be terminated prior to its expiry by *force majeure*.[514] It should be noted that *force majeure* renders the performance impossible while in cases of frustration, there is possibility to continue with performance with additional or increase in obligations. That is why section 32 of the labour code has made provision for suspension of contracts of employment.

6.2.4.1 Terminations by Frustration

This refers to a situation where without the fault of either party, the contract has become impossible to perform because the circumstances in which performance is called for would render it a thing different from that which was undertaken by the contract.

In labour law, when unforeseen circumstances beyond the control of both parties occur making it impossible for the employer and employee to perform their contractual obligations as was initially agreed, or if performed, it will be radically different from what the contracting parties had envisaged,[515] the contract will be seen as frustrated. Employment contracts will be frustrated where the occurrence was due to no fault of either party.[516]

---

513 Gifis, S.H.,*Barron's Law Dictionary, op. cit.* at p. 326.

514 This mode of termination of employment does not weaken the security of service since such terminations are realistically inevitable in the nature of things.

515 Rideout, R.W.,& Dyson, J., *op. cit.* at p.177-179.

516 Per Lord Brandon in *Paal Wilson & Co A/S v. Partenreederci Haanah Blumenthal* [1983] 1AC 854, 909.

The doctrine of frustration at common law occurs when the law recognises that,

> "without default of either party a contractual obligation had become incapable of being performed because the circumstances in which the performance is called for would render it a thing radically different from that which was undertaken by the contract."[517]

Frustration kills the contract with the effect that the parties to the employment are discharged from their contractual obligations.[518] Uvieghara[519] has argued that the contract law position of the principle of frustration identified by Lord Radcliffe above is applicable to employment law. According to him, this occurs where the changes in the circumstances of employment are such that it will render the further performance of the contract impossible or where the obligations undertaken by the parties under the contract have become radically different. It is in this wise that it is contended here that a contract of employment can be terminated by frustration upon long illness of employee, imprisonment of the employee or death. This mode of termination occurs as a pure function of the law which should in the natural course in the business be expected and planned for. It clearly does not impact negatively on the security of service. Although the Labour Code is mute as to this doctrine, it cannot be gainsaid that as a general common law principle the doctrine of frustration in employment contracts is applicable here on the basis of section 156 of the Code.

6.2.4.1.a Terminations by Frustration due to Ill Health

At common law,[520] the illness of an employee per se does not automatically bring a contract of employment to an end.[521] It is only where a worker is struck by occupational disease or industrial accident, which makes it impossible for the employee to take up his/her service permanently that

---

517 Per lord Radcliffe in *Davies Contractors Ltd v. Fareham U.D.C* [1956]A.C. 696.

518 Per Viscount Simon L.C. in *Joseph Constantine Steamship Ltd v. Imperial Smeltimg Corporation Ltd* [1942] A.C 154.

519 Uvieghara, E.E., *op. cit.* at p. 47

520 See for example the case of *Warburton v. Co-operative Wholesale Society LTD* [1917] 1 KB 663. Where the court of Appeal held that 'it has long been settled that a contract of service is not terminated by incapacity to work by reason of temporary illness, and that upon return to work, the man can recover his wages during the period of his absence' due to ill health.

521 Yanou, M.A., *op. cit.* at p. 85-86.

the contract of employment can be said to be terminated by frustration due to incapacity.[522]

This common law position is codified in section 32(c) of the Labour Code which provides that a contract of employment shall be suspended;

> "during the worker's absence in the cause of ill health duly certified by a medical practitioner approved by the employer or one belonging to a hospital establishment recognised by the state, for periods not exceeding six months... shall be extended until such time as the worker is replaced."

It is further provided in section 32(g) of the Code that a worker's contract will be suspended during any period of unavailability following an industrial accident or occupational disease. Since section 89(3)(a) –(b) actually sees these periods of incapacity as periods of leave, it follows that this 'leave' cannot at the same time amount to a termination of the employment by frustration. The issue is made clearer by the second limb of section 32(g) which extends the six months period of sick leave indefinitely to ' such a time as the worker is replaced.' Does it therefore mean that for security of service, a worker who has been incapacitated for more than six months whose work rule or collective bargaining agreement is silent can sue for wrongful dismissal if he is terminated because of absence from work due to ill health if he has not been replaced? It is contended that from a literary understanding of this phrase, such a worker can sue for wrongful dismissal.

It is important to draw the fine line, which separates frustration of a contract of employment due to ill health from dismissals by reason of disability as was done in the *TRAPP Groupement d'Entreprise v. Che Guza Cletus.*[523] Here, the plaintiff was employed as a welder for the stone crushing machine of the defendant who were road constructors. He developed ear problems later on in the course of employment and a declaration to this effect was sent to National Social Insurance Fund.

Following the defendant's physician's report that the plaintiff had developed ear problems that needed continuous medical attention, the plaintiff was transferred from his post as welder to that of general labour. However, the defendants on economic grounds subsequently terminated him. The plaintiff brought an action for wrongful determination. The plaintiff argued that his termination was not for economic reasons but was rather due

---

522 This then gives the employer the right to employ another in place of the incapacitated employee.

523 Appeal No. BCA/2.1/98 (unreported).

to the occupational disease he suffered as a result of the defendant's failure to give him proper medical care. His termination according to the plaintiff was a disguise, which enabled the defendant to escape the issue of wrongful dismissal.

After reviewing the above facts, the trial judge held that the worker's redundancy was wrongful and entered judgement in his favour. This decision which was confirmed upon appeal to the Bamenda Court of Appeal, enhances security of tenure in that in finding that the worker was wrongfully dismissed (although the worker's contract with the employer had ended), gave room for his entitlement to accrued wages and damages for wrongful dismissal. Had the Appeal Court not arrived at a decision of wrongful dismissal, Che would have been entitled only to redundancy benefits which would have been by far lower than the entitlements he got.

The facts of this case show that although there was a general redundancy in the enterprise, the entire construction work had not been completed. It is therefore obvious that the worker was dismissed as he contended because he could no longer render the services for which he was employed. As a skilled worker, had he not suffered the injury, he would have been kept in employment until the end of the construction work.[524]

Since the facts of this case reveal the fate of many workers who are discarded under the camouflage of economic reasons, it is for reason of security of service imperative to distinguish at all times between terminations due to frustration and terminations on economic grounds. This is because in the latter, the employer has to pay only compensation, while in wrongful dismissals, the employee is entitled to damages and /or other forms of remedies.

The author adopts the position of Phillips J. in *Eggs Stores (Stamford Hill) Ltd v. Leibovici*[525] which puts forward a nine point non-exhaustive guidelines which should be considered, before a decision on frustration is taken viz; i) the length of employment ii) how long the contract was supposed to last, iii) the nature of the job, iv) the nature and length of the illness, v) the needs of the employer in the work to be done, vi) the risk of the employer in

524 See Tabe *op. cit.* at p.40. in the case of *Mofa Ngoe David v. Plantation Du Haut Penja* Suit No. HCF/L.001/04-05, 37 (unreported) at p. 41, the defendants have themselves contended that the plaintiff was dismissed because his output had dropped. Forbang J, held this to be a serious violation of the plaintiff's rights, whose performance dropped as a result of two accidents suffered while serving the defendant and not because the company was in any economic difficulty.

525 [1997]1CR 260 at p. 265.

acquiring obligations in respect of redundancy payments or compensation for unfair dismissal to the replacement of employee, vii)whether wages have been continuously paid, viii) the acts and the statements of the employer in relation to the employment, including the dismissal of, or failure to dismiss, the employee's prospects of recovery, and ix) whether in all the circumstances a reasonable employer could be expected to wait any longer.

The application of these criteria can be done although it will be difficult to situate their application in the context of the Labour Code. The criteria may be applied in the context of a common law the same way civil law courts in Francophone Regions Cameroon interpret the Labour Code under the influence of the civil law.[526] It is certain that the application of the criteria in the interpretation of retirement will substantially strengthen employment.

6.2.4.1.b Terminations and Frustration Due to Imprisonment

Although at common law a contract of employment can be frustrated by imprisonment, section 32(i) of the Labour Code merely provides that where a worker is under preventive detention or police custody, the contract of employment may be suspended, but not terminated. Reading the *expression unio est exclusio alterius* rule (stating one thing excludes the others) alongside section 32(i) of the Code, where a worker is given a prison sentence, the contract of employment may be terminated by frustration without the need for compensation to be paid by either party to the contract.

The Cameroonian position as stated above is different from that in English common law. Under the latter, it is uncertain whether there is conflict as to whether imprisonment actually frustrates a contract of employment. The decision of the National Industrial Relations Court in *Hare v. Murphy Brothers*[527] held that the plaintiff's sentence of imprisonment was not a frustrating event because it was brought about by his own act in committing the offence for which he was imprisoned. Upon appeal to the English Court of Appeal, Lord Denning MR held that the sentence of imprisonment did frustrate the contract of employment because of the length of time he would be away from work and the importance of his position to his employer as a

526 See Yanou, M.A., *Labour Law Principles and Practice in Cameroon, op. cit.* at p.42. Note also that their application may be justified under section 156 of the Code which allows procedural issues not covered by the Code to be applied in cases.

527 [1974] 1RLR 342.

foreman.[528] It may be observed that Lord Denning in this decision made an analogy with a case where the contract of employment of a worker who is incapacitated for eight months as a result of accident would be frustrated even though the contract was determinable on short notice

6.2.4.1.c Termination and Frustration Due to Death

At common law, the death of any of the parties to an employment contract will terminate the contract. This common law position though not incorporated in the Labour Code expressly may be applied in Cameroon where the employee dies. This is so because contracts of employments are contracts of personal service by virtue of section 31 of the Labour Code which cannot survive the death of the worker.

However, it is contended that the death of the employer does not necessarily bring the employment contract to an end. Obviously, an employer that is a company cannot automatically terminate its employment because of economic difficulty leading to the compulsory liquidation of the company. Clearly therefore, the parties are not discharged of their contractual obligations only on the basis that the company has gone into liquidation unlike in cases of frustration. The employer in the former case will have to pay the employee certain benefits like the lump sum payments for redundancy. It is for this reason that the death of an employer which is a company or a partnership is sometimes not seen as frustration. Rideout[529] argues that the dissolution of a partnership will operate as a breach of contract and not as an effective termination of it. In the same light, she further observes that although an order for compulsory winding-up of a company operates as a notice of dismissal to the worker,[530] voluntary winding up does not automatically terminate the contract of employment since the receiver is acting as an agent of the company if it is still an on-going concern.

Frustration, a doctrine that determines contract of employment, must be treated with caution because of its potential to negatively affect the security of employment. It is ill advised for the court to arrive at a decision that frustration

528 Stevenson LJ in the same case observed that a sentence of imprisonment did terminate an employment and it did not matter whether the termination was labelled a frustrating event, repudiatory conduct, a breach going to the root of the contract of employment or impossibility of performance.

529 Rideout, R.W., *Rideout's Principles of Labour Law, op. cit.* at 180-181.

530 *Re General Rolling Stock Co.* (1866) L.R. 1 Eq. 346

has occurred without more since to do so will provide the courts with an easy escape from its obligations of investigation of the entire situation to see whether the employer acted reasonably. This approach is consistent with the demands to ensure that employments are secure.[531]

6.3 Termination on Economic Grounds[532]

Termination on economic grounds refers to a situation where workers lose their job because the employer has ceased or intends to cease to carry on business[533]. It could also result from diminished business activity.[534] When terminations are triggered by economic difficulties, the worker is said to have been made redundant or retrenched by the employer. In practice, this occurs when there is either a closure of the employer's business,[535] reduction in staff for better economic management of the enterprise so long as it is not capricious. It could also occur where the employer's business is transferred or substantially changed.

Section 40 (1) of the Labour Code defines this specie of termination as:

> "any dismissal, effected by the employer for one or more reasons not inherent in the person of the worker and resulting from an abolition or transformation of posts or an amendment to the contract of employment consequent on economic difficulties, technological changes or internal re-organisation."

Terminations hinged on the inability of a worker to adapt to work which has become faster, more demanding or because of the application

531 See generally Hepple, R., "Restructuring Employment Rights," 1986, 15 ILJ 69 and Collins, H., *Justice in Dismissal*, Oxford, Oxford Clarendon Press, 1992. p. 44-45.

532 Professor Grunfeld observes that redundancy is based on the policy that unnecessary workmen should not be retained in any industry but should be released so as to be free to take employment elsewhere; *Hawkins v. Thomas Foreman and Sons Ltd* [1967] ITR 59, 61. Professor Grunfeld, *Law of Redundancy*, 3rd Edition, 1989, p. 2. This is acceptable where jobs are easy to come by. But, in times of economic crises, jobs are most precious and each employee will want to keep.

533 CorneliBen describes this as objective job insecurity as opposed to subjective job insecurity which is a workers perception of job loss and the consequences of such a loss on him/her. CorneliBen, T., *Flexibility and Security in the Labour Market, Labour Market Institutions and Perceived Job Security in Europe*, Budapest, International Labour Organisation, 2007, p.7. see also on this Klanderman, B., and Van Vuuren, T., "Job Insecurity: Introduction", *European Journal Of Work and Organisational Psychology*, 1991, Vol. 8, p. 145-153.

534 Rideout, R.W. *op. cit.* at p. 269.

535 *John Anagho v. Agip Cameroon S.A.*, Suit No. WC/11A/69 HC (unreported).

of new technology, cannot be attributed to redundancy. It is a function of incompetence. To qualify as redundancy, retrenchment must result from the economic difficulty experienced by the enterprise. The dividing line between terminations caused by re-organisation of work and those indirectly and undeniably caused by reduction or creation of new jobs may be very difficult to draw.[536] What is certain, however, is that the termination and/or re-organisation based on economic difficulty must have been prompted by the employer's need to save his/her enterprise through re-organising it for more business efficiency.

Generally, the dissolution or compulsory winding-up of a firm at common law does operate to terminate the contract of employment[537]. This is so since the employing company would no longer have an on-going business that can employ. However, with voluntary winding-up[538] where a liquidator is employed, the contract does not automatically come to an end as the liquidator may want to carry on business as an on-going concern. This invariably means the employer will continue with the workers who want to stay on.[539] The receiver in such a case acts as the agent of the company.[540]

Section 40(1), read subject to section 34 of the Code, requires the employer to inform the employee in writing of the termination of the contract in the event of economic difficulties. Section 40(3) requires the employer to first convene a meeting with staff representatives in the presence of the local labour inspector. The provisions encourage the employer to adopt measures like the reduction in working hours, shift work, reduction in wages, staff strength including the downward review of benefits to salvage the enterprise from collapse.

Indeed, the strength of these provisions lie in the fact that the employer was not left alone in taking the vital decision about whether the measures have succeeded or not. The usual self-interest of the employer which is driven by profit and conducive to mass terminations cannot occur as the decision is to be taken in consultation with the Labour Inspector who must endorse the

536 Whincup, M., *Modern Employment Law*, 8th edition, London: Butterworth, 1995, p. 207.

537 In such situations, the contract of employment will be said to have been terminated by operation of law.

538 Koning, P. "Unilever,Contract Farmers and Co-operatives in Cameroon: Crisis and Response," *The Journal of Peasant Studies*, Vol. 26, No. 1, Oct 1998, p. 122-123.

539 Workers who do not accept the new work conditions and measures are dismissed with pay in – lieu of notice and severance pay as provided for in section 40(5) of the Code.

540 In any given dissolution of a company it is important for security of service purposes the difference between these two types of liquidation in order for the worker to know who his employer is in fact.

decision. This, to an extent, strengthens security of tenure because although some workers will lose their jobs, it salvages the company from total collapse, which invariably implies job security for many more workers than otherwise. This was the kind of agreement which the Fako Agricultural Workers' Union Signed with CDC management on the 6th of January, 1990, that has kept CDC afloat as an on-going business till date.[541]

Since contracts of employment are based on consensus, the position at common law is that an employee who refuses 'unreasonably' to accept the new dispensation will not be eligible for redundancy payment. This position has been incorporated into the Labour Code, as a worker who does not accept the new dispensation is dismissed and may not qualify for redundancy payment. He is however entitled to pay-in-lieu-of notice and severance pay.[542] The Code does not include the notion of 'unreasonableness' in the refusal to accept the new working condition but rather insists on the requirement that the employer should be seen to have exhausted all the avenues prescribed in section 40(3) to keep the employment contract. The notion of unreasonableness in the refusal should be included in the Labour Code, as the current position under section 40 is 'cut and dry' leaving the worker with little or no option. The worker is therefore subtly cajoled to accept the new agreement, which may in some way fundamentally affect their job specification, other incidental terms and conditions of work or face dismissal, which is not an option most workers in Cameroon would want to take. As observed above, what is taken home by the employee depends on whether it is a dismissal or a redundancy. Although this is better than losing a job, poverty of the worker will be fostered.

In Britain, for example, a worker is supposed to be given due warning besides, being consulted about the redundancy. According to this thinking, the gravity of termination on the redundant worker makes it such that failure to consult is a criminal offence punishable with a fine. It is obvious that criminalisation does enhance security of tenure but at too severe a cost. Employments which are civil arrangements should not casually lead to the possibility of imprisonment of one of the parties.

541 Initially, the workers had taken a resolve that CDC be liquidated and all of them paid-off. Thanks to the relentless efforts of the President of Fako Agricultural Workers' Union who convinced the workers otherwise, the workers subsequently agreed to the plan to keep CDC afloat as an on-going business by making enormous financial sacrifices. See in addition the letter drafted to the CDC Management by Vewessee on the 9th March 2000 on the "Imminent Privatisation of CDC, the situation of Staff and employee."

542 Section 40(5)of the Labour Code.

For purpose of employment security, the checks introduced in section 40(3) of the Code are commendable. For an employee to be made fairly redundant, the criteria for selection listed in section 40(6) of the Code must be rigorously adhered to. The selection of workers for redundancy must not therefore be arbitrary or based on personal prejudices. The Supreme Court held in *Namadina v. Grand Travaux de l'Est*[543] that an employer, who alleges reduction in staff in order to frustrate a worker's entitlement to the length of service, is liable for wrongful dismissal necessitating claims for damages under section 39(4) of the Code by the aggrieved worker.

It is always possible for economic hardship to be used as a disguise to terminate workers when the employer wants to escape liability for wrongful dismissals. In *Mofa Ngoe David v. Plantation du Haut Penja*,[544] the plaintiff had suffered serious injuries in the course of employment leading to the drop in his output. Relying on economic difficulties, the defendant decided to retrench workers who were above 54 years and those who accepted to go on voluntary retirement. Although the plaintiff did not fall in any of the categories he was terminated. All arguments by the defendants that the retrenchment was for economic grounds were punctured by the fact that the defendants had conceded that the plaintiff's output had dropped. Justice Forbang on the facts of this case held that the decision to terminate was based on the person of the employee rather than the considerations spelled out in section 40 of the Code. The worker's dismissal was considered wrongful entitling him to general damages assessed on the basis of section 39(4) of the Code which amounted to 768.000FCFA, being his fixed salary of 64.0 00 multiplied by 12years of service. However, his claim of the salary he would have earned from date of termination to date of retirement was dismissed as puerile and purely speculative.

As depicted above, these protective measures put in place to cushion the effect of the crisis in order to protect the worker have not been scrupulously applied with the effect that security of service has suffered. Many workers have been thrown out of work without the payment of their dues in the guise of privatisation.[545] Sometimes these workers are terminated even after enormous sacrifices made by them to keep the company on-going in a bid to secure their job. The common law position of last in first out should have been adopted to curb

543 C.S. Arret No. 37/S du 15 Avril 1976, Bulletin des Arrets No. 9, 1976, p. 4691 and also the Supreme Court in *Affaire Cluzelle Christian* Suit No. Arret 81/S du 18 Janvier 1996, which took a similar decision.

544 Suit No. HCF/ L.001/2004-2005, 37. See also the *TRAPP case* discussed above.

545 This in a bid to avoid liability for breach of contract (wrongful termination).

the arbitrariness or prejudice in the selection of workers to be made redundant sometimes adopted by the employer in spite of section 40(3) of the Code.

The entitlement for redundancy pay arises irrespective of whether or not the employee gains immediate employment with another employer. However, for a worker to be eligible for redundancy pay, the worker must have been employed in the same establishment or its successor for a period of at least two years otherwise they go away with nothing.[546] This provision in our opinion weakens security of service as the amount of redundancy pay is based on the fact of having worked for a period of at least two years in the enterprise and not the age of the worker. In the cases provided in section 32 of the Code, if a worker is suspended and subsequently his/her employer runs into economic difficulty during the period of suspension, can the period of suspension of the contract of employment be counted toward the two years? The relevance of the period of two years to the employee is that, it is only after this period that an employee would have acquired the necessary seniority qualifying him/her for certain entitlements.[547] It weakens security of service to leave this question to the discretion of the judge. It should have been addressed squarely by the law to avert haphazard interpretation. It is contended that since the suspension does not go to the substratum of the contract, justice dictates that this period of suspension should be included in the two years.

What if the business is sold to another, like the case where CDC sold its Tea sector to CTE? Whincup[548] observes that if there is no transfer of business in the legal sense (transfer of all the assets, business, rights and liabilities) the old employer must be responsible for the redundancy payments. Employees therefore deserve to know how similar the new business is to the old, in order to ascertain who takes responsibility for the redundancy payments in case of termination on economic grounds.

The sale of a business in company law constitutes the death of an employer and the birth of another.[549] Notwithstanding the fundamental common law rule that a contract of employment cannot be assigned, section 42 (1) (a) of the Code provides that in the event of any sale, amalgamation, financial reorganisation or transformation into a partnership or company, all contracts of employment in force shall subsist between former employees and the new institutions. However, by section 42 (1) paragraph 1 of the Labour Code, should

---

546 Section 40(9) of the Labour Code.

547 This is the period from which seniority is counted entitling the redundant worker to severance pay as per section 37(1) of the Code.

548 *Op. cit.* at p. 214.

549 Whincup, *op. cit.* at p. 214.

the company change its activities, its contracts may not be assigned. This is however subject to the fact that a worker who expresses the desire to terminate to the local Labour Inspector may do so, although his/her benefits can only be paid according to old rates. Section 42 is an important provision with regard to the security of tenure because it gives the worker the added assurance that in the event of any change in ownership, etc, of the enterprise, the subsistence of their contract of employment is guaranteed. Unfortunately, this provision was ignored in the Cameroon Tea Estate saga where the employers 'deliberately' made employment difficult for the employees by unilaterally imposing new employment terms and forcing majority of the workers to quit.[550]

Contracts of employment are amendable by either party to the contract. As provided in section 42(2)(a), an employer can substantially amend contract terms and he/she will be justified to do so if it is in the 'interest of the enterprise'. This provision strikes a devastating blow on the security of service when it insists that a worker who rejects the amendment may be legitimately terminated. The provision may be criticised for encouraging employers to amend contracts in a manner which they know will be unacceptable to their workers under the pretext that it is in the interest of the enterprise to do so. The provision is a lot more damaging to the security of service because it fails to define the phrase 'interest of the enterprise.'[551] This leaves too much discretion in the hands of an already powerful employer with its potential for dangerous abuse.

6.4 Dismissal of a Worker

This section shall dwell on the concept of dismissal and its effect on private sector employment.

6.4.1 The Concept of Dismissal

Dismissal is the sudden determination of a contract of service without due notice[552] usually due to a misconduct by the employee and not minding

550 Yanou, M.A., & Fonyam, J.B., *op. cit.* at p.28-29.

551 Even if the phrase is seen as in the interest of the community, government, workers and the enterprise (that is stakeholders).

552 Where there is no reason for dismissal, the worker will be said to have been wrongfully dismissed at common law. Where there is a statutory provision requiring that the reason for dismissal be founded and the employer fails to show such justification, the dismissal becomes unfair. In such a situation therefore there is a breach of contract requiring general and special damages as well as other equitable remedies.

the wishes of the other party.[553] Although dismissal is fault connected, it could occur where there is a failure to renew a contract of fixed term on the same terms or if the employer constructively determines the employee's contract by repudiating it.[554]

Although the Labour Code has not directly defined dismissal, its conceptual nature may be gleaned from section 36(2) of the Code. This provision ties the definition of dismissal to gross misconduct. Although the Code has not defined gross misconduct, it is clear that it refers to any conduct of the employee which prevents further satisfactory continuance of relationship. Such conducts will include; wilful disobedience of a lawful order,[555] dishonesty,[556] theft,[557] use of violence, disclosure of trade secrets, habitual, serious and persistent neglect of service, carelessness or laziness, etc.[558] The list is non-exhaustive. According to the second arm of section 36(2)

---

553 See Yanou, M.A., *Labour Law, op. cit.* at p.72. At common law, where a worker is terminated summarily for no just cause, such a dismissal is termed wrongful and the employee is entitled to the normal protection and remedies afforded by common law such as an action for breach of employment contract. Unfair dismissal is a concept introduced by various statute that seek to give protection to employees.

554 This is a situation where a worker leaves his job voluntarily, but because of pressure from his/her employer. Collin, P.H., *Dictionary of Law*, Peter Collin Publisher, 3rd Edition, p.80.

555 *Pepper v Webb* [1969] 2 All ER 216, where a servant wilfully refusal to obey lawful and reasonable orders of his employer after numerous complaints of inefficiency and 'dumb insolence' was held to be gross misconduct warranting the summary dismissal of the employee. See in contrast the case of *Laws v London Chronicle (Indicator Newspapers) Ltd* [1959] 1WLR 698.

556 See the case of *Omog Etien v. CAMAIR* Suit No.HCF/ L.53/2000-2001 where, the plaintiff, an employee of the defendant, defrauded the latter causing them great loss. The High Court did not hesitate to hold that the employee's summary dismissal was justified. In *Denco Ltd v. Johnson* [1991] 1RLR 63, the Employment Tribunal held that the employee's deliberate use of an authorised pass word to enter the employer's computer which was known to contain information which the employee was not entitled to was gross misconduct which justified the summary dismissal.

557 *Victor Oyebog v. Cameroon Development Corporation* Suit No. HCF/ L.1/1997, 33 (unreported), where the plaintiff in this case who had worked for the defendant since 17th June 1976 was dismissed summarily in 1996, when in the course of execution of service as foreman at the Mukonje Factory, some building materials which he had personally collected from Tiko went missing as they were never received by the store keeper at the receiving estate (Mukonje) as per CDC Regulations. Instead it was the Plaintiff who received the goods on grounds that he was the foreman. The plaintiff did not report to the management of the missing items. After investigation and a letter of query to the plaintiff he was summarily dismissed. The dismissal was justified on grounds that the plaintiff either acted in complicity with, to cause loss to the defendant or was too negligent causing the defendant to suffer loss.

558 According to the decision in CS. Arret No. 32/s of 24th December 1997 and Professor Pougue Commentaries on *Code du Travail Annote* p. 60-65, it is trite law that negligence cannot form the basis of summary dismissal. Lesser misdemeanour would require the employer to give warning as to future behaviour before dismissing. It was observed by Painter that a combination of such misdemeanour may lead to a justified dismissal. Painter, R.W, Holmes, A.,& Migdal, S. *Cases & Materials on Employment Law*, Hampshire: Blackstone Press Ltd, p. 350.

of the Code, it is for the competent court to determine whether the conduct of the employee was grave enough to warrant summary dismissal even when it has been alleged by the employer.[559]

A dismissed worker loses the entitlement to both contractual and statutory minimum notice as well as certain benefits and gratuities. Equally damaging is the fact that a dismissed staff losses the opportunity to vindicate his/her name including all the statutory protection given to workers once the 'just cause' has been established.[560] Once dismissed, a worker definitely finds it a lot more difficult to get another employment. It was for these reasons that it was held by Ademola CJN in *Irem v. Obubra District Council*,[561] that a

> 'a dismissal from the service carries such infamy that a termination does not carry.'[562]

The decision in *Irem's Case* is consistent with the views of Voize-Valayre who contended that because dismissals are laden with social consequences, they could not be compared with terminations and resignations which to him barely inconvenience the employee.

It is apparent from the above analysis that dismissals are different from terminations, retirements and resignations both conceptually and the incidents they carry. Yanou[563] has for this reason observed with regret that, these distinctions have been ignored by the Labour Code in Cameroon which uses the notions interchangeably. This notwithstanding, the position of the legislator can be justified by the fact that the certificate of service that is delivered to the worker in case of determination does not carry the reason for the determination, and so third parties will not know the reason for the determination.

6.4.2 Dismissals for Trade Union and Staff Representative Activities

Following the country's international obligations as a member of the ILO,[564] and the preambular provisions of its Constitution which gives all workers and employers the right to freely create and join trade unions, section

559 Per Mokwe J in the *Oyebog Case* (supra).
560 Uvieghara, E.E., *op. cit.* at p. 75.
561 [1960] 5 FSC 24.
562 *Ibid dem* at p. 27.
563 Yanou, M.A., *op. cit.* at p. 63.
564 Cameroon signed and ratified ILO Convention No 87 (1948) on Freedom of Association and Protection of the Right to organize especially articles 1-4. Article 22 of the International Covenant on Civil and Political Rights also gives everyone the right to form and join trade unions for the protection of his/her interest.

4 of the Code guarantees the right and freedom of workers and employers to freely join any trade union of their choice in Cameroon. Indeed, section 4(2) categorically protects a worker who joins a trade union from anti-union activity or discrimination, including punitive dismissals for union activity. Clearly, section 4(3) of the labour Code provides what can be described as the most powerful protection of employment in Cameroon when it declared that any dismissal for union activity is null and void.[565] Yanou[566] has in this regard concluded that any worker dismissed in disregard of section 4(3) of the Code is entitled to be reinstated to his employment. It is clear from this conclusion that the security of service of workers active in trade union matters is comparatively stronger than those who are not unionised.

Can an employer dismiss a worker who is a trade unionist or staff representative and is involved in gross misconduct? The answer to this question is clearly in the negative as section 130(1) of the Labour Code insists that a staff representative who is involved in gross misconduct can only be dismissed with the prior authorisation of the local labour inspector who must be convinced that the said dismissal is not because of the latter's involvement in union activities. Yanou,[567] had relied on the analysis of Mbeng JCA's decision in *SODEPA Dumbu v. Bienbu Martin Nfang*[568] to argue that a staff representative enjoys greater security of service. Here, the judge held that the dismissal of a staff representative for gross misconduct in violation of the employer's obligation under section 130 of the Code was unlawful. Although the Court of Appeal judge did not order the worker to be re-instated, he stated obiter that this was possible, noting categorically that the dismissal was void in spite of the gross misconduct of the staff representative.[569]

---

565 In same light, article 5(a) of the ILO Convention 158 which Cameroon ratified in 1988 provides inter alia that a worker cannot be dismissed for being a member of a trade union or actively participates in union activities during or after working hours, or for seeking office as worker's representative or for having acted as one.

566 Yanou, M.A. *op. cit.* at p.87. Also, Anderman is of the same view as he opines that a worker who is dismissed for union activity is given the right to intermediary relief pending a decision from industrial tribunal. Anderman *op. cit.* at p.264

567 Yanou, M.A., *Labour Law Principles and Practice in Cameroon, op. cit.* at p.70.

568 BCA/71/2006 (unreported).

569 The Labour Code position is similar to what obtains in France. In France, such a dismissal is possible upon approval of the trade union (work council) and a fiat from a labour inspector of the Ministry of Labour.[569] Article 436-1 of the *Code de Travail* 1973 makes it difficult to dismiss employees' representative even six months after the end of his/her mandate as a staff representative. In Britain, although a worker is protected from dismissal by section 152(1) (2) of the Trade Union and Labour Relations (Consolidation) (TULRCA) Act 1992, for union membership, he/she may be dismissed for gross misconduct.

In spite of the protection offered by section 130(1) of the Code to the security of service, some employers attempt to circumvent by avoiding to go through the required procedure. A case in point is that of Jean Marie N'Di, the Secretary General of the *Federation des Syndicats de la Sante, Pharmacie et Assimiles* (health and pharmaceutical workers' union); FSESPAC, an affiliate of Public Services International (PSI) who was fired in June 2006 by the *Fondation Medicale* AD-LUCEM, because of union activities, without going through proper procedure.[570]

6.4.3 Constructive Dismissal

This is a simple breach of a contract of employment by the employer in such a manner that the other party is entitled to treat himself/herself as discharged from the contract. Although constructive dismissal applies to either party to the contract of employment, it has been defined in the dictionary of law as a situation where a worker leaves his job voluntarily, but because of pressure from management.[571] This occurs when the employee or employer commits a breach of his/her contract obligations which goes to the root of the contract showing that the employer/employee no longer intends to be bound by one or more of the essential terms of the contract. Rideout[572] defines constructive dismissal as a situation where the employee terminates the employment contract with or without notice, in circumstances such that he is entitled to terminate it without notice by reason of the employer's conduct.

It is a feature of this phenomenon that the conduct of the employer/employee must be sufficiently serious to entitle the other party to leave at once. The innocent party must therefore act promptly, since if he/she continues in the employment for any length of time without leaving, he/she will be

570 In same manner, in January 2006, 163 workers of a road constructing firm, working on a road connecting Yaounde and Moundou in Chad were fired for organizing a strike in protest against their working conditions and for making demands on accommodation allowance. Their leader was arrested and detained in Yaounde on May 22nd 2006. See generally, National Labour Law Profiles: Cameroon, accessed on 25th September 2009. See also ILO NATLEX Cameroon.

571 Collin, P.H., *Dictionary of Law*, Peter Collin Publishing, 3rd Edition, p. 80.

572 Rideout, R.W. *Principles of Labour Law, op. cit.* at p. 185-186. Whincup calls it implied or indirect dismissal. He defines it as a situation where the employer for example expressly requires the employee to resign or face dismissal, or when he unilaterally changes the terms of the contract of employment in some fundamental way which gives the employee no choice than to resign. See generally Whincup, *Modern Employment Law*, p. 145-148.

regarded as having elected to affirm the contract and thereby lose the right to treat himself as discharged from the contract.[573]

It is clear that where a worker for no good reason is put on technical leave for three months and upon expiry he/she reports for work and is told to go and wait for an indefinite period, such a worker can assume that the contract has been constructively terminated.[574] This principle was illustrated in the case of *Njoko Jean Claude v. Societe SOFIDEX & Njoh Francois Maurice*.[575] The plaintiff who had served the defendant for fifteen months without any problems was in June 2004 put on a technical leave of three months by the defendant. The plaintiff duly reported to work upon expiry of the technical leave but was told to go and wait indefinitely. This waiting lasted for two years when he again approached his employers. After this second phase of waiting, his employers simply did nothing. Forbang J. held that the only logical thing to do is to invoke the doctrine of specific performance since the defendant is still their employee until such a time that the defendants formally terminate the plaintiff's service. The defendants were jointly ordered to pay the plaintiff 16.913.260 FCFA being salary, severance pay, other wages and damages.

Although this case may be applauded for its strong stance with regard to security of service, it leaves many questions unanswered. It appears to conflict with the principle vividly captured in the Court of Appeal decision in *Assurance Des Provinces Reunis v. Tiogum David*[576] which rather held that the plaintiff had been wrongfully dismissed. The respondent an employee of the appellant company, sued the latter for wrongful dismissal. The respondent who had assumed duty in Bamenda was requested in writing to meet the General Manager of the appellant company in Douala for purpose of sorting out some matters related to the respondent's services with the company. The respondent made four trips to Douala to this effect and on each occasion he was told that the General Manager could not attend to him. He was subsequently barred from entering his office in Bamenda and his salary stopped. The court on the facts held that the respondent had been wrongfully dismissed. Jani JCA

573 Painter, R.W, Holmes, A., & Migdal, S., *Cases and Materials on Emplyment Law, op. cit.* at p. 385.

574 The correct thing for such an employer to do is to pay damages to the aggrieved worker and get an alternative job. But in a situation where jobs are hard to find, this will not only cause him insecurity of service but will make him loose out on seniority and the knowledge and professional expertise he would have acquired had he been regularly given work.

575 Suit No. HCF/L.020/2006-2007 (unreported).

576 1998 1 CCLR PART 4, 662-64.

in delivering the unanimous decision of the Court of Appeal North West[577] pointed out that;

> 'Where an employer by such conduct forces his employee to abandon his service, the employer has constructively terminated the contract of employment.'[578]

Note that in the *Njoko Jean Claude Case* above, the high court did not hold that the plaintiff had been wrongfully dismissed as in the latter case of the Court of Appeal in Bamenda.

6.4.4 Summary Dismissals

This is sudden and precipitated determination of a contract of service without the service of proper notice for justifiable reasons usually related to the conduct of the employee in the course of employment.[579] It is trite law that a worker who engages in activities which are incompatible with his contract of service, leaves his/her employer with no other choice than to dismiss him/her.

Although the Code has not given any direct definition of dismissal, it can be gleaned from section 36 that, it is determination without notice caused by serious misconduct, subject to the findings of the competent court.

The employer is under section 39(3) required to state the reason for dismissal and prove that the grounds for dismissals alleged by him/her are well-founded. This provision of the law has been given judicial approval in the Supreme Court of Cameroon Case of *Societe Shell Cameroon v Kemayou Henri*.[580] It follows quite naturally that a sudden and precipitate dismissal of a worker for gross misconduct is legal. It is thus plain from this analysis that summary dismissal is a concept under the Code. Although a rather drastic move, section 39(3) of the Code which places the burden of proof of the misconduct alleged on the employer, enhances security of service in the context of the country. *Agbor Mathias Arrey v. National Social Insurance Fund*[581] is a case in point. Here, the plaintiff had been the defendant's employee from1987 to July 2006 when he was summarily dismissed for alleged complicity

577 Citing in approval *Cours Supreme du Cameroun Oriental* 15th December 1964, Bulletin p.936.

578 1998 1 CCLR PART 4, 662-64 at p. 663.

579 Yanou., M.A., *Labour Law, Principles &Practice in Cameroon, op. cit.* at p. 72.

580 Appeal No. 79/5/2004-05 of 12th May 2005. This position has been followed by Ngassa J, in *Kalndjel Mathieu v. SIAC Brasseries Isenbeck S.A, SIAC Distributors SNC & SIAC Taurex SNC* Suit No. HCF/101/N/2001-2002, at p. 59.

581 HCF/L.0004/2009 (unreported).

to defraud the plaintiff. The plaintiff had never received any query and had always been highly rated by his superiors. A criminal investigation prompted by the defendant was instituted in which preliminary inquiry discharged the plaintiff of the allegations against him. Having done so, it became incumbent on the defendant to discharge the burden placed on them by section 39(3), to prove the soundness of their decision to summarily dismiss the plaintiff. The High Court of Fako held that failure of the defendant to establish as required under section 39(3) of the Code the soundness of their decision to summarily dismiss the plaintiff, made the plaintiff's dismissal wrongful.

Dismissal of a worker for gross misconduct is a central feature of employment relations. The principle that dismissal should be for gross misconduct which by section 36 of the Labour Code has to be ascertained by a competent court protects workers from the excessive advantages that employers derived from unrestrained liberalism and unequal bargaining power.[582] This is because from a capitalist perspective, an employer is seen not only as the sole manager of the enterprise but also as the sole arbiter of the enterprise's best interest and good function. Where therefore in the employer's opinion, an employee no longer conforms to the productionist and protectionist ideals of corporate interest, it is right for the employer to dismiss him/her.[583] However, with the rise of activism by international labour associations, ILO Recommendation 119 on the termination of employment was adopted to ensure that all dismissals be subject to a valid motive. This recommendation was designed to encourage a worldwide spirit to enhance security of service in employment.

In the case of Cameroon, the 'valid motive' referred to above is "serious misconduct," which is incorporated into section 36(2) and section 37(1) of the Code. This requirement now contained in most modern labour legislation is most welcomed. One's career is not only his /her human capital but it is also his/her property particularly when one has become skilled in the art of his/her profession.[584] Although dismissal may only be valid when resorted to for gross misconduct, the code has not expressly defined misconduct. It has failed to provide any guidelines as to how this may be ascertained either. This lacuna in the Labour Code, which was enacted as a detailed statute with the ultimate objective to address the crisis in the labour sector during and after the economic crises, leaves much to be desired given the severity of

582 Voize-Valayre *op. cit.* at p. 544.

583 Konings, P.,*Labour Resistance in Cameroon, op. cit.* p.135-141.

584 Sugeno, k.,& Suwa, Y., *op. cit.* at p. 98-101.

dismissal and its consequences on security of service.[585] Fonjock JCA in the North West Court of Appeal decision in *SODEPA Dumbu v. Biebu Martin Nfang*,[586] after arguing that, it is at the discretion of the individual judge to determine the gravity of the misconduct for purposes of dismissals, noted that gravity is a function of each individual case since it varies from case to case.[587]

The Supreme Court has authoritatively held[588] that gross misconduct does not include professional error but relates to the intentional act of the worker in the performance of his contract.[589] The definition excludes the personal inconveniences of the employer. Since gross misconduct invoked by the employer must be the immediate and direct cause of the summary dismissal, it must necessarily be something which is impliedly or expressly a repudiation of a fundamental term of the contract of employment. Although the Supreme Court[590] had held that gross misconduct need not necessarily cause loss to the employer, Fonjock JCA in the *SODEPA Dumbu case* quoting another Supreme Court decision noted that gross misconduct is intentional misconduct or negligent misconduct of an employee which causes considerable loss (grave prejudice) to the employer[591].

It is not enough therefore for the employer to dismiss a worker on allegation of misconduct. The employer must prove in cases of dismissals that the dismissal of the employee was justified and well founded. It was thus held in the case of *Societe Shell Cameroun SA v. Kemajou Henri*[592] that, a worker sacked on grounds of loss of confidence without more had not been guilty of gross misconduct. Noting that the phrase was a vague ground for dismissal, the court held that the failure of the employer to prove that the employee caused him to lose 1900000 FCFA was fatal to his case.[593]

In spite of what was said in the *Kemajou Case*, an employee who fails to follow lawful instruction like the refusal to go on transfer can be dismissed.

---

585 Voize-Valayre argues that this is a negation of workers' right as a worker must know with certainty what will amount to an act which will warrant their summary dismissal. Voize-Valayre *op. cit.* at p. 546.

586 BCA/7L/2006 (unreported).

587 See Pougoue., P.G., *Code du Travail du Cameroun Annote*-P.U.A, 1997 at p. 64-65.

588 Arret No. 97/s of 12th September, 1985.

589 Yanou, M.A., *op. cit.* at p. 73.

590 Arret CS No.30/s of 29th December 1967.

591 BCA/7L/2006 unreported at p.4.

592 Appeal No. 79/8/04-05 of 12th May 2005 (unreported).

593 Yanou, M.A. *op. cit.* p. 77.

In *Ndongo Fred Ebanja v. The Chamber of Agriculture*,[594] Ngassa J of the High Court of Fako after citing with approval the decisions in *Poissonerie Populaire du Cameroon v. Shey Ndi John*,[595] held in spite of the plaintiff's claims that his transfer was bad in form, that the persistent refusal of the plaintiff to go on regular transfer like any reasonable worker would despite several warnings amounted to gross misconduct justifying his summary dismissal.[596] It is contended that the fact that the conduct attracts summary dismissal does not mean that there is no security of employment. Workers engaged in conducts incompatible with their contracts of employment are themselves responsible for the insecurity of their service. This is because the contract of service is a contract of subordination that must be executed within the meaning of sections 1(2) and 23 of the Labour Code. A worker therefore who fails to assume this subordination by accepting to surrender his/her labour under the management and control of the employer is by his own action jeopardising his security of employment.

It must be observed that orders must be reasonable and related to the functions of the employee otherwise their disobedience will not amount to acts inconsistent with the contracts of employment, especially as there is nothing more basic to employment which strengthens security of service employment. It was thus held in *Laws v. London Chronicle*[597] that the plaintiff who was dismissed for the disobedience of an order not connected to his duties was wrongfully dismissed.

It is perhaps necessary to ask whether a single misconduct can justify dismissal of a worker. Lord Evershed MR in the *Laws case* held that,

> ....one act of disobedience or misconduct may justify dismissal only if it is of a nature which goes to show (in effect) that the servant is repudiating the contract, or one of its essential conditions.....the disobedience must at least have the quality that it is wilful: it does (in other words) connote a deliberate flouting of the essential contractual conditions.[598]

---

594 Suit No. HCF/L.42/03-04 (unreported).

595 2 CCLR 244-251. in which *Education Board Of Cameroon Baptist Convention v. Robinson Fai Fominyen* BCA/3L/92 (unreported) and *Emmanuel J. Ngwayi v. CDC* quoted and held that refusal to go on transfer was gross misconduct warranting dismissal.

596 See also *Ayuk v. Mamfe Rural Council* CASWP /L1/95 (unreported) where the Courts confirmed the dismissal of the plaintiff a driver who refused to follow lawful instructions of his employer. See also *Catholic Education Secretary v. Mary Masone* Suit No. CASWP L1/ 04-05.

597 [1959] 1WLR 698.

598 [1959] 1WLR 698 at p. 701.

Yanou,[599] on the other hand, argues that no straight answer can be given as to whether a single act can justify summary dismissal noting that it will depend on the circumstances of each case. The principal consideration is the gravity of the misconduct. Where the misconduct is such that it goes to the core of the contract, the worker can be dismissed. It was thus held in *SODEPA Dumbu v. Biebu Martin Mfang*[600] that there need not be multiplicity of acts to justify summary dismissal, as one single intentional or negligent act is sufficient where it could ruin the enterprise. It follows from the above Court of Appeal decision that a misconduct which does not strike at the root of the contract cannot be good reason for dismissal. This apart from strengthening employment security it is reasonable as are the other less drastic disciplinary measures which may be used to sanction such an erring staff. It is important to know with certainty the party responsible for determining an employment as well as when the employment effectively ended.

Does the contract end when the repudiating act occurs?[601] There are two schools of thought, one holding that the repudiatory breach by an employee automatically ends the contract; and the other, the elective theory, insists that the contract ends only when the innocent part elects to accept the breach. It is contended that the former cannot be true otherwise, contracts of employment will be determined upon the commission of a fundamental breach although the breach is unknown to the employer.

Applying this automatic theory to for example, the *Catholic Education Secretary v. Mary Masone, Mary Masone*,[602] the head teacher who siphoned examination fees automatically sacked herself by her behaviour even though the repudiating act (siphoning of examination fees) was still unknown to the Catholic Education Secretary, her employer. The proper position is articulated in *Thomas Marshall (Export) Limited v. Guinle & Others.*[603] Here, it was held that such a breach will amount to repudiation only if the party breaking the contract intended to bring the contract to an end. This therefore gives the initial choice to terminate to the guilty party. This is illustrated in the *Njoko Jean Claude v. Societe SOFIDEX & Njoh Francois Maurice*[604] discussed above. Although a case on constructive dismissal, Forbang J. noted that the contract was still subsisting 'until such time that the defendant shall formally

---

599 Yanou, M.A, *Labour Law Principles and Practice In Cameroon, Op. cit.* at p.79.
600 BCA/7.L/2006 (unreported).
601 Even though they all lead to the same consequence.
602 Suit No. CASWP L.1/ 04-05. (unreported).
603 [1979] 1Ch 227.
604 Suit No. HCF/L.020/06-07 (unreported).

terminate the plaintiff.' This therefore gives the choice to terminate to the guilty party.

The automatic theory is founded on the precept that a fundamental breach of contractual term goes to the root of the contract and so the parties are dismissed without further need of acceptance by the innocent party (in this case the employer).[605] That act must be a complete and intended withdrawal from the contract by the innocent party.

The alternative school of thought which propagates the elective theory, insists that the contract ends only when the innocent party elects to accept the breach. This theoretical approach is similar to the Labour Code's position in section 36(2) in combination with section 39(3). Under these provisions, the employer relies on the repudiating conduct of the employee (dishonesty, incompetence, disobedience, etc) to justify the summary sacking, which otherwise would have been wrongful. By electing to choose the repudiating act as reason for dismissing the worker, the Labour Code position in section 36 and 39(3) strengthens security of service better than the automatic theory which is often used under the common law.

Indeed, these provisions are consistent with Templeman L.J.'s judgment in *London Transport Executive v. Clarke*[606] where the court did not see why a contract of employment should be determined by repudiation and not by acceptance of the repudiation[607] noting that it is of little practical importance, since self-dismissal and acceptance of repudiation lead to the same consequence. However, under the Code a tribunal must first ascertain whether the fundamental breach amounted to a self-dismissal by the worker. Otherwise, the employer must show that the employee's dismissal was in fact fair.[608] It would seem that this common law position has been incorporated

---

605 Per Blackburn J in *Poussant v. Spiers & Pond* [1876] 1QBD 410, at 414-415.

606 [1981]1CR 355.

607 A fact which Lord Oliver in delivering judgment in the House of Lord's case of *Rigby v. Ferodo LTD* [1988] 1CR 29, clearly concurs with as it held that as a general rule, an unaccepted repudiation leaves the contractual obligation of the parties unaffected.

608 Lord Denning MR in his dissenting judgment in the *London Transport Executive Case supra* argues that it is wrong to think that a contract of employment can never be discharged by a breach of contractual obligation no matter how fundamental – unless it is accepted by the other party. Such automatically leads to a breach without any need for acceptance. He used the *Laws Case* above to explain that although the plaintiff's conduct of disobedience was wrong, it did not justify her dismissal since, it did not go to the root of the contract. He distinguished this case from *Pepper v. Webb* where, the gardener's callous retort to his employer after he was instructed on his job obligations left the master with an option whether or not to dismiss him. He elected to and his dismissal was justified dismissal. Lord Denning further explained that, in such situations, the employer's conduct of his job obligations is bad enough to justify the employer dismissing him but the choice to dismiss is left with the employer. See Generally Painter *et al op. cit.* at p. 360-362.

into section 39(3) of the Code which places an inflexible obligation on the employer to show that the grounds for dismissal alleged by him are well founded.

It is necessary to address the theory of efficient breach that argues that it is sometimes economically beneficial and efficient for a party to breach a contract and pay damages if the breaching party will retain profits after paying expectancy damages to the aggrieved party. Warkol[609] posits that this should be encouraged although it works against the security of service employment.[610] To advocates of this theory, it is economically beneficial to the society as the breaching party will re-invest the net gains from the breach thus increasing goods and services leading to the creation of more stable jobs. Although in the short-run this may seem bad for security of service, it is good in the long run if more jobs will be secured in the future.

This thinking is in the opinion of the candidate suspect. What about the security of tenure of the worker whose job has been sacrificed for the sake of long term societal benefits? It is because of these questions that Warkol himself has in an attempt to rationalise this view argued that there is lack of recognition of the value of morality in contracts in general and that of employment in particular which in the main, depends on good faith that each party will perform their part of the contract and not breach it. In addition, the theory does not consider the fact that not all damages are economic which makes it difficult to quantify and compensate.[611] It is for this reason that as strong as the arguments for this theory may be, it definitely does not strengthen security of service. This conclusion accounts for the reluctance of its application by American judges, after more than 70 years since Holme's ideology[612] was formalised into the theory of efficient breach.

Acceptance by an employer of a repudiatory breach of a worker who still wants to continue with the contract is what determines the contract of employment. Nevertheless, there is still an unresolved controversy at common

609 Warkol, C., "Resolving the Paradox Between Legal Theory and Legal Fact: The Judicial Rejection of the Theory of Efficient Breach", 1998, *20 Cardozo Law Review*. p. 324-330.

610 The author concedes that judges still do not decide cases based on the merits of this theory. *Ibid* at p. 321. Also, see for example the case of *Merk v. Jewel Food Stores* 945 F. 2d 889(7th Cir. 1991), *ibid* at p. 340.

611 *Ibid* at p 343.

612 In 1897 Oliver Wendell Holmes, judge of the Supreme Court Justice stated that: "the duty to keep a contract at common law means a prediction that you must pay damages if you do not keep it, and nothing else. Olive Wendell Holmes, the Path of the Law, 10 Harvard law Review, 457, 458 (1897) in Warkol, C.S., 'Resolving the Paradox Between Legal Theory and Legal Fact: the Judicial Rejection of the Theory of Efficient Breach,' *Cardozo Law Review*, September, 1998, p. 323.

law whether the contracts of employment are now *sui generis* so that an employee who is wrongfully dismissed by his employer must first accept the repudiation.[613]

Whatever the case, it is opined that where the repudiatory conduct takes the form of direct abrogation of a fundamental contract obligation, the elective theory has no place since the worker has sacked her/himself. Therefore, cases of self-dismissal (out-right dismissal or walk-out), must be distinguished from those cases where the worker does not sack himself but is guilty of breach, entitling the employer to elect to dismiss. This common law distinction which is a fine one has not been adopted in Cameroon. Based on the above reasoning, it is argued that the automatic theory will strengthen employment relationship if it is applied in cases of gross misconduct only as contemplated in section 36(2) of the Code.

---

613 Per Lord Ralph Groom LJ in *Boyo v. London Borough of Lambeth* [1995] 1RLR 50, a case where Boyo a an accountant of the Borough of Lambeth was summarily dismissed for gross misconduct (fraud). The Borough of Lambeth tried to terminate the contract on grounds of frustration to no avail as Boyo refused to accept the termination and continued to make himself available for work although he was barred from entering the work place.

CHAPTER 7

REMEDIES FOR WRONGFUL DISMISSAL

The value of a justice system lies in the effect of the decision arrived at in court. The decision's real value depends on whether justice[614] is seen to have been done to the plaintiff, the defendant and the society. Clearly, to determine this in labour actions, one needs to evaluate the remedies a worker gets in cases of dismissal. It is in the context of employment law necessary to begin this discourse by stressing that the labour justice of a worker dictates that the remedies available to an aggrieved worker who has been wrongfully dismissed should not only be limited to *restitutio in integrum*.

7.1 The Concept of Wrongful Dismissal

Wrongful dismissal otherwise known as unfair dismissal in common understanding is the determination of a contract of employment for no just cause, requiring the employer to pay damages or for the worker to be re-instated or re-engaged. Collin[615] defines the notion as 'removing someone from a job for a reason which does not justify dismissal and which is in breach of the contract of employment.'

Although the ILO Convention No. 158[616] does not specifically define wrongful dismissal, it could be gleaned from the definition of termination in its article 4 of same[617] that wrongful dismissal is dismissal without valid reason. It is observed that article 5 of the same Convention provides, *inter alia*, that

---

[614] Justice in this context is the "constant and unceasing will to render to each one his due." Elegibo, J.M., *Jurisprudence*, Lagos: Spectrum Law Publishing, 1994, p.360.

[615] Collin, P.H., *Dictionary of Law*, Peter Collin Publisher, 3rd edition, p. 396.

[616] ILO Convention No. 158 on the Termination of Employment Convention, 1982. This treaty which Cameroon ratified in 1988 takes precedence over all national laws as per the constitution of 1996 as revised.

[617] Art 4 of ILO Convention No. 158 provides that; 'the employment of a worker shall not be terminated unless there is a valid reason for such termination connected with the capacity or conduct of the worker or based on the operational requirements of the undertaking, establishment or service.'

membership or participation in trade union activities shall not constitute a valid reason for dismissal. Neither will participation in legal proceedings against an employer who has violated regulations in force nor dismissals because of race, colour, sex, marital status, family responsibilities, religion, political leaning, social origin, national extraction or pregnancy, constitute valid reasons for dismissal.

Clearly, it is apparent from sections 36 (2) and 37(1) of the Labour Code that dismissal occurs where employment is determined for a valid reason[618]. A dismissal for reasons not made out is wrongful. Dismissals based on bad faith,[619] dismissals contrary to the provisions in the Labour Code,[620] dismissal contrary to terms in collective agreement including constructive dismissal,[621] are wrongful. It is apparent from the tenor of section 39(1) of the Labour Code that dismissals not based on objective grounds are considered wrongful. Quite clearly, dismissals are under the spirit animating the Labour Code in section 39(2) prima facie considered as wrongful unless justified by the employer before a properly constituted labour court. Where the courts find that the justification provided by the employer is not enough, the dismissal will be wrongful.

The notion of dismissal in the context of the Labour Code is considered consistent with dismissal as defined under the common law. The common law's view of dismissal was vividly captured by Justice Forbang's decision in the High Court of Fako Case in *Goreh Andrew v. Cameroon Baptist Convention Education Board.*[622] Here his lordship defined wrongful (summary) dismissal as a dismissal without just cause, without authority, illegal or malicious. The learned judge added rightly that even when originally legal, a dismissal will become wrongful if done in tacit disregard of due process.[623]

---

618 See generally Sama-Lang, I.F.," Are Dimissals under section 36(2) of the Cameroon Labour Code of 1992 a breach of the Principle of *audialteram partem*?" *African Journal of Law and Politics, L'Harmattan*, Issue 1 - No.1,47-62.

619 For example in the Supreme Court Case of *Namandina v. Grand Travaux de L'Est* C.S Arret No. 37/s du 15 Avril 1976, Bulletin des Arrets No. 9, 1976, p. 4691, the Court adopted the view that if an employer undertakes a reduction in staff strength in order to frustrate a worker's entitlement to length of service an action, the employer will be liable for wrongful dismissal, giving rise to an action in damages at the instance of the aggrieved worker.

620 For example dismissal because a woman is pregnant in *contra distinction* with the second limb of section 84(1) of the Labour Code 1992 which provides that; 'Any pregnant woman whose pregnancy has been medically certified may terminate her contract of employment without notice and without being obliged on that account to pay the compensation provided for in section 36 above. During such period, the employer shall not terminate the employment contract of the woman concerned because of the pregnancy.

621 See generally Anyangwe, C., "Wrongful Dismissal: the *Cameroon Development Corporation v. D.N Embola*," *Cameroon Law Review*, 2nd Series, No. 26, 1983, p.28.

622 Suit no. HCF/L.16/2000-2001, 44-52(unreported).

623 *Ibid* at p. 50.

Although the court did not expressly say so, this common law definition of wrongful dismissal has the basic conceptual ingredients of dismissal captured by the Labour Code. Both regard dismissal not effected for valid and objective reason as wrongful. The common law approach has apparently recognised the fact that although an employer may be justified in dismissing a worker, the adoption of wrong procedure will make the dismissal wrongful.

The minor distinction between the common law approach and the Labour Code's is the fact that under the former, the adoption of a wrong procedure makes the dismissal wrongful. There is clearly no provision of the Labour Code which encapsulates this principle as stated in the *Goreh Andrew* case..

7.2 Damages for Wrongful Dismissals

At common law, the most common remedy for wrongful dismissal is damages. Damages can be defined literally as monetary award by a judge in a civil action to assuage the legal injuries suffered by the person instituting the claim. Black's Law Dictionary[624] defines damages as money claimed by, or ordered to be paid to, a person as compensation for loss or injury. Although there are different types of damages, the Labour Code recognises only two types; general damages (specific amount of money which is calculated as the loss suffered)[625] and special damages (also known as particular damages, these are damages which are alleged to have been sustained in the circumstances of a particular wrong, which must be specifically claimed and proved).[626] Both species of damages proceed on the idea that the plaintiff be put in the position he would have been if the dismissal had not taken place.

Damages have been defined under the common law as the monetary compensation that is given a dismissed worker representing what he would have earned had the contract been properly terminated.[627] This sum also

---

624 *Black's Law Dictionary*, West Group, 1999, p.393. Gahan defines it as the sum of money which a person wronged is entitled to receive from the wrongdoer as compensation for wrong. Gahan, F., *The Law of Damages, in Black's Law Diction, op. cit.* at p. 393. Collin defines it as money claimed by the claimant from a defendant as compensation for harm done or money awarded by a court as compensation to a claimant Collin, P.H. *op. cit.* at p. 99. Black's law Dictionary

625 Also termed direct damages or necessary damages, *Black's Law Dictionary* defines it as damages that the law presumes from the type of wrong complained of, which need not be specifically claimed or proved to have been sustained. *Black's Law Dictionary, op. cit.* at p. 394.

626 *Black's Law Dictionary, op. cit.* at p. 396. These are damages of a kind which are not presumed by law, but must be specifically pleaded together with the facts on which the person pleading relies must be proved-*CDC v. Isa Bongam* Suit No. CASWP/74/96, CCLR PART 3 at p. 263.

627 Rideout, at p. 176.

takes into consideration any accrued dues as of right. The concept proceeds on the assumption that a wrongfully dismissed worker is merely entitled to compensatory damages, that is, loss which can readily be proven to have been sustained which the worker should be compensated for, as of right. The measure of damages is based on the extent of the legal obligation of the employer, which has been breached. Under this principle the law is:

> concerned with legal obligations only,... created by mutual agreement between contractors-not with expectations, however reasonable......[628]

It is plain from the above legal principle that not everything that flows from a wrongful act can be taken account of in the calculation of damages. Indeed, according to Lord Wright in the case of *Liesbosch Dredger v. Edison*,[629] it will be infinite for the law to judge the cause of causes or consequences of consequences. This principle is predicated on the argument that in the varied web of affairs, the law must abstract some consequences as relevant, not perhaps on grounds of pure logic, but simply for practical reasons.

This common law position above has been incorporated into the Labour Code. The principle in section 39(4)(b) of the Labour Code which prescribes that a worker who is dismissed is entitled to damages of "not less than three month's salary or more than one month's salary per year of service" has its foundation on the above common law principle. It can be argued that this compensation model ought not to be accepted. This remedy provided by the Labour Code is grossly inadequate that it cannot act as a deterrent for arbitrary dismissal. Yanou[630] has in fact argued that it on the contrary, appears to lead to the temptation to discard workers at the absolute pleasure of the employer which is fundamentally prejudicial to security of service.

Section 39(1) of the Labour Code 1992 provides that every wrongful dismissal may[631] entail damages. Although the Code in section 39(1) has identified three instances where a worker's dismissal will be seen as wrongful, Anyangwe[632] argues that cases based on the instances stated in section 39(1) are very rare and workers have been wrongfully dismissed for other reasons. That

---

628 Per Diplock L.J in *Lavarack v. Woods of Colchester Ltd* [1967] 2QB 278, at 292.

629 [1933] AC 449, at 460.

630 Yanou, M.A., *Labour Law Principles & Practice in Cameroon, op. cit.* at p. 90.

631 The use of may instead of shall implies that remedies are not the only remedies for wrongful dismissals.

632 Anyangwe, C.N., "Wrongful Dismissal: The *Cameroon Development Corporation v. D.N Embola*," Cameroon Law Review, 2nd Series No. 26, 1983, p. 28.

notwithstanding, since dismissal strikes at the core of employment relations, the remedies available must ensure security of service of the worker.[633]

According to section 39(4) of the Labour Code 1992;

> Damages shall be assessed with due regard to all parties indicating that prejudice has been caused and all factors determining the extent of such prejudice, and in particular, with due regard:
> a). where the worker is responsible, to his qualification and post;
> b). where the employer is responsible, to the type of employments worker's seniority with the employer, his age and any vested rights. However, the damages shall not be less than three months salary or more than one month's salary per year of service in the enterprise.

It is noted here that section 39(4)(a) and (b) are imports from section 41 of the old Labour Code 1974 where damages were at large judges having wide discretionary powers to award damages to the employee. The impact of section 41 of Labour Code 1974 on the security of service was two folds. On the one hand, the employers were kept in check, as they could not easily dismiss a worker, since they were aware of the cost of such dismissals on their business if it turned out to be wrongful. On the other hand, such previously wide discretions given judges and the exaggerated damages they awarded created room for workers to scheme for their dismissals in order to benefit from the high damages regime. This did not strengthen security of service. It was because of the excessive and exaggerated damages awarded employees that triggered revision of the 1974 labour Code, especially its section 41.

Njie Njonga Manfred v. Office National des Ports du Cameroun (ONPC)[634] is a case in point. The respondent was an employee of the

---

633 For the remedy of damages to be available, the wrongfully dismissed worker must have gone through due process of law. He/she must first submit their case to the local labour inspector who must enter a resolution of conciliation, partial conciliation or non-conciliation, as required by section 130 of the Labour Code, under pain of nullity as was the case in *Me Penda v. Evina Joseph.* C,S Judgment No. 30/s of 21st January 1982. See also *Pectin Cameroon Company v. Agbornah Tataw James* Suit No. CASWP/ LP/90.

634 Suit No. CASWP/L.8/2001 (unreported). See also the case of *The General Manager BICI C v. Chief Ngoh Deah John* CASWP/L.7/87(unreported). In which the lower court in Kumba had awarded the respondent 86.104.680FCFA for wrongful dismissal. The Court of Appeal South West remitted the case to the lower court for retrial.

defendant (appellant) who was prematurely retired in August 1988 before he attained the age of 60 which is the statutory retirement age.[635] Counsel for the plaintiff noted that since the premature retirement violated statutory laws in force, it was null and void. Besides, despite orders issued to the Director General of National Ports Authority by the Minister of Labour and Social Insurance that the employees of the defendants retired before the age of 60 be re-instated, the defendant continued to flout such order, arguing instead that their internal rules gave them authority to retire the plaintiff as they did.

Based on these facts, the High Court of Fako held that the premature retirement in flagrant disrespect of statutory laws in force and ministerial orders calling for re-instatement was wrongful. The court awarded ten million one hundred and sixty four thousand eight hundred and seventy eight francs as special damages, sixteen million as general damages and eight hundred and thirty five thousand one hundred and twenty two francs as cost to the plaintiff, giving a grand total of twenty seven million francs. The defendant appealed against the ruling on the grounds that the twenty seven million francs damages awarded the plaintiff was exaggerated and violates principles of public policy and is in total disregard of the cardinal principle in the case of *Ben Oluwole v. Lagos State Development Corporation*[636], thereby rendering the decision illegal. It was contended that the special damages were unproven and so lacked any legal basis. However, the correct basis for the award of damages is contained in section 39(4) (b) paragraph 1which states that

> "....damages shall not be less than three months salary or more than one month's salary per year of service in the enterprise."
> This provision which was not included in the old Labour Code of 1974, gives clear guidance for the award of damages.

Clearly, the circumstances in which the code was passed influenced Parliament to adopt this almost insignificant amount of damage thus giving the employers' the right to dismiss at will and especially as seemingly, other remedies are not available. The Code was passed when Cameroon was undergoing biting economic crisis marked by street marches and ghost towns, which hampered the performance of most businesses. The government

---

635 As provided by article 9(1) Law No. 84/007 of 4th August 1984 Instituting a regime of Old Age Pension in Cameroon.

636 MCA/L/50/78 (unreported).

has an obligation to support the viable enterprises[637] which could salvage unemployment in especially the private sector. At that time, what was necessary was the protection of the job provider in order to guarantee job security for a few regardless of abuses. The only way to do this was to curtail the wide discretion given judges in the award of damages.

The provisions of section 39(4)(b) of the Labour Code should be revisited, in order to protect the employee. This is so because the insignificant amount of damages payable for wrongful dismissal does not dissuade an employer from dismissing without valid reason.

Notwithstanding the clear position adopted in section 39(4) of the Code, some judges still award excessive damages. A case in point is the *TRAPP case.* Tabe[638] contends that the judge's decision to award two million to the plaintiff in this case was not only excessive but a gross exaggeration. He argued that had the judge followed the calculations in section 39(4) (b) of the Labour Code, the plaintiff who had not worked for the defendant for up to a year would not have been awarded two million francs as damages.[639] According to him, because of this, the trial judge and the Court of Appeal in confirming the award of damages erred. He further contended that damages[640] and compensation are different[641] and so the court ought to have issued damages under section 39(4) and afterwards dealt with the issue of notice and compensation under section 34(1) and 36(1) of the Labour Code. The whole aim of the award of damages is to put the legally injured party as far as possible to the place he ought to have been had the contract been properly executed. It is therefore reparation[642] and not an exaggerated gift.

His position is correct. These workers are reduced to used articles, which are used and dumped when the owner no longer find use for them.

---

637 This observations have been supported by Charles Mbide Kode, the judicial secretary of Fako Agricultural Workers' Union in an interview granted on 11/3/2011, in which he explained that the Code was passed during the economic crises with the view of encouraging foreign investors especially. Unfortunately, in so doing, the code makes the workers victims in front of the powerful employer especially as the amount of damages payable does not take into consideration the amount of prejudice the worker suffers as a result of the wrongful dismissal.

638 Tabe, S. T., *op. cit.* at p.42.

639 It is such exaggerated payment which were abusive of the discretion given judges that forced the drafters to lower limit the quantum of damages to not less than three month or more than a month's salary per year of service. As observed by Yanou, it is these kind of exaggeration, whether or not intended, that scare off foreign investors badly needed to jump-start the ailing economy.

640 Which Yanou defines as pecuniary satisfaction awarded by a judge in a civil suit for a wrong suffered by the plaintiff who in labour relations could either a worker or employer.

641 Given that labour justice is an adjunct of security of service.

642 Per Lord Blackburn in *Livingstone v. Rawyard Co* (1880) AC 25, at 39.

This is especially so where the sole reason of their dismissal is low output occasioned by occupational disease[643]. Such a worker ought to have back his job if he is in good health to continue. Che's (the plaintiff in the *TRAPP Case*) plight is the situation of many workers in Cameroon, whose employers in a bid to escape the payment of social insurance compensations for industrial or occupational diseases to such workers, will rather pay the damages for wrongful dismissal.

Not withstanding the yardsticks to be considered in the award of damages, Yanou[644] contends that the yardsticks given in section 39(4) of the Code become significant in assessing damages for contracts spanning between 1-2 years. In his analysis of Mbeng JCA's judgment in *Union Camerounaise de Brasseries v. Baiye Afue Joseph*,[645] he opined that the yardsticks ought not be used in determining the general damages.[646] This stance of the Court of Appeal is correct as it is trite law that where a claimant specifically alleges that he/she has suffered special damages,[647] he must per force prove it.[648]

Generally, the labour courts in Cameroon grant two types of damages, namely; general or special damages. General damages are liquidated damages awarded where a worker has suffered prejudices due to the wrongful determination of employment. The court assesses the general damages once a case of wrongful dismissal has been established pursuant to the provision of section 39(4) of the Labour Code. On the other hand, special damages are actual losses suffered as a result of the breach. Special damages carry known monetary values. Special damages must be discernible and quantified and

---

643 Once the occupational disease has been certified by a physician indicating the degree of disablement, the worker must be compensated accordingly after the employer has notified the National Social Insurance Fund as per section 17(6) of Decree No. 77/11 of 1977. Failing which the employee has to take upon himself to so declare within three years or be time barred. See article 46 of Decree No. 77/11 of 1977.

644 *Op. cit.* at p. 92.

645 CASWP/L.17/2000 (unreported).

646 This is the stance taken in the courts in the Britain, where the courts held severally that, damages are not payable for distress, vexation, frustration, including consequent ill-health. Or difficulty of obtaining another job. See for example the case of *Addis v. Gramophone Co. LTD* [1909] AC 488, *Cox v. Philips Industries Ltd* [1976] 1WLR 638, *Bliss v. South East Thames RHA* [1987] 1 CR 700 and also, *O'Laoire v. Jackel Ltd.* (No.2)[1991] 1CR718, 730-731. This notwithstanding, this traditional approach was not adopted in New Zealand where the High Court there in the case of *Whelan v. Waitaki Meats Ltd.* [1991] 2N.Z.L.R.74 awarded damages for mental distress, anxiety, humiliation, loss of dignity and injury to feelings.

647 These monetary entitlements have become due to the worker as a right in the course of employment.

648 Per Forbang J in the *Mofa Ngoe David case (supra)* citing with approval Pats - Acholonu JSC in *Neka Manufacturing Ltd v. ACB* Nigerian Quarterly Report Jan-March 2004 at p. 243.

must not rest on a puerile conception open to speculation, approximation or estimate.[649] It must be proven, otherwise it will not be awarded.

Special damages in the context of the Labour Code must be itemised in the claim of the party and incorporated in the state of non-conciliation or partial conciliation, as the case may be.[650] These usually include pay in lieu of notice, severance pay, leave allowance, salary arrears, bonus and seniority, etc. As a rule, special damages include all the worker's claims that had become due before termination. It was thus held in *University of Buea v. Mbua Teke*[651] that salaries which would have been earned had the employment not been terminated cannot be claimed as damages special or general.

If the special and general damages are well founded, then the employee will be entitled to:

- Severance pay.[652] These are compensations based on length of service payable to an employee upon determination of contract of employment[653]. If such a worker has at least two consecutive years of seniority in his/her employment, they will be entitled to tis redress.
- Pay–in-lieu of Notice.[654] These are compensations given to an employee for the employers failure to serve him/her with appropriate notice before determination of the contract of employment.
- Leave pay.[655] These are monetary awards to a worker on leave to cover the cost of travel for him/her and his/her family to their village of origin.
- Repatriation Allowance.[656] This is a monetary compensation given to an employee to transport him/her to the place where he/she was recruited or place of origin.

649 Per Justice Forbang in *Mofa Ngoe David v Plantation du Haut Penja*, Suit No. HCF/L.001/04-05, 37 at p. 43.

650 The employee must not only give particulars of the special claims, but also strictly adduce evidence that he actually suffered the special damages he/she is claiming, *Oshinjinrin v. Elias (1970)* All NLR 153.

651 CASWP Appeal No. 16/S/2002-2003.

652 Mindeful of section 37(2), This is calculated according to Ministerial Order No. 016/MTPS/SG/CJ of 26/5/1993, fixing the method of granting and calculating termination benefits. The distribution is as follows; indemnity for the first 5 years equal to 20% of salary; indemnity for the six to ten years equal 25% of salary; indemnity for eleven to fifteen years equal 30% of salary; indemnity for sixteen to twenty years equal 35% of salary and indemnity for twenty one years and above is 40% of salary.

653 *Webster's Collegiate Dictionary*, p.1078.

654 Calculated according to Ministerial Order No. 015/MTPS/SG/CJ of 26th May 1993, to determine the conditions and duration of notice of termination.

655 Calculated according to section 89 and 90(3) of the Labour Code.

656 Calculated according to Decree No. 93/573/PM of 15th July 1993 determining the allowance to be given any displaced or terminated worker. See also section 94(1) of the Code.

- Seniority Bonus and personal Wages Incremental Position, following rightful categorisation.
- Any wages like unpaid salary, housing allowance, accommodation, utility, etc that is due.

Sometimes, the employer may be justified in dismissing the worker but irregularities by the employer during the tenure of employment will warrant that certain damages be paid the aggrieved worker. A case in point is *Mafany Godlove Namme v. Mbonge Rural Council.*[657] The plaintiff in this case was employed by the defendant on a salary of 24.920 FCFA under a contract for specified duration. He however continued to work for the defendant after this period had long expired until the 14th February 1995 when he was dismissed for absence from work. During the tenure of employment, the defendants failed to register and make contributions for the plaintiff with the National Social Insurance Fund despite the fact that they retained part of his salary for this.

Apart from causing the plaintiff the loss of family allowance, safe delivery allowance for his four children and old age pension, the defendant also failed to issue a table of accessible wages. The court held that the worker was entitled to special damages because having so failed to contribute, the defendants were bound to step into the shoes of the National Social Insurance Fund and pay the plaintiff what he would have gotten had he been registered. He was awarded special damages as follows;

- Delivery allowance for four children - 151.200FCFA
- Family allowance for four children - 1.468.000FCFA
- Old age pension calculated on 2.8% Of the plaintiff's monthly contribution of 24.920frs for 17 years of service - 414.462FCFA
- General damages for the inconveniences caused the plaintiff based on salary for the past 17years - 5.966.338FCFA
- Total - 8.000000FCFA.

It is important to note that this worker could still have claimed this from the National Social Insurance Fund under articles 1 and 5(3) of Decree no. 76-321 of 2nd August1976, which is vested with all powers of payment for workers insurance coverage.

[657] Suit No. HCF/L.001/03-04 (unreported).

Where the ground for the claim of any of these heads by a wrongfully dismissed worker has been proven, but it turns out that the amount given is exorbitant or low as to lead to a conclusion that there was an error in the calculation, upon appeal, the decision will be reversed.

The compensation model adopted in the Labour Code does not enhance labour justice and social security of a worker. The measure of damage under section 39(4) is not strong enough to act as deterrent for a determined and malicious employer who would rather pay the meagre damages than be saddled with the employee. Section 39(4) of the labour code is hinged on the fact that labour law does not recognise any property right in employment.[658] Would it not be better for the worker if exemplary or punitive damages are introduced which are stiff enough to deter out rightly abusive determinations. The policy behind damages is to put the injured party in the position he would have been in but for the breach. The compensation model in section 39(4) (b) of the Labour Code definitely does not restitute the aggrieved. The revision of the Code would, be consistent with the philosophy that conceptualises a worker's career as his/her property which they have invested time and money to acquire. Such a conceptualisation also means that a compensation regime that is limited to only monetary payment is inappropriate redress since social security justice would not be achieved.

7.3 Specific Performance in Employment Relations as a Remedy

Specific performance is an equitable remedy available when the party's remedy at law is inadequate, consisting of a requirement that the party guilty of breach undertake to perform or complete the performance of his/her contract obligation.[659] The importance of this remedy to the thesis lies in the fact that it will enforce the execution of the contract according to its terms. Since its enforcement is by the power of the court, disobedience of the decree is seen as contempt which makes the offender (employer) liable to imprisonment, until he/she is willing to comply with the decree.[660]

---

658 This opinion ought to change especially with the concept of career is property, labour law should start recognizing the property rights in employment.

659 Gifis, S.H., *Barron's Law Dictionary*, Barron's Educational Series, Inc, p. 449. *Black's Law Dictionary* defines specific performance as a court ordered discretionary remedy in equity which requires precise fulfilment of a legal or contractual obligation when monetary damages are inappropriate or inadequate. *Black's Law Dictionary, op. cit.* at p. 1407.

660 Keeton, G.W., *An Introduction to Equity* 304 5th edition in Black's Law Dictionary, *op. cit.* at p. 1407.

Common law has over the years refused the remedy of specific performance so far as they relate to re-instatement[661] or re-engagement[662] of a dismissed worker.[663] Rideout[664] contends that from this mind set, the law developed the attitude that the making of anything other than an enforceable recommendation was valueless.

She contends further that, the courts continue to ignore the power of a command (order of specific performance) over that of a recommendation, which the other party (employer) may chose to ignore. This inhibited the consideration of other available remedies with the result that the law continues to fail to give ultimate job security. In spite of what Rideout says, it is opined that emphasis be put more on the enforcement of labour contracts. In this wise, the labour courts ought to move from the primary remedy of damages to specific performance and injunctive relief especially as the compensation model contemplated by section 39(4) is grossly inequitable. The unfairness makes labour law in Cameroon unjust. In terms of this, Eso J's contention that,

> "...for law to be justified in any society, it must be just, it is justice that enables law to appear in any society as an acceptable norm, or an agreeable concept, and it is justice that could give law a socially and culturally high significant meaning...........it is the concept of justice, which could be attainable thereby, that gives the concept (law) life....,"[665]

Only go to strengthen the call for natural justice and equity to be applied.

As earlier indicted, specific performance is an equitable remedy which in the context of labour law involves orders for re-instatement and re-engagement. The former deals with the situation where a worker is taken back in service as if he was never dismissed while the latter refers to the situation where the worker is given back his job but not necessarily the position he /she had held. The value of the orders of specific performance where a worker is re-instated, his/her fellow workers see the power of labour law protection. The employer is deprived of the fruits of his illegal behaviour and suffers serious

661 The employee is taken back in service as if he had never been dismissed. To place in former position, to restore. *Black's Law Dictionary, op. cit.* at p. 1290.

662 The employee is taken back in employment comparable to that from which he was dismissed or other suitable employment.

663 Rideout, *op. cit.* at p. 254, Whincup, *op. cit.* at p. 188, Painter *et al, op. cit.*

664 Rideout, *op. cit.* at p. 254.

665 Eso, J., "Wither Nigerian Jurisprudence, Volkgeist ?" Lecture delivered at Faculty of Law, University of Ibadan, March, 1986. In Sagay, *A legacy for Posterity*, The Work of the Supreme Court 1980-1988, Lagos, p. 119.

erosion of absolute swing within his plant. This will be a major disincentive to the employers who intend to flout the employment contracts.[666]

It is contended that section 39(1) of the labour code does not rule out other remedies. Indeed by providing that 'every wrongful termination of a worker may entail damages,' gives judges the discretion to provide other remedies which include re-instatement. It is only when an order of re-instatement is made in appropriate circumstances that one can conclude as Oputa JSC did that:

> "The judge should appreciate that in the final analysis at the end of law is justice. He should therefore endeavour to see that the law and justice of the individual case he is trying go hand in hand. The spectacle of law triumphant and justice prostrate should be to him a very sorry spectacle indeed.... He should know that all said and done the law is, or ought to be a handmaid of justice."[667]

Quite apart from the above analysis of section 39(1) re-instatement as a remedy is not alien to Cameroon labour law. Section 4 (2) and (3) of the Labour Code 1992 read together provide that where a worker is dismissed for union activities, such a dismissal is purely null and void. This means that the dismissal is invalid, non-existent and for this reason, the worker must be re-instated. Section 4(3) is a command which is not subject to variation. The judge in such a case must order specific re-instatement of such a worker.

Although section 39(1) of the Labour Code provides that the dismissal of workers because of their opinion, membership or non-membership of a trade union is wrongful, section 130(1) of the Labour Code provides that a staff representative can only be dismissed with prior approval of the local labour inspector. The latter provision indicates the willingness of the government to protect staff representatives.[668] Section 130 (3) provides that the dismissal of a staff representative without prior consent of the labour inspector is null and void. However, in cases of gross misconduct, section 130(4) of the Code provides that the staff representative may be temporarily suspended pending

666 Weiler, C.W, "Promises to Keep:Securing Workers' Rights to self-Organisation under the NLRA," *Harvard Law Review*, June 1983, p. 1791.

667 Oputa, C.A., "Access to Justice,' A lecture delivered at the University of IFE, June 1988, in Sagay, *A Legacy for Prosperity. The Work of the Supreme Court 1980-1988*, p. 120. See also Eso, J. "Wither Nigerian Jurisprudence, Volgeist?" Lecture delivered at the Faculty of Law, University of Ibadan, March, 1986, in Sagay, *op. cit.* p. 119.

668 Yanou, M.A., *Labour Law, op. cit.* at p. 103.

a decision from the local labour inspector. Should the authorisation of the labour inspector not be granted, the staff representative will be re-instated with full pay for the period he/she was suspended.

As Yanou points out, section 130(4) does not only lend support to section 130(3) but goes on to provide that a dismissed staff representative in such circumstances must be re-instated, since the dismissal is null and void. This beyond all doubts strengthens the security of service of the worker.

This was the basis of the decision of the House Lords in *Vine v. National Dock Labour Board.*[669] Here, the House of Lords declared dismissal of a dock worker a nullity, because the local board had no jurisdiction to delegate its power to a committee which dismissed the worker.

The House held that since the removal of the plaintiff's name from the register was, in law a nullity, and hence an invalidity, the worker must be treated as a registered dock worker with all the benefits attached. This principle is also the basis of the decision of *Tatah Ndiwa Faison v. Cameroon Development Corporation.*[670] Here, the plaintiff was employed as general labour of the defendant who through in house training became security guard of the defendant under a contract of unspecified duration. He was subsequently promoted to the rank of chief of security post of one of the departments of the defendant company. Sometime in January 2006, he arrived at his job site to discover that an arch welding plant under his charge had been stolen. He and other workers of the department were arrested and detained but subsequently released, pending criminal proceedings at the Limbe Court of First Instance. The plaintiff appeared before the defendant's disciplinary board and was dismissed from service alongside others who were subsequently re-absorbed. The plaintiff was also a staff representative.

Counsel for the plaintiff argued that the plaintiff was dismissed because of theft of the defendant's property by an unknown individual which theft occurred when the plaintiff was not on duty. The counsel noted that of all the co-accused workers, the plaintiff was the only one summarily dismissed. He argued that his client being a staff representative had been dismissed in flagrant disrespect of the procedure in force and for that reason the plaintiff's dismissal is null and void.

On this basis, the court held that the dismissal was wrongful as the extent of the plaintiff's culpability is still pending before the court in Limbe.

---

669 [1956] 1 Q.B. 658.

670 TM/28L/06-07 (Unreported)

The defendant's dismissal of the plaintiff was not only premature but was 'discriminatory and an abuse of the plaintiff's human right to work.' The dismissal was declared null and void and in addition to cost of one hundred thousand francs, general damages of one million francs and special damages of two hundred and six thousand seven hundred and forty two francs, the defendant was ordered under section 130(3) of the 1992 Code to re-instate the plaintiff immediately and to regularise his salary and all his dues. The plaintiff had since resumed duty.

This ruling of the Court of First Instance Tiko, shows the extent the courts can go in the protection of workers. It also shows that a worker who has received proper legal counsel, fully aware of his rights will not back down in the face of a powerful employer like the CDC but will insist on his/her rightful remedy. Although the plaintiff's claim above was only limited to general and special damages for wrongful dismissal, the counsel pushed through for the ultimate remedy provided in section 130(3) of the Labour Code which is re-instatement. The enforcement by Court of the remedy provided in the Code strengthens security of service.

The ILO Convention 98[671] in its article 1 does provide adequate protection against workers who are dismissed for union activities. Gernignon[672] observed that it is insufficient in the light of article 1 of ILO Convention 98 to allow termination by according statutory compensation payable for unjustified dismissal. Such dismissals are a violation of a fundamental workers' right and so compensation should be in full and comprehensive. According to him, reinstatement of the dismissed worker with retroactive compensation is in this context clearly the most appropriate means of resolving acts of anti-union discrimination.

During the economic crisis period, in a bid to portray itself as trade union friendly, the government had to pass laws or adopt measures that protect the security of service of trade unionists and staff representatives. That is why against the back drop of street marches and workers' strikes it had to pass laws to defend trade unions and their members. As dictated by social security and social justice and the protection of the fundamental rights to work of a worker,[673] there is a shift in paradigm toward the protection of ordinary

---

671 On the Right to Organise and Collective Bargaining 1949. Cameroon ratified this on the 3rd September 1962.

672 Gernignon, B., "ILO Convention 98: An Instrument still topical 50years after Adoption," http://www.training.itcilo.org/ils/ils_freedom/t.... accessed on the 10/3/2011.

673 Protected by the United Nations Declaration of Human Rights, International Covenant on Economic Social and Cultural Rights article 6, the ILO and its Decent work Agenda, the Constitution of Cameroon 1996 and section 2 of the Labour Code 1992, just to name a few.

workers and not just the protection of unionists and employers. The remedy of specific re-instatement should be extended to all workers whether or not they belong to trade unions or are still staff representatives.

Indeed Epuli J (as he then was) in his ruling in *Linonge v. Six International*,[674] took this bold first step when he affirmed that a labour court has powers to re-instate dismissed workers who may not be staff representatives. This he observed he would have done in the case under review had the defendant's activities not been completed. Although this view can be applauded, the order should only be considered if the employee so wishes.[675] This is so as a court has no jurisdiction to grant a relief not specifically asked for.

Forbang J in *Agbor Mathias Arrey v. National Social Insurance Fund*[676] unconditionally awarded the equitable remedy of specific performance to an ordinary worker who is not a staff representative. The plaintiff was employed by the defendant in 1987. The plaintiff had always been highly rated throughout his twenty years of service. He had never received a query from them. However, he was accused by the defendant of complicity to defraud them and for violation of article 23 of the internal regulations and collective convention which forbid staff from involving in acts of dishonesty or receiving any form of gratification. A criminal investigation prompted by the defendant was instituted which led to the arrest and detention of the plaintiff. A preliminary inquiry discharged the plaintiff of the accusations in 2008, a ruling which was never appealed against. This notwithstanding, a disciplinary meeting convened subsequently by the defendant dismissed the plaintiff summarily.[677] The plaintiff sued for wrongful dismissal after the defendant's refusal to reinstate him.

Since the defendant failed to discharge their statutory obligation under s. 39(3) of the Labour Code 1992, mindful of the fact that the decision of a properly constituted court remains binding on even the defendant and takes precedence over the decision of a disciplinary meeting, considering the fact that the plaintiff had been well rated professionally and had not suffered

---

674 HCF/L. 20/1987 (unreported).

675 Aldous J in *Alexander v. Standard Telephones & Cables Ltd* [1990] 1 C R 29, at p. 307, held that all matters must be taken into consideration, including who the employer is, the nature of the work, the ability of the employee, the past history of the employment, the relationship of the employee with the other employees and whether there is work for the employee to do.

676 HCF/L.0004/2009 (unreported).

677 The Bamenda Court of Appeal in *Nkututoh Tifu Micheal v. Kom Area Cooperative* Suit No. BCA/271/80 (unreported), had ruled that the dismissal of the appellant for allegedly misappropriating stocks belonging to the employer after a preliminary inquiry, the judge had ruled that there was no case against the appellant was wrongful.

any professional problems until his dismissal, the court found the plaintiff's dismissal wrongful and null and void. On this basis[678] and on the basis of equity and natural justice, the Court ordered immediate and unconditional reinstatement with all accrued benefits. In addition, the defendant was ordered to pay the plaintiff's accrued salary since July 2006 in the sum of 328.000FCFA x 60 months, making a total of 19.680.000FCFA.

Although these equitable remedies strengthen security of service, common sense dictates that they ought not to be insisted upon where to do so will in the long run be negative to security of service.[679] This argument is based on the fact that contracts of employment though personal are not slave-like and are based on mutual trust and confidence. The dismissal of the worker destroys trust and confidence to the extent that it is sometimes difficult for the worker to accept to continue to work with the employer. Where the worker is dismissed, it is in the first instance gleaned that these might have died and insisting on the worker and employer to be stuck with persons that they do not really want to work with may instead lead to under production and the waning of the employer's authority on other workers.[680] In dispensing justice, therefore, care must be taken to ensure that the worker's interest, which one is seeking to protect, is not jeopardised. The same is not the case with the employer who is invariably an enterprise without a face or emotions.

---

678 The measure of damage is section 39(4) Labour Code 1992.

679 Weiler contends that it is one thing to order for re-instatement and another to try to reconstruct an employment relationship that has been torn apart. He argues that an employer who breaks the law by wrongfully dismissing a worker is wont to feel quite vindictive when forced by an order of re-instatement to take back a dismissed employee. Such an employer may start looking for excuses to get rid of the worker again. Fully aware of this fact, the dismissed worker may not want to return for fear of reprisal. He adds that time is very much of the essence in re-instatement orders. In this wise, the worker is most unlikely to accept the offer of re-instatement if he/she has gotten another job in the interim. The reluctance to return is rooted in the grim prospects at his old job given the poor relationship prevailing between the two. Weiler, P.C., *op. cit.* at1791. In the same light, Megarry J. in *Giles & Co.Ltd v. Morris* [1972] 1. W.L.R. 307, held that ' In general, no doubt, the inconvenience and mischief of decreeing specific performance of most of such contracts will greatly outweigh the advantages, and specific performance will be refused. But, I do not think that it should be assumed that as soon as any element of personal service or continuous services can be discerned in a contract the court will, without more, refuse specific performance.

680 Yanou argues that it is the employer who usually does not want to re-instate or re-engage the employee because of the ridicule and wrong message this might send to other workers. He contends that a worker who sues for re-instatement shows enough evidence of his/her willingness to go back to his/her employment. See generally Yanou, M.A., *Labour Law, op. cit.* at p. 107. In an interview with Raymond Tabe a labour inspector, he explained that, that even where the labour inspector wants to grant specific re-instatement, the employees, prefer to receive damages.

7.4 Injunctive Relief

An Injunction or injunctive relief according to *Black's Law Dictionary* is a court order commanding or preventing an action.[681] In labour law, the remedy may be awarded by a judge prohibiting an employer from violating his/her obligation under the employment contract. Although interlocutory, labour injunctions are particularly useful as they often help to stop the dismissal of a worker arbitrarily.

Section 42 (2) (a) of the Labour Code provides that a worker who refuses to accept amendments to contracts of employment may be dismissed which may be justified if the amendment is in the interest of the undertaking. A worker about to be dismissed for refusing to accept an amendment can apply for an order of injunction restraining the employer from dismissing him pending the determination of whether the amendment is indeed in the interest of the employer. In *Robb v. Hammersmith and Fulham London Borough Council*,[682] the Court granted an injunction restraining an employer from summarily dismissing an employee until requisite steps in the disciplinary procedure had been completed. This was so despite a 'genuine' loss of confidence in the employee who had been summarily dismissed in breach of contractual disciplinary procedures.

Labour injunctions could also be used to restrain employers from dismissing employees in breach of contract terms[683] especially during redundancy selection procedure or under the guise of economic difficulties, etc. In such situations, the award of an injunctive relief is preferred to waiting and getting dismissed particularly as damages will not be adequate recompense for a worker who was dismissed in such circumstances.[684] Denial

---

681 It could also be defined as a writ framed according to the circumstances of the case, commanding an act which the court regards as essential to justice, or restraining an act which it esteems contrary to equity and good conscience; as a remedial writ which courts issue for the purpose of enforcing their jurisdiction. *Black's Law Dictionary, op. cit.* at p. 788. According to Gifis, it is a judicial remedy awarded, requiring a party to refrain from doing or continuing to do a particular act or activity Gifis, S.H. *op. cit.* at p. 170

682 [1991] 1RLR 72. See also Chadwick J in *Jones v Gwent County Council* [1992] 1 RLR 521.

683 See for example *Irani v. Southampton and South-West Hampshire Health Authority* [1985] 1 CR. 590, where it was held that injunctive relief could be granted if there is still complete confidence between the employer and employee; secondly, if the employee is dismissed in breach of procedural provisions in the contract of employment and thirdly, in the circumstances of the case damages will not be appropriate. Cf *Ali v Southwark L.B.C* [1988] where the question of confidence played a prominent part in the court's refusal to grant injunctive relief.

684 Also in the *American Cynamid Co v. Ethicon LTD* [1975] A.C. 396 where the granting of interlocutory injunction developed and also *R.v. Secretary of State for Transport, ex parte*

of such a remedy in situations as explained above will, in the words of Warner J. in *Irani v. Southampton Case*,[685] 'be a right to employers to snap their fingers at the rights of their employees under the contracts of employment'.[686] After all, the measure of damages under the Labour Code is just a small token which employers do not 'mind' losing.

Therefore, it would be incorrect to assume based on the forgone that the laws within the present legal framework are adequately adapted to provide security of employment in the face of terminations, dismissals or redundancies. This is especially so with the compensation model provided in section 39(4) of the Labour Code 1992, which most judges assume, damages ought to be the sole remedy to recompense a worker who has been wrongfully dismissed.

Factortame Ltd (No. 2) [1991] 1 AC 603, 671-683 where it was held that an employee need not show that there is a prima facie case to answer. All that is necessary is for him/her to show that there is a serious issue to be tried. Once this has been ascertained, the courts will then consider the granting of an injunction is damages will not be appropriate. See generally, Ewing, K.D., *op. cit.* at p. 429-30.

685 [1985] 1CR 590, at 604.

686 See also Forbang J in the *Njoko Jean Claude Case* above.

CHAPTER 8

TRADE UNIONS

The concept of freedom of association is born out of the idea that man is a social being[687] whose impact cannot be felt if he operates alone given the inequality in society. The decision in the United States in *NLRB v. Jones & Laughlin Steel Corpn*[688] has held that since a single employee ordinarily depends on his daily wage for the maintenance of himself and family, alone in front of his employer, he is helpless should the employer refuse to pay him for what he thought fair, supports the above theoretical conclusion.

From this premise, trade unions are essential in giving workers the opportunity to deal with their employers on common ground.[689] Indeed, it is in recognition of workers' helplessness that promoters[690] of workers' rights stressed the need to conceptualise the freedom of workers to associate unconditionally as a core labour right. The ILO's Declaration on Fundamental Principles and Rights at Work and its follow-up of 18th June 1998,[691] reaffirmed freedom of association as one of the four universal rights of a worker. Clearly, when seen from the present philosophical standpoint, freedom of association is a basic feature of industrial relations in modern democratic states.

Juan Somavia posits that "social justice is the best way to ensure sustainable peace and eradicate poverty," noting that he believes "in people coming together organizing, joining forces, making their voices heard."[692] This

---

687 Trade unions were born out of the inequality in the negotiating strength between employers and employees.

688 30, U.S. 1, 33 at 34.

689 Tabb, M., "Employee Innocence and the Privileges of Powers Reappraisal implied Contract Rights," *52 Missouri Law Review*, Fall 1983, 808.

690 The International Labour Organisation.

691 1998 Declaration. www.ilo.org/declaration/thedeclaration/textdeclaration/lang-en/index.htm accessed on the 20th July 2010.

692 Juan Somavia, ILO Director General. http://www.ilo.org/global/About_the_ILO/Mission_and_objectives/lang--en/index.htm accessed on 1/17/2008. Indeed in a recent study by CorneliBen of the ILO office in Budapest on Central and Eastern European Countries, he emphasises that social dialogue has an important role to play in flexible forms of employment and in the improvemrnt of worker's employment and social protection. CorneliBen, T., *Flexibility and Security in the Labour Market, Labour Market Institutions and Perceived Job Security in Europe*, Budapest: International Labour Organisation, 2007

statement of the Director General of the International Labour Organisation (ILO) lends credence to the first paragraph of the Preamble of the ILO constitution, that, "universal peace can be established only if it is based on social justice."[693] From this perspective, it is opined that labour justice can be secured only where workers' rights and obligations are preserved and respected. Clearly lasting peace can be established only when workers receive decent treatment.

The right to belong to trade unions is secured by article 23 of the Universal Declaration of Human Rights (UDHR), 1948, article 6 International Covenant for Economic Social and Cultural Rights (ICESCR), 1966, article 21 of the International Covenant on Civil and Political Rights 1966, the ILO Convention No. 87 of Freedom of Association and the Protection of the Right to Organise, 1948[694] and ILO Convention No. 98 on the Right to Organise and Collective Bargaining Convention, 1949.[695] This right is equally secured locally in the preamble of the 1996 Constitution of Cameroon as revised, which guarantees the "freedom... of association, and of trade unionism, as well as the right to strike, under conditions fixed by law."[696] The Labour Code 1992, which is the specific law regulating labour in the country provides in section 4 that: "every worker and employer shall have the right to join a trade union... of his own choice in his occupation or kind of business." In say doing, they shall be protected from anti-union discrimination in their employment[697] and any practice that tie their employment to membership or non-membership to a trade union or that may result to their dismissal or undue prejudice as a result of their membership or non-membership in any trade union.[698] Kahn-Freund has argued that[699] freedom of association only means two things, viz, the absence of prohibitions or restraints, and the presence of positive guarantees for its exercise. It is necessary to review the notion of freedom of association from this perspective with the view of examining how the idea contributes to the protection of employment security. Apart from reviewing the nature of trade unions with the above in mind, this chapter examines

---

693 http://www.ilo.org/ilolex/english/iloconst.htm accessed 1/17/2008.

694 Ratified by Cameroon in 1960.

695 Ratified by Cameroon in 1962.

696 According to Art 65 of the 1996 Constitution, provisions in the preamble have the same force like provisions in the constitution.

697 Section 4 (2) (a) Labour Code 1992.

698 Section 4 (2) (b) Labour Code 1992.

699 Kahn-Freund, O., *Labour and the Law, London: Stevens*, 1972, p. 167.

the historical evolution of trade union, the procedure for the creation of trade unions, staff representatives, Collective bargaining and function of trade unions in modern democracies.

8.1 Evolution of Trade Unions in Cameroon

This section analyses the evolution of trade unions in Cameroon from the period of German rule through to the post – independent Cameroon.

8.1.1 Evolution of Trade Unions in German Kamerun

During the German occupation of Cameroon,[700] the administration's attitude towards trade unions was to a large extent informed by the policies of the German firms operating in Cameroon. These firms generally did not involve workers in defining the content of these policies for fear that it would empower workers and put them in a position where they could challenge German employers who at that time treated labour as a mere factor of production subservient to capital. On the contrary, German planters simply co-opted union leaders as intermediaries or brokers in the control structure over labour in the plantations.[701]

This, notwithstanding, trade unions developed during this period in Cameroon when workers who were engaged in these German firms,[702] naturally teamed up to discuss their common problems. Although these associations started off as ethnic associations, they soon gained roots in most of the German plantations leading to agitations in some of the plantations for better pay and work conditions.[703] However, because of the hostile management structure of German colonialism, these associations were in the main underground movements which could not in any significant way impact on the security of tenure.

---

700 1896-1914.

701 See generally Hyman, R., *Maxism and Sociology of Trade Unionism*, London: Pluto Press Ltd, 1975 in Konings, P. *Labour Resistance in Cameroon, op. cit.* at p. 107.

702 Konings, contends that the workers appear to have become gradually aware of their limitations of individualistic, informal actions and spontaneous and often localized, collective actions in their struggles against control and exploitation. Konings, P., *Labour Resistance in Cameroon, op. cit.* 107.

703 See generally, Ebune *op. cit.* at p. 68-70.

8.1.2 Trade Unionism in British Cameroons

Although as early as September 1930, Lord Passfield[704] insisted on the legalization of trade unions in the then Southern Cameroons, it was not until after the passing of the Trade Union Ordinance No. 44 of 1938, that trade unionism gained roots. Inspired by the success story of trade unions in Nigeria and the concessions gained from their concerted labour action, plantation workers went on strikes from 11-19 July 1945 and 7-17 August 1945 leading to work stoppages.[705] Following these, the colonial administration and plantation management realised the need for the establishment of trade unions which they could control. Negotiations between the workers and their employers eventually led to the founding of the Cameroon Development Corporation Workers' Union.

Although the union later became the Cameroon Plantations Workers' Union (CPWU) in 1947 under the leadership of the late Dr. E.M.L Endeley, this union was only formally recognised in 1948 after its registration. It is significant to note that these trade unionists were not paid employees of the corporation but rather paid employees of the workers who were employed through election by the workers.[706] This is fundamental in that it made the unions to be free from pressure from the corporations to whom they owed no obligations.

It was clear that the primary aim of this union was the security of employment of the workers and the conditions of employment of its members. Mbille[707] has observed that in 1949, the daily wage of a worker was one shilling and six pence which could not cater for a worker's basic needs. In a bid to improve on the slave-like living standards of the workers, the trade union in 1949 resorted to the longest strike of the corporation which resulted in the corporation yielding to the union's demands.[708] Other trade unions like the Likomba Plantation Workers' Union, Tombel Banana Union and the Bakweri

---

704 Also known as Sydney Webb was the Secretary of State for the Colonies in the Labour government of Britain.

705 Konings, P., *Labour Resistance in Cameroon, op. cit.* at p.108-109.

706 Mbille, N.N. *Cameroon Political Story, Memories of an Authentic Eye Witness, Limbe*: Presprint, 2000, p.29-30.

707 *Ibid* at p. 30.

708 Salaries were increased to one shillings and ten pence daily wage, general positive revision of salaries for monthly paid workers, schools, hospitals and workers' shops were established and weekly rations of workers were also subsidised. The number of Africans in senior positions also increased, *Ibid* at p. 36-37.

Cooperative Farmers' Union were subsequently registered with practically the same interests.[709]

Konings[710] has observed that the British Trusteeship Authority introduced a model of "free but responsible trade unionism" aimed at controlling the militancy of trade unions and ensuring that the unions pursued a moderate, productionist and a-political policy especially with the emergence of nationalist movements and political parties. In this regard, the CDC, the largest private employer instituted a military-like command structure[711] which used loss of jobs, fines and physical punishments to brow beat workers into towing the corporation's line, while those who kept company rules were highly rewarded.[712] This state of affairs meant that unions in the corporation could not significantly contribute to the security of service amongst workers in the company.

Furthermore, the introduction of free and responsible trade unionism as against the militant trade unionism meant that the workers were wont to solving industrial disputes amicably rather than through strike actions. This approach to dealing with industrial disputes had minimal effect on the capacity of unions to strengthen security of service. Strike and work disruptions, which in fact cause industrial instability were and still are strong tools in the hands of the unions. When deployed to achieve security of service these are a lot more successful.[713]

Furthermore, the administration pursued a policy of persistent ideological indoctrination of the workers. They appealed to the good conscience of the workers whom they encouraged to make sacrifice for the sake of national development. Workers were encouraged to regard their relationship with their employers as that of an elder brother and a younger

---

709 See generally Ebune *op. cit.* at p.68-83.

710 Konings, P., *Labour Resistance in Cameroon*, Leiden: African Studies Centre, 1993, p. 108.

711 In CDC plantations where trade unionism gained grounds, the Germans had put in place a hierarchical structure where at the helm of the estate was/is the estate manager with field assistants as his immediate subordinates. He was/is accountable to the Group manager. Konings opines that these managers demanded strict obedience of constituted authority. Since most of these managers were mainly rank and file workers with little or no basic education and who in the main were trained in their career by CDC, they owed their career and job security to CDC. For this reason, their loyalties laid with the management, rather than to the workers. Konings, P. *Labour Resistance in Cameroon, op. cit.* at p. 81 - 85. With this reality, Such indigenous management staff could not jeopardize their job security for the 'simple pleasures' of protecting the job of another, especially as these top positions came with a lot of financial and social benefits.

712 *Ibid* at p. 94.

713 Article 5 of the ILO Convention 87, which Cameroon ratified in 1960 does not make registration a condition *sine qua non* for the existence of trade unions.

one. The management likened the work place to a family set up where each member has a responsibility to see it succeed for their common good.[714] In this wise therefore, workers were cajoled into putting state and plantation interest first before their own job benefits which would have come with their persistent demands. This paternalistic and national development ideologies preached by the administration which continued even after independence and re-unification to a large extent punctured the militancy of the trade unions that had emerged, with of course significant negative impact on the security of tenure.

8.1.3 Trade Unionism in French Cameroon

On August 27th 1944, immediately after the legalisation of trade unionism in East Cameroun, the *Confederation Generale du Travail* (CGT), the largest communist dominated trade union in France, was extended to this overseas territory. This was closely followed in September of the same year by *Union des Syndicats Confederes du Cameroun* (USCC). By July 1945, the union activities had gathered enough momentum to challenge certain aspects of the Labour Code of 18th July 1945 drafted according to the dictates of the Brazzaville Conference of 1944 for overseas territories.[715]

The CGT called for strikes in protest of the mistreatment of indigenous labour force. The activities of the *Jeunesse Camerounaise Francaise* (jeucafra)[716] and the effect of the International Forced Labour Convention of 1946[717] domesticated in Cameroon through Law No 52/1322 of 15th December, 1952, did not only proscribe forced labour in French Cameroun but also abolished the division of laws into *indigenes* and the *assimiles*.[718] These combined and concerted efforts through veritable trade unions strengthen job security, as well as restitute the dignity of the natives.

---

714 See generally, *ibid* at p 91.

715 It held between January 30-8th February 1944 to revise relationship between France and its colonies in Africa. The aim was to abolish forced labour, to make policy for the native population to be employed in public service positions within the colonies and carry out economic reforms to diminish exploitation of the natives by the colonialist. Furthermore, citizens of French colonies would have equal rights with French citizens and the natives will have the right to vote. See generally, http://www.ask.com/wiki/Brazzaville_conference_of_1944, accessed on the 12th November 2010.

716 A political party which called for the africanisation of cadre.

717 Which was executed by Act No. 46-645 of 11th April 1946.

718 Le Vine, *op. cit.* at p. 142-143

8.1.4 Trade Unionism in Post-independence Cameroon

In the then West Cameroon, trade unionism was introduced from Nigeria and modeled along independent lines consistent with the Anglo-saxon philosophy of freedom. On the other hand, unionism in East Cameroon began as a workers' revolution that metamorphosed into syndicates and was integrated into the *Union des Populations du Cameroun* (UPC) political struggle against the colonial power.

After the formal ending of multi-party politics in 1966 and the coming into being of the Cameroon National Union (CNU), the government of Ahidjo was bent on bringing autonomous trade unions under his grip, in a bid to kill militancy and foster his hegemonic control.[719] In the CNU congress in Garoua, Ahidjo called on trade unions across both sides of the Mungo to sink their differences and form one union for the sake of 'national unity' and development. Konings[720] notes that Ahidjo argued that in a country like Cameroon with no class conflicts, where the state strives for labour justice, the trade unions must be more constructive rather than contentious. According to this view, workers should only make demands in the light of the possibilities available in an economy where there was sacrifice by persons of all walks of life. After elaborating on the quadrupule pronged role of the trade unions,[721] he enjoined the unions to break away from the international associations like the International Confederation of Free Trade Unions, (ICFTU).

Following the emphatic demands that had been made for the unity of trade unions, the West Cameroon Trade Union Congress founded in 1962[722] joined the *Federation Syndicale du Cameroun and the Union des Syndicats Croyants du Cameroun to form the Union des Travailleurs du Cameroun* (National Union of Cameroon Workers - NUCW) in 1972. They immediately elected a central bureau to manage its affairs. Article 3 of the Statute of NUCW provided that the new union will carry out its activities according to the dictates of the CNU. To guarantee that this was followed, the Political Bureau of the CNU was represented in all branches of the NUCW.

---

719 According to Bayart, Ahidjo aimed beyond the establishment of a one party system to make trade unions subordinate to the party. See Bayart, J-F., *L'Etat en Afrique: La Politique du Ventre*, Paris Fayard, in Konings, P., *Labour Resistance in Cameroon, op. cit.* at p. 135.

720 Konings, P., *Labour Resistanc in Cameroon, op. cit.* at p. 135-136.

721 Now contained in Article 9 of the Statutes of NUCW i) To ensure the enforcement of labour laws and application of labour discipline at the work place; ii) To contribute to the professional training of members and to educate them in development problems; iii) To mobilize the masses for the task of nation building and iv) To assist government efforts to improve the workers' living standard.

722 Which had rather preferred trade union unity instead of trade union political integration.

Furthermore, to ensure the complete demise of free trade unions, the Labour Code 1967 was passed introducing staff representatives within companies which were easily manipulated in West Cameroon. It is worth noting that staff representatives already existed in the then East Cameroon. Strikes were completely outlawed and in matters of labour disputes, compulsory arbitration was prescribed. This gave opportunity for the state and its elites to have control over capital accumulation and total control over civil society with the barest of opposition. From then onward, workers' representatives acted in accordance with party discipline and not workers' interest.[723] Under this labour dispensation, issues of the security of workers' employment were relegated to the background by the CNU controlled trade union which was pre-occupied with the political survival of the Ahidjo one party regime. It is regrettably true that this kind of ideological slant still exist even in 2011.

8.2 The Concept of a Trade Union

Black's Law Dictionary defines a trade union as an organisation formed to negotiate with employers, on behalf of workers collectively, about job-related issues such as salary, benefits, hours, and working conditions.[724] This definition is similar to that proffered under common law by Sir Donaldson in *Midland Cold Storage Ltd v. Turner.*[725] Here, his lordship defines a trade union as an association consisting wholly or mainly of workers with the principal objective of regulating the relationship between workers of that description and its employers.[726] Both definitions have as a basic definitive feature a

---

723 Konings, P., *Labour Resistance in Cameroon, op. cit.* p.135-141.

724 Black's Law Dictionary, Garner,B.A (ed), West Group, 1999, p.1532. Webster has defined a trade union as an organisation of workers formed for the purpose of advancing its members' interest in respect to wages, benefits and working conditions. *Webster's New Collegiate Dictionary*, Merriam – Webster INC Publishers, p. 668. Gifis defines it as any association of workers whose main purpose is bargaining on behalf of workers with employers about the terms and conditions of employment. Gifis, S.H., *Barron's Law Dictionary*, Barron's Educational Series, INC p. 260.

725 [1972] 1CR 773.

726 Section 1 of the British Trade Union and Labour Relations (Consolidation) Act 1992 defines trade unions as an organization which consists wholly or mainly of workers of one or more descriptions and whose principal purposes include the regulation of relations between workers of the description or those descriptions and employers or employers' associations; or which consist wholly or mainly of constituent or affiliated organizations which fulfill the above requirement. Section 1(1) of the Trade Unions Act, Cap. 437, Laws of the Federation of Nigeria, 1990, Defines trade unions as any combination of workers or employers, whether temporary or permanent, the purpose of which is to regulate the terms and conditions of employment of workers, whether the combination in question would or would not, apart from this Act, be an unlawful combination by reason of any purposes being in restraint of trade and whether its purpose do or do not include the provisions of benefits for its members.

collectivity of workers dedicated to issues touching on their welfare and job security.

Section 3 of the Labour Code[727] has not comprehensibly defined a trade union. However, it could be gleaned from this section that workers and employers who without prior authorisation freely associate for the study, defence, promotion and protection of their interests, particularly those of an economic, industrial, commercial or agricultural nature, are rightfully seen as trade unions.

Although the concept of trade union is most often erroneously seen as an association of workers, it is clear from the above that both workers and employers can form trade unions of their own, the workers and the employers cannot come together to form a single association. They both are forbidden from entering into each other's activities.[728]

As captured in section 3 of the Labour Code, the association is formed solely for the study, defence, promotion and protection of the socio-economic, cultural and moral advancement of its members. This is therefore the basic objective for the creation of the association, although it is not expressly so provided, it can be inferred from the reading of the second limb of section 3 which expressly prohibits any unconnected activity of such an association which is not in line with these objectives.

The right to freely unionise belong is a right guaranteed and secured in the preamble of the 1996 Constitution of Cameroon as revised. Any attempt therefore by an employer to prevent or prohibit employees from joining a trade union whether or not based on any law[729] will be an infringement of the worker's right. This may for instance include for instance signing a contract on the part of an employee not to belong to any trade union.

Membership to worker's trade unions is available only to persons who are gainfully employed at the time of joining the union. In other words, eligibility is only for workers as defined in section 1(2) of the Labour Code although persons who had ceased to be gainfully employed may continue to be a member if he has carried on with his occupation for at least six months,

727 According to this section, "the law recognises the right of workers and employers, without distinction whatsoever, to set up freely and without prior authorization(trade unions or employers'), associations for the study, defence, promotion and protection of their interests, particularly those of an economic, industrial, commercial o agricultural nature, and for the social, economic, cultural and moral advancement of their members"

728 Section 5(2) Labour Code 1992.

729 Section 4 (3) Labour Code provides that "Any act contrary to the provision of this section shall be null and void".

is engaged in union activity or holds a position of responsibility established by law.[730] Non–national wish to belong to trade union in addition to being gainfully employed must have resided in Cameroon for not less than five years.[731]

Although it goes without saying that the right to unionise is a constitutional and basic right of a worker, no worker is compelled by law to join if they do not wish to. At common law, there is however, a recognition of the right of unions to establish and maintain a closed shop as per Sargeant J in *Reynolds v. Shipping Federartion Ltd*,[732] "for many years past no one has questioned the right of a trade union to insist, if they are strong enough to do so, under penalty of a strike that an employer or a group of employers shall employ none but members of the trade union.

The independence of trade union requires positive guarantee of a right to freely organise and associate as a union without prior authorisation. This has been guarantees by the ILO Convention No. 87 which gives them right to draw up their constitutions, elect representatives, formulate their programs without the interventions of the public officers who may restrict or impede these right and such unions are not be dissolved safe as is provided for in section 1 of the Labour code 1992.

Trade unions as viewed from an Anglo-saxon perspective must necessarily import the idea that the organization is independent. This distinguishes trade unions from similar associations set-up by the employers of the workers with no direct interest in challenging management's power, which in labour parlance are known as 'sweet-heart unions'.[733] This explains why section 5 of Trade Union and Labour Relations (Consolidation) Act 1992, an English statute, defines independent trade unions as that which is not under the domination or control of an employer or any such group or association tending towards such control and is not liable to interference by the employer or any such group.

Lord Denning in *Squib UK Staff Association v. Certification officer*[734] held that to ascertain if an association is indeed a trade union, there must be a probe to see the strength of the employer, the pressures the employers can bring to bear against the staff association and the facilities the employers can

730 Section 7 Labour Code 1992.
731 Section 10 (2) Labour code 1992
732 [1924] 1 Ch 28 at pp. 39-40.
733 Painter *et al op. cit.* at p. 610.
734 [1980] 1RLR 431.

withdraw which can affect the association. Where a workers' trade union is weak to the extent of being exposed to the vulnerability of interferences, then such a workers' association will not be seen as being independent. Although independence is not a formal requirement for the existence of trade unions, the autonomous character of a trade union impacts positively in favour of the worker for the reason that unions which are autonomous can best fight without fear or favour for workers' rights and employment security.

8.2.1 Procedure for Registration, Status and Cancellation of a Trade Union

This section discusses the procedure for registration and cancellation of a trade union.

8.2.1.i Procedure for Registration

Although section 3 of the Labour Code expressly provides for existence of a trade union without prior authorisation, section 6 (1) of same clearly provides that no trade union whether employer or worker, shall have a legal existence if it has not received a certificate of registration from the registrar of trade unions. As a consequence, any person who operates such a union without a priori authorisation shall be punished with a fine of from 50.000frs to 500.000frs.[735]

The applicant in this regard shall motivate and send to the registrar of trade unions a complete application for registration of the union duly signed by at least 20 members (in case of worker's union) indicating their titles together with two copies of the rules.[736] Such applicant or member of administration of the union must be in possession of their civic right or must not have been convicted of any offence laid down in section 30 (1), (2) and(3) of the.Penal Code of Cameroon. After acknowledging receipt of the application documents, the Registrar shall examine and register same within one month. After this time lapse, the applicant is right to assume that the registration has been effected.[737]

---

[735] See in this regard section 6 (2) and section 166 Labour Code 1992.

[736] Section 11 (1) (a).

[737] Section 11 (1) (b) Labour Code 1992.

8.2.1.ii Capacity and Functions of a Trade Union

According to section 16 of the Labour Code, a duly registered trade union must have an office to which all notices and correspondences shall be addressed. The address of such office must be communicated to the Registrar of Trade Unions within 30 days and in case of any subsequent change, the registrar must be duly notified within 30 days of the change under pain of being punished with a fine of from 50.000-500.000frs.

Once a trade union is registered, it becomes a legal entity with rights and prerogatives. Although it is not an incorporation, it enjoys the major character of a corporate personality as it has express powers conferred to it by section 17 of the labour code to acquire both moveable and immoveable property by way of donations or outright purchase and by section 18, it can sue and be sued. It therefore has a proprietary right to the registered name of the union and so is freed from bringing derivative or representative actions as is the case with most unincorporated association. In this regard therefore, a trade union is different as is noted by Lord Keith in *Bonsor v. Musician's Union*[738] from an unincorporated association in that it is unnecessary to consider who were the members at any particular time. For instance, it is immaterial who were the members at the time that any cause of action arose, or what members have joined the union since the cause of action arose. The Registered trade union may be said to assume a collective responsibility for all members past, present and future, in respect of any cause of action for which it may be made liable…….. irrespective of the date of action. On the other hand, the judgment creditor can look only to the funds of such trade union to satisfy his debt, and to the extent to which these may be augmented from time to time by contributions of member, whether new or old, they will still be available for the unsatisfied judgement creditor.[739]

The role of trade unions as partners in development[740] and the third sector of the society cannot be over-emphasised. Ewing[741] has observed that trade unions have numerous functions some of which are more prominent than others, depending on the period in history, economic orthodoxies and

---

738 [1956] AC 104.

739 *Ibid* at pp. 149-150.

740 Sama-Lang, I.D.F, "Trade Unions: Ensurers of the right to work and Development in Cameroon," *Annales de la Faculte des Sciences Jurisdique et Politique*, University of Dschang, Tome 12, 2008, pp. 119-209.

741 *Ewing, K.D., 'The Function of Trade Unions,' 34 Industrial Law Journal,* March 2005, p. 1.

the political party in power. In other words, the functions of trade unions are not stable but move with time. In order to function as a collectivity for the regulation of relations between workers and employers, Ewing[742] identified five basic functions.

A service function[743] which involves the provision of services and benefits to its members for example, health and unemployment benefits, the provision of services which are not work related, ensuring the enforcement of rules and laws in force. Although Ewing notes that this function is the activity of a 'fledging and immature organisation,'[744] in line with this service function section 18 of the labour code, trade unions may also, set aside resources for the construction of houses for its members or buy farm land or sporting grounds for the wellbeing and recreation of workers of their members. In furtherance of the occupation or trade of the members, the trade union may establish, administer or make grants to institutions serving the trade or occupation such as provident schemes, solidarity funds, laboratories, experimental farming stations, schemes for scientific, agricultural or social education, courses and publications in matters concerning the trade or occupation[745]. They may make grants to producer or consumer cooperatives as well as enter into agreements with other associations, companies undertakings and persons.

In addition as provided by the rules and provided they do not distribute to members any profits made, the trade may purchase for hire, lending, distribution to their members anything that is necessary for their trade or occupation including tools, implements, machinery pants, animals. They may also provide free service for the sale of products derived exclusively from the personal labour or holding of members and promote sale by means of exhibition, advertisement, publication, group orders and deliveries even though such is not done in the name of the union.

A workplace representation function,[746] which simply means that the trade unions will represent the interests of its members in the workplace, for example, providing professional support and a lay advocate for handling of individual disputes, it extends to consultations and bargaining for the workforce. Section 18 (1) (a) of the Labour code expressly gives power to the trade unions to take action which directly or indirectly cause prejudice to the

---

742 *Ibid* at p. 3.

743 *Ibid* at p. 5-8.

744 *Ibid* at p.3.

745 Section 18 (1) (c).

746 *Ibid* at p. 9-12.

collective interest of the trade or occupation which they represent. In defence of its member's right, the trade unions paly important consultative role apart from participating in negotiations through collective bargaining, they can assist members in court in addition to initiating court action on their behalf as was seen in the case of *SYNES v. Dr. Njeuma.*[747]

Ewing opines[748] that ancillary to the representation at workplace is the manner in which the representation is to be carried out through partnership, which calls for cooperation between employers and employees through their unions. This view is supported by section 22 of the Labour code which permits partnership through into federations with companies, employer's association of any kind and under any name so long as it does not violate the objective of section 3 of same.

Partnerships function compliment flexibility with action to improve employment security in the workplace, since it focuses on quality of work life. It leads to improvements of terms and conditions and more opportunities for employees to participate at decisions about their work as well. It is in this regard that trade union activists will want establishments with trade union partnerships to look and perform better than those which do not.[749] This is so because the partnership helps the trade unions play an active role in developing organisational policy and strategy[750] through which the unions can push through their mission of ensuring that workers dignity in labour.

The sustained collaboration between trade unions on behalf of their members and the management is fundamental in the survival of the establishment and continuous employment of workers. A case in point is the active partnership between the CDC and the Fako Agriclutural Workers Union.

In 1989, following the collapse of the market for primary products, there was immediate need for steps to be taken in order to keep the corporation afloat. In collaboration with the trade union, the management came up with a package, which the trade union had negotiated with the workers to stabilize the corporation's finances and to improve on its cash flow situation. The Board of Directors rejected the package. The precarious situation of the corporation deepened to the extent that management was informed that the corporation would not escape liquidation if things did not change. The workers and staff

747 Suit No. CASWP/13/2006 (unreported).
748 Yanou, M.A., "Rules for the Registrationof Trade Unions in Cameroon," *op. cit.* at p. 9-10.
749 Trade Union Congress, *Partnership in Depth*, www.tuc.org.uk/pi/partnership.htm.
750 *Ibid.*

representatives resolved that the corporation be liquidated and all workers be paid off. However, the Fako Agricultural Workers' Union after rejecting this approach[751] embarked on a mission through all the corporation's plantations to reach a different agreement where workers were expected to mandatorily save 15% of salary, which would increase the cash flow of CDC. The workers bought the union's idea with the effect that they raised within a short time 3.5 Billion FCFA that kept the corporation afloat and saved it from liquidation.[752] This improved financial situation of the CDC influenced the government's decision to list CDC as one of the States Corporation to be privatised.[753] Although fringe benefits were slashed, the workers' sacrifice under the union's leadership salvaged the company and saved thousands from losing their jobs.

The regulatory function[754] which is a function that arises mainly from the scope and extent of the bargaining process. It is concerned mainly with rule making and collective bargaining which set terms and conditions of work for an industry or industrial sector. This function of the trade union which is one of the eight fundamental tenets of the ILO,[755] has been preserved by the ILO Convention No. 98.[756] Article 4 of this Convention provides that appropriate conditions shall be taken where necessary to encourage and promote full development and utilisation of machinery for voluntary negotiation between employer and employees with the view to regulation of terms and conditions of employment by means of collective bargaining. This is re-enforced and strengthened by article 6 of the ICESCR 1966 on the overall right to work which is the foundation on which the security of service employment is built. The United Nations Economic and Social Council General Comment 18[757] expressly recognizes the role trade unions play in the regulation of activities

---

751 Interview with Vewessee on the 30/1/2008. See also Letter from Vewessee to the Provincial Delegate of Labour and Social Insurance, Buea dated 13th May, 1992. See also Report of the Divisional Inspector of Labour, on Mass Meetings with the workers of the CDC Estates/Services in connection with the economic crisis, in file MESP/SWP/BU.134/Vol. IV, CDC General Correspondence in Konings, P. "Plantation labour and Economic Crisis in Cameroon," *op. cit.* at p.532.

752 See Letter from FAWU president to General Manager of CDC on Imminent privatisation of CDC, CCTU/FAWU/3/V.5/2366 of 9th March 2000, p. 2.

753 *Ibid dem* at p. 3.

754 *Ibid.*

755 http://www.workinfo.com/free/htm accessed on the 12th May 2011. The ILO recognises the right of human beings to work and freely associate. See also article 8(1)(b) of ICESCR 1966. The right to freely associate is also a core human rights enshrined in the International Covenant on Civil and Political Rights.

756 On the Right to Organise and Collective Bargaining 1949, was ratified by Cameroon in 1962.

757 The right to work adopted on 24/11/05 by the Committee on Economic, Social and Cultural Rights Herein referred to as Comment 18.

in an establishment. It observed that, "trade unions play a fundamental role in ensuring respect for the right to work at the local and national levels and in assisting state parties to comply with their obligations under article 6 ICESCR 1966. The role of trade unions is fundamental and will continue to be considered by the committee in its consideration of reports of state parties." Although this document is merely a comment with no strong legal binding force, it nevertheless is important in showing the link between trade unions.

The public administration function.[758] These last two functions require unions to engage with governments in order to secure legislation that will enable them perform their other functions. This requires unions to be involved in the development, implementation and delivery of government policy. The government function is important as the trade unionists rise through the ranks to the extent of assuming government functions.

8.2.1.iii Refusal to Register and Cancellation of Registration

The registrar may decline registration of an association with identical name to that already o the roll. If the application does not comply with the conditions for registration, the Registrar shall communicate his observation to the applicant together with a request to re-submit. Upon receipt of the re-submission, the Registrar may within thirty days either issue a certificate or refuse to register giving clearly the reasons for doing so.[759]

The Registrar has powers conferred to it by section 13 of the Labour Code 1992 to cancel the registration of the trade union even after it has been issued and after the service of a two months' notice clearly specifying the reason for such a cancellation[760] if it can be established that the certificate of registration was fraudulently obtained,[761] that the registered union has wilfully violated any provision of the Labour Code[762] or has carried out a non-statutory activity of the union or that the registered union has ceased to exist[763]. The Registrar must in this regard publicise the fact of cancellation.

Any member of such a union aggrieved by the decision to cancel the registration has a period of thirty days from the date of notification

---

758 *Ibid* at p. 5.

759 Section 12 Labour Code 1992.

760 Section 13 (2) Labour Code 1992.

761 Section 13 (1) (a) Labour Code 1992.

762 Section 13 (1) (b) Labour Code 1992.

763 Section 13 (1) (c) Labour Code 1992.

of cancellation to refer the matter to the competent court. In this case the competent administrative court without prejudice to any further appeal to the competent superior court.[764] This is because it is an action against an administrative act of an administrative officer - the Registrar.[765]

8.2.2 Staff Representatives Distinguished From Trade Unions

Staff representatives are workers of an establishment elected by their peers for a period of two years renewable to carry out the functions clearly spelled out in section 128 of the Labour Code.[766] They are by this provision expected to refer the collective demands of the workers relating to conditions of employment, workers' protection, application of collective agreements, classification of occupations and wage rates not acceded to by their employer.[767] They are further required to refer to the inspectorate of labour laws and regulations which is within their competence to enforce.[768] ii) to ensure that safety and hygiene rules of workers are enforced and that social insurance is observed, as well as make recommendation in this regard to the employer.[769] iii) to make useful suggestions to the employer for improving the output of the enterprise.[770] And iv) to submit grievances and suggestions of workers directly to the employer.[771]

The above functions of the staff representatives especially section 128(a) of the Labour Code which ensures the respect and protection of workers' conditions of employment are *prima facie* commendable. However, it is observed that the role of a staff representative is more like a conduit as section 128 requires the staff representatives to either refer or submit claims, complaints or grievances to the employer and does not involve any form of negotiation of better employment conditions *per se*. The staff representatives, like trade unions, are supposed to work with the employers to foster and protect the interest of the workers whom they represent. This, notwithstanding, it is apparent that it is not usually the case in practice. Viewed from this perspective, although the intention of the functions in sections 128 might have

---

764 Section 14 Labour Code 1992.

765 See section 3 and 14 of Law No. 2009/022 of 29th December 2006 to lay own the organization and functioning of the administrative courts.

766 The Labour Code has not given any definition of who staff representatives are.

767 Section 128 (a) Labour Code 1992.

768 Section 128 (b) Labour Code 1992.

769 Section 128 (c) Labour Code 1992.

770 Section 128 (d) Labour Code 1992.

771 Section 129 Labour Code 1992.

been for the ensurance of workers' security, it can be contended that because the staff representatives are bank rolled by the employer, their independence is jeopardised and for this reason, they tend to rather serve the interest of the employer rather than the workers whom they represent, thereby weakening the security of employment of the workers they are supposed to be protecting.

This is prevalent in establishments where trade unions do not exist, which could have ensured that their nominees[772] are elected as staff representatives, thereby fostering and enforcing the trade union's stands on not only collective bargaining but the protection of labour rights and by extension the security of employment.

Staff representatives as defined above are different from trade unions in the context of this thesis. The state had to create staff representatives in every establishment and push trade unions to divisions in order to create a void. This was a subtle way of co-opting the staff representatives into a 'hegemonic alliance'[773] which will pave the way for the state to maximise its efforts at capital accumulation and labour control. In other words, the state through the staff representatives would have gotten what the trade unions have persistently refused to give them. C.P.N Vewessee, President of Fako Agricultural Workers Union,[774] has observed that limiting trade unions to a

772 In an interview (Limbe 12th May, 2011) with Charles Mbide Kode, the legal adviser of FAWU, he explained that in establishments where trade unions exist, the trade unions nominate eligible workers who are also members of trade unions for election as staff representatives. Where these workers are elected, they become the eyes and ears of the trade unions in that establishment. The enhancement of labour rights and the security of employment is guaranteed in such establishments. It is only where trade unions do not exist that staff representatives are elected from outside the ranks of the trade unions. This views of the legal adviser FAWU was confirmed in an interview (Buea,13th May, 2011) with Tabe Raymond, labour inspector Delegation of Labour and Social Insurance, South West Region.

773 Konings, P., *Labour Resistance in Cameroon, op. cit.* at p. 155.

774 Interviewed by this researcher on the 30/01/2008, in Limbe South West Region, Cameroon. Vewessee has been a permanent official of CDC Workers' Union since 1973. He has taken several courses on labour relations and trade unionism in the Harvard University Business School amongst others. When the workers' (staff) representative replaced trade unions in 1967, after the harmonized Labour Code became law, the workers' representative had jurisdiction over workers in a given division. That is how the trade unions were divided into divisional unions. Founded in 1972, Fako Agricultural Workers' Union headed by Vewessee since 1974 is a product of this Law (the issues of staff representatives was also taken up in Order no. 10/MTPS of 17 June 1968, articles 131-137 of the 1974 Labour Code, Order no 21/MTPS of 28 October 1981 and Order no. 24/MTPS of July 27 1987. The difference between the staff representatives and the trade unions is that all important decisions are now taken at the national level. These divisional unions are no longer concerned with collective bargained and collective agreements. They are concerned with the implementation of decisions taken by the National Union of Cameroon Workers in collaboration with the National Labour Council and the National Joint Bargaining Board for Collective Agreements and Wages.

division[775] is a divide and rule tactic on the part of the government to limit the strength of an already disorganised labour association.

This assertion is buttressed by the provisions of section 6(2) of the Labour Code which requires prior authorisation for trade unions to function in spite of the country's international obligations under the ILO Convention No. 87. This fragmentation is a heavy blow for unionists who cannot now harness the synergies of concerted effort from a wider pull larger than that of a division to protect the security of employments.[776]

Article 2 of ILO Convention No. 87, 1948[777] require trade unions to be created without prior authorisation in tandem with sections 3 and 11(b)[778] of the Labour Code 1992. These lend credence to the fact that no prior authorisation is required in Cameroon for the creation of trade unions. However, the decision of the Court of Appeal South West case in *National Union of Teachers of Higher Education (SYNES) v. Dr. Dorothy Njeuma*[779] and the provisions of section 6(2) of the Labour Code 1992 which criminalises the operation of trade unions without prior registration points to the contrary[780]. Here, the applicant's case was dismissed for lack of competence due to no registration.[781] The courts arrived at this decision even though SYNES had complied with the requirement of especially section 11(1) (b) of the Labour Code 1992 that a trade union comes into formal existence after a period of one month after formal application has been sent to the registrar of trade unions. This is a strong indication that the law in Cameroon requires prior authorisation for a trade union to be formally in existence. This is so despite the fact that the Administrative Tribunal of the ILO in *SYNES v. The*

---

775 Section 125 of the Labour Code.

776 It is clear that the only connection between staff representatives and trade unions is only as they relate to the insurance of the protection of conditions of employment and therefore security of employment.

777 Ratified by Cameroon in 1960. Art 45 of the Constitution of 1996, places this treaty in a higher position than the Labour Code and any other local legislation.

778 Yanou, explained that a simple interpretation of section 11 of the Labour Code require that thirty days after acknowledgment of receipt of application of registration of trade unions, that trade union shall be considered as registered. In order words, the trade union is considered as being in existence after lapse of 30 days. See Yanou, M.A., "Rules for the Registration of Trade Unions in Cameroon," *International Journal of Comparative Law*, Vol. 25, Issue 4, December 2009, p. 350.

779 Suit No. CASWP/13/2006 (unreported).

780 There seem to be a confusion between creation caught by section 3 and legal existence of trade unions in Cameroon as captured by section 6, which is a *sine qua non* condition for the trade unions to have legal personality.

781 See generally Yanou, M. A., "Rules for the registration of Trade Unions in Cameroon," *op. cit.* at p. 351-352.

Government of Cameroon[782] held that the trade unions had legal existence since they had applied for registration and the thirty days requirement had lapsed.[783]

Furthermore, such insistence gives government an upper hand as to which trade unions should be formally recognised. In this candidate's view, it is another way of killing trade union freedom and autonomy and a direct intention of subjugating trade unions to state control. The fact that section 5(4) of the Law on Freedom of Association[784] provides that trade unions and political parties shall be regulated by a different law shows the government's intentions to bring trade unions under tight control. In so doing, only 'sweet heart' unions which are stooges of the government will be created. The third sector of the society and collective bargaining which the ILO insists on will not be effective.

The days when workers' trade unions were regarded as vanguard of factory gates are long gone. In legal and social dynamics of development, trade unions are active players, which must not be ignored if the society wants to grow. It is the fact that individuals, enterprises and governments ignore the unions that drive them to radicalism, anarchy and political activism,[785] a far cry from the original intentions of the unions. It is only a dictatorial regime that wants to breed anarchy that will refuse to collaborate with trade unions for the development of the workers and the security of their tenure. In the view of the ILO, the main route out of poverty is work. He, who talks work, must talk collective bargaining through unionism and not staff representatives who cannot fit into the model of trade unions as conceptualised above to fight for workers' rights and job security.

8.3 Collective Bargaining Agreements

This section explains how worker's union bargain for better working conditions from a legal perspective.

---

[782] Case 1699 ILO Administrative Tribunal.

[783] Yanou, M. A., "Rules for the registration of Trade Unions in Cameroon," *op. cit.* at p. 354

[784] Law No. 90/053 of December 19th 1990.

[785] Lenin and the Bolsheviks based their strategy on the teachings of Max and Engel so that each time there was a strike by workers, the Bolsheviks established contacts with the strikers and helped them to win partial demands. With time, such economic struggles turned into political struggles which culminated in the 1917 Bolshevik Revolution.

8.3.1 Introduction: Negotiation of Contracts of Employment

Section 23 (2) of the Code provides that contracts of employments are a product of free negotiations between the parties with the parties in *consensus ad idem*.[786] This concept[787], which was profoundly influenced by the economic philosophy of laissez faire, is premised on the idea that the freedom to negotiate employment promotes economic self-interest, as the parties would bargain to obtain the maximum social wealth of the society. The doctrine of freedom and sanctity of contracts of employments were no longer based on religion and social status of the worker but on decisions of two free and voluntarily consenting minds. To this extent, once the employer and employee have entered into such employment contracts, each must abide by it unless relieved by the other. However, with the changing times, the sanctity of the individualist theory could no longer hold in the face of changing social, political or economic circumstances. The laissez-faire idealism was supplanted by social security, which suggests status rather than the contracts so that there is a compulsion to protect the contractual parties against economic and social exploitation in the guise of liberty to contract.[788]

8.3.2 Collective Bargaining: Legal Position

Collective bargaining[789] is a process, a mechanism for negotiation between one or more trade unions and employer or employers' association regarding conditions of employment and wages (family benefits, training,

---

786 According to Napier, this liberal approach to employment contracts may produce an illusion of equality between employer and employee. Although equal rights on paper may comfort the employee, one can correctly question the textbook assertion that employer and the employee have the same rights. See generally on this Napier, R.W., in Voize-Valayre, "The French Law of Dismissals," *23 New York University Journal of International Law and Politics*, 1991, p. 520.

787 According to Atiyah, judges of the 18th century believed that classical contracts take root from theories of natural law which provide that man have inalienable rights to own property (in this case his labour) and so has authority to make his own arrangements to sell his labour through proper employment contracts with no interference from government. This in a bid to enable contracting parties realize their wills irrespective of the justice or fairness these ideals of laissez-faire will mean to an imprudent and weaker employee. See generally Atiyah, P.S., *Introduction to the Law of Contract*, Clarendon Law Series, 5th edition, p. 8. Also as per Lord Cairns in *Cundy v. Lindsay* (1878) 3Cas 459 at p. 459, for there to be a valid contract there must be consensus of mind.

788 See generally chapter two for detailed analysis.

789 Art 2 of Collective Bargaining Convention No. 154, 1981 defines collective bargaining as " all negotiation which takes place between an employer and a group of employers or one or more employer's organisations, on the one hand and one or more worker's organization on the other

working hours, health, retirement, time-off, insurance, work environment and equipment, pay, leave). It could be seen as the right of workers to meet, harmonise and uniformly negotiate their basic rights and interest with their employer. As a form of industrial democracy, the main objective here is to settle terms and conditions of employment. The right to collectively bargain is rooted in the ILO Constitution 1919 as a core right. Art 23 of the Universal Declaration of Human Rights 1948 (that is given impetus by art 65 of the 1996 Constitution of Cameroon as revised), ILO Convention No 98 on the Right to Organise and Collective Bargaining, 1949. This Convention Provides that appropriate measures be taken nationally where necessary to encourage and promote the full development and utilisation of machinery for voluntary negotiation between workers and employers. Indeed the ILO's Declaration on Fundamental Principles and Rights at Work and its follow-up of 18th June 1998, reaffirmed collective bargaining as one of the four universal rights of a worker.

When combined with a strong freedom of association, sound collective bargaining practices ensures that employers and workers have equal voice in negotiations and that the outcome of such negotiations will be fair and equitable. It therefore negotiates a fair employment relationship and prevents costly labour disputes.

Even though collective bargaining is a by-product of laissez faire, it cannot accomplish by contract, what the law prohibits. For example, collective bargaining agreements cannot deprive workers of benefits they would otherwise have enjoyed under the law or waive obligations imposed by law. E.g, employers cannot use collective bargaining to reduce the safety standards at work.

Collective bargaining is a group action, it is therefore bipartite, a continuous process that does not end with one agreement and it is a process which means it involves a number of phases/steps and the end product of collective bargaining is collective agreement. It starts off with the preparation stage through the discussion, proposal phase, bargaining phase to the settlement phase when the contract is concluded. The workers are often represented in this bargaining process by trade union and involves their negotiating with management of the employer company. Such may be

relations between employers and workers and or regulating relations between employers and their organisations and worker's organization. Collective bargaining also includes negotiations with the worker's representatives.

between a single employer and a single trade union - single plant bargaining. Or between a single firm with different branches where workers are employed. Here the representatives of the workers in these different branches bargain with the common employer - multiple plant bargaining, where unions of same industry bargain through their federation with employer's federation of that industry - multiple employer bargaining. It is dynamic and complementary since one party needs something that the other party already has and it is industrial democracy at work, where workers' union represent the workers in negotiations with the employers.

For there to be effective bargaining, there must be

- A strong trade union or workers' representative that believes in the settlement of grievances through negotiations. Ewing notes that trade unions have five functions; which are the service function, representative function, regulatory function which extends to partmership and government function.
- The existence of fact finding approach and willingness to use new tools and methods to solve industrial unrest.
- Avoidance of unfair labour practices and bad faith in the negotiation

This supposes that there must be recognition of the negotiating parties to the extent that if one is not recognised, they will not have *locus standi*. The negotiations are therefore bilateral agreements rather than unilateral decision making by the employer. An employer cannot incorporate such agreements negotiated by the association into his employee's contracts. Difficulties arise as to how to decide which terms are incorporated.

Collectively bargained agreements are not enforceable except it is expressly incorporated into contracts of employment of an employee so that it becomes terms in his contract enforceable against and by the employer individually - *N.C.B v. Galley*[790] (employee) bound by national agreement requiring overtime work. An employee whose contract does not bear expressly inclusive terms of collectively bargained agreements may not be bound by the collective agreement. By just simply implying these terms into the contract without more may lead to the employee rejecting that he had ever accepted to be bound by the terms. Once incorporated to the contract, it shall maintain its position as a clause in the contract until properly amended or removed. What happens to the collective agreement that ceases to be relevant? can

---

790 [1957] EWCA CIV Jii27-1.

amendments of the collective agreements amend the individual contracts it hitherto applied to unilateral amendments by either party cannot affect the contract.

Secondly, the agreement or term could be binding out of mutual acceptance by both parties. It is likely that aspects of an agreement burdensome to him (employer) will necessitate some relatively immediate and directly related action on his part. Acceptance by the employee cannot be so convincingly demonstrated because it must often be implied from indirectly related conduct, mindful of fact that the employee may have only constructive notice of these collectively bargained term in other words, an employee may not necessarily be bound by a term that he has no knowledge of simply because he had accepted the job except there is an established custom and practice of widespread acceptance by an individual. silence cannot be deemed to be consent and it will be too facile an assumption that a worker who continues to work without protesting despite the fact that he is aware of the new agreements will be deemed to have accepted. - *Duke v. Reliance Systems ltd*[791] Browne-Wilkinson J insists on knowledge as a prerequisite of consent and that custom and practice cannot be a reason for unilateral implication unless it can be shown that the practice is drawn to the attention of the employee or has been followed without exception for a considerable period.

Thirdly agreement could also be incorporated by long standing observance of the collective agreement by both sides

Forth, where it is negotiated by the union as agent for its members, the member can then enforce it as a principal. There is an assumption that trade unions are agents for whom it bargains. Does it mean that in industrial relations, the courts may be free to invoke agency for all employees? The significance of this question lies in the appreciation of whether the trade unions can be said to be agent for non-union members? Are such members bound by the collectively bargained agreements as if they were members of trade unions? If they are not, a potentially chaotic contractual differentiation will arise. Put it another way, can an agency arise without the agreement of the principal (employee)? Can such an agency hold good in the face of express rejection by the principal. There could be a presumption of agency with opting out options for non-consenting members - *Singh v. British Steel*;.[792] Agency principle grew out of specific issues that the trade unions had to negotiate for small group

---

791 [1988] 1 All ER 626.

792 [1974] 1RLR 131 See also *Edwards v. Skyways Ltd [1964]* 1 WLR 349.

of employees. This principle has been dismissed in *Holland v. London Society of Compositors*[793]. In this case, a member of a provincial trade union brought an action to enforce an agreement between his union and its London based counterpart that he would be received into membership by the latter when he moved to London. The agreement was designed to benefit individuals but the learned judge held that the unions must nevertheless be regarded as acting for their own interests and not those of individual members meaning therefor that the unions intended an agreement between themselves alone. In *Burton Group Ltd v. Smith*[794], Arnold J. averred that there is no reason why an agency cannot be created between trade unions and its members although such an agency would not be implied simply from the fact of membership in a trade union. Not withstanding, agency will be assumed where there is a specific agency.

Although in some Common Law jurisdictions like Britain collective agreements prima facie do not have contractual force, section 18 (1) (e) of the Labour Code 1992 makes collectively bargained agreements part and parcel of the terms of the employment of a worker in Cameroon. This provision gives statutory recognition to a trade union's capacity to enter into collective agreements with the employer on the workers' behalf. This, notwithstanding, trade unions in practice are rarely involved in the collective bargaining process in companies or enterprises. Indeed, in Cameroon, until early 2010 when the Minister of Labour and Social Security signed two collective agreements for the private sector banking and hydrocarbons corporations, there were virtually no such agreements in the country. Even these agreements are objectionable because the minister should not be involved with them. Government participation definitely brings pressure on the trade unions as well as gives the collective bargaining process a tripartite quality, distorting its original bilateral character (trade unions and employers). It clearly turns the collective bargaining process into a regulatory transaction on the obvious basis that the negotiations may not be free in the circumstances of government interference.

In addition, although it is correct to assume as Atiyah rightly points out that employment contracts are relational and for this reason different from simple classical contracts, this does not however mean that everything about them has to be negotiated and agreed upon. Since the employer may amend some aspects of the employee's obligations without his/her agreement, this gives an upper

---

793 [1924] 40 TLR 440.

794 [1977] 1RLR 351.

hand to the employer who may jump at the opportunity to negatively amend the contract against the interest of the employee. A combination of this common law position and section 42 (2) of the Labour Code 1992 weakens employment by giving the employer the discretion to sack a worker under the pretext of 'economic reason' should the worker reject changes made by the employer.

This feature of Cameroon's labour law shows that it evolved out of a capitalist system that accommodates the interest of those who hold power in the country. This philosophy insists on allowing employer/entrepreneur the liberty to manage the enterprise to maximise profit. This philosophical foundation makes the employer/entrepreneur to develop monopolistic and clientelist tendencies creating a situation of 'take it or leave it' contracts of service. It is opined that, the freedom to negotiate under section 23 (2) of the Labour Code 1992 is a mirage with grave consequences on the security of employment in the country. Statutes have always regulated the relationship by establishing minimum terms and conditions of employment.

8.3.3 Benefits of Collective Bargaining

Where collective bargaining is practiced and highly co-ordinated, the workers will less likely have inequality in wages, lower and less persistent unemployment and fewer and shorter strikes than countries where collective bargaining is less established. In *Facilities Subsector Bargaining Association v. British Columbia,*[795] it was observed that "the right to bargain collectively with an employer enhances the human dignity, liberty and autonomy of the workers by giving them the opportunity to influence the establishment of work place rules and thereby gain some control over a major aspect of their lives, namely their work. Collective bargaining is not simply an instrument for pursuing external ends.... Rather it is intrinsically valuable as an experience in self-government with a view to the regulation of terms and conditions of employment by means of collective agreement.

Collective bargaining improves on the quality of the life of the worker by increasing their pay. It improves on the cost of worker benefits as will be shown in the output of the work, consistency with productivity and set of standards which every worker can be held to while in the work place. Employees who collectively bargain have better working conditions, higher wages and better benefit packages than employees who don't.

---

795 [2007] 2. S.S.R. 391.

Collective bargaining gives a larger voice to the worker than when workers act as individuals. In such dispensations it becomes difficult to negotiate with an employer. Many non-union workers are faced with take it or leave it contracts (quaere what about flexicurity?) when workers band together into larger groups, they create a louder voice that can help provide one another with a mutually beneficial outcome. It gives a platform for worker's grievances to be heard and acknowledged.

Collective bargaining improves on the worker's life and also worker's safety and working conditions. This adds up to overall quality of life for the workers. This improves on the dignity of the worker and promotes mutual respect in the workplace. It can help in the avoidance of industrial actions by workers due to a breakdown of negotiation

It creates employment consistency as all workers are placed at same level according to experience, qualification, longevity, etc.

Collective bargaining are done in good faith with the belief that the parties will honour them. They also open up proper communication channels in the employment leading to stability and industrial peace.

The down side of collective bargaining is that it reduces individuality and it can be costly to both parties.

It may require non-members to be bound by the agreement

It is not always a process of fair representation

It creates significant potential for polarisation between employer and employee. It can change the work environment and turn it into a politically charged one.

It restraints management ability to deal effectively with troubled employee individually.

It may not necessarily guarantee a good deal for either party. Without a good negotiator, it becomes possible for one group to create one sided agreement.

CHAPTER 9

MIGRANT WORKERS & EMPLOYMENT RELATIONS

In the past and at present, the world is witnessing an increase in migration and displacement of people owing to conflicts and human rights violations,[796] poverty as a result of unemployment or underemployment, the economic and social gaps between industrialised and developing countries, amongst others. In 2015 for instance, more than 90% of migrants worldwide constituted migrant workers,[797] and it is estimated that the number will go up to 405 million international migrants globally by 2050.[798] The ILO estimated

---

[796] Like the present socio-political crisis in Cameroon that has led to the movement of many Cameroonian to other states such as Nigeria, Ghana, USA, Belgium among others. See generally V. Chetail., *Code of International Migration Law*, Brussels, Bruylant, 2008, in C. Papinot., 'International protection of migrant workers' PhD thesis, Paris West University Nanterre, 2014, P14.

[797] See ILO., *International Labour Migration and Development: The ILO Perspective*, Geneva, International Labour Office, 2007, P.1, See also International Organisation for Migration (IOM) 'World Migration Report', 2018, P. 3.

[798] The main statistics of international migration are offered by the United Nations, Department of Economic and Social Affairs (UN DESA), the United Nations High Commissioner for Refugees - The UN Refugee Agency (UNCHR), the Organization for Economic Cooperation and Development (OECD), and the International Organization for Migration (IOM),. Based on these migration databases, statistics show that, globally, the total number of migrants has increased from 94 million in 1970, to 153 million in 1990, reaching around 244 million in 2015 as seen above, from the total world population of about 7.3 billion people (meaning 1 person in every 30 people). Still, as a share of the world's population, the migration flow is relatively steady, representing 2.3% in 1970, and 3.3 in 2015. Around 75% of international migrants in 2015 (almost 157 million) targeted the "high-income economies . . . compared with 77 million foreign-born who resided in middle-income countries (about one-third of the total migrant stock) and almost 9 million in low-income countries in the same year." Out of 244 million migrants in 2015, the largest share was for Europe (over 31%), Asia (almost 31%), and North America (over 22%). In Europe, the highest migrants' allocation was for Western Europe (36%) and Eastern Europe (26%) with a total of 76 million migrants in 2015. The most preferred European countries by migrants in 2015 were: Germany (12 million migrants), the United Kingdom (8.5 million), France (7.8 million), Spain (5.9 million), Italy (5.8 million), Sweden (1.6 million), Austria (1.5 million), Belgium (1.4 million), Denmark (572 thousand), and Finland (315 thousand). The main origin countries of migrants into European regions were the Russian Federation (over 6 million), Poland (3.6 million), Romania (almost 3 million), and Morocco (2.5 million). For 2016 compared to 2015, the migration flows increased by 30% in Germany, 4% in France, 7% in Belgium, 18% in Spain,

that in 2010 migrants represented 214 million people or 3% of the world's population.[799]

The popular destinations for these migrants, especially the migrant workers are the USA and Europe. In Recent times, because of the availability and the sustainability of jobs in some Southeast Asian countries such as Malaysia, Singapore and Thailand,[800] and some Arabic Gulf countries for instance Saudi Arabia, Qatar, Bahrain, United Arab Emirates[801] amongst others, most unemployed, especially the youths from mostly the African and Asian countries, are now attracted to these economically stable countries.[802]

In accordance with the understanding that migration for work in itself is not a bad practice as it is associated with consequential benefits to both the country of origin and the host country on the one hand, and the migrants themselves,[803] and amidst the Spread of xenophobic and racist movements

---

26% in Sweden, and decreased by 6% in the UK (mainly due to the BREXIT vote in June 2016), and by 5% in Denmark. See generally G. Noja *et al.*, 'Migrants' Role in Enhancing the Economic Development of Host Countries: Empirical Evidence from Europe', *Journal of environmental, cultural, economic, and social sustainability of human beings (Sustainability)*, 2018, P. 2, PP.2-20.

799 ILO, "ILO Study on International Labor Migration", Geneva, 2010, P. 201.

800 According to Mauro and others, Malaysia, Singapore, and Thailand constitute immigration hubs in the South East Asia with most migrants coming from Cambodia, Myanmar, Indonesia, The Philippines and Vietnam. See generally T. Mauro *et al.*, *Migrating to Opportunity: Overcoming Barriers to Labor Mobility in Southeast Asia*, 2017. Available at https://doi.org/10.1596/978-1-4648-1106-7-ch1. Accessed on 15-9-2021.

801 These workers travel mainly to the countries of the Arabian Gulf and also to Jordan and Lebanon. The six states of the Gulf Cooperation Council (GCC), Bahrain, Kuwait, Qatar, Oman, Saudi Arabia, and the United Arab Emirates (UAE), host approximately 10 million foreign workers, with the largest number (8.8 million) in Saudi Arabia. In several cases, the number of foreign workers in the country exceeds the native population substantially. See generally G. S. Manseau 'Contractual Solutions for Migrant Labourers: The Case of Domestic Workers in the Middle East', 2006, P.26. Available at http:// beta. nottingham. ac.uk/ hrlc/ documents/ publications/ hrl commentary 2006 /migrantlabourers.pdf. Accessed on 15-9-2021.

802 Since the 1970s, migrant labourers, especially those who perform domestic work, have been in high demand in the Middle East. Currently, approximately 10 million migrant workers, primarily from Southeast Asia, South Asia or Africa, live and work in these countries. Their native countries benefit greatly from these workers' remittances and encourage migration; the host countries also benefit from cheap labour but provide almost no protection against abuse of workers by the private sector that hires them. The workers themselves flock to the region for the promise of high salaries, but as temporary workers tied to their employers, they are frequently placed in positions of extreme vulnerability with little recourse to justice. It is contended in this study that one solution to the problem of abuse of migrant workers generally and domestic workers, particularly in most of these Middle East countries, is to establish and enforce a standard working contract for all migrant workers in various domains. See generally Manseau *ibid* at P. 27.

803 Temporary work overseas may be very beneficial to workers since jobs in the Middle East offer wages that eclipse those available in sending countries, and /or provide employment opportunities which may not exist at home. Increased financial stability available to workers after working for several years in the Middle East may enhance a worker's social status at home and provide a

against foreigners, and the persistence forced labour perpetrated especially on foreign domestic workers; this chapter seeks to critically examine the extent to which migrant workers are protected in Cameroon. In doing so, we have conceptualised migration for work, critically assessed the protection of migrant workers under the Cameroonian legal framework (which comprises a blend of both national and ratified international instruments), as well as Inter-governmental and bilateral agreements touching on migrant workers, and concluded by discussing the principle of States sovereignty and the enforcement of migrant workers' rights in Cameroon.

9.1 The Conceptualisation of a Migrant Worker

Migration is a term that covers a wide variety of movements and situations involving people of all walks of life and backgrounds including workers. More than ever before, migration touches all States and people in an era where the world is almost becoming a global village. Migration has helped improve people's lives in both origin and destination countries and has offered opportunities for millions of people worldwide to forge safe and meaningful lives abroad.[804]

Though there are several[805] definitions of the term 'Migrant worker,' unfortunately there is no universally acceptable definition of this term. It is impossible to draw a sharp line between 'migration for work' and 'migration.' In this light, Chetail argues that 'migration,' all types of migrations combined, is commonly perceived as 'a movement of people leaving or

means of support for children, education and investment that would be inaccessible otherwise. See generally Eelens, Schampers and Speckmann., *Labour Migration to the Middle East: From Sri Lanka to the Gulf*, London, Routledge, 1992, P. 1.

804 See G. D. Lieto., 'International Legal Realities of Migrant Labour Rights,' *Journal of Identity and Migration Studies*, Vol. 9, No. 2, 2015, PP. 86-109, in Akamin P., 'The Protection of the Core Rights of a Worker in International Law: An Assessment of the Cameroonian Situation' PhD Thesis, Department of English Law, University of Buea, 2020, P.245

805 Article 2 (1) of the UN Convention on the Protection of the Rights of All Migrant Workers and Members of Their Families 1990, defines "migrant worker" in general terms. The definition includes any person who is to be engaged, is engaged or has already been engaged in a remunerated activity in a State of which he or she is not a national. Excluded from the above definition are personnel of international organizations, persons who are employed by a State outside its territory, investors, refugees and stateless persons, students, trainees, seafarers and workers on an offshore installation provided that they have not been admitted to take up residence and engage in a remunerated activity in the State of employment. On its part article 11 (1) of the ILO Convention No. 97 on Migration for Employment (revised), 1949 defines a migrant worker as a person who migrates from one country to another for the purpose of employment. This definition includes any person who is regularly admitted as a migrant for employment.

leaving a State, to enter another State in order to reside on a permanent or temporary basis.'[806] This definition, therefore, covers emigration (departure or travel), immigration (arrival in the host country), and residence and possibly return. In a more general terms, a migrant worker can be defined as 'a natural person who leaves or who has left the country in which he/she is resident with the intention of moving to another country, of which he/she does not have nationality for the purposes of employment.'[807] As such it is not required that the 'work' or the 'employment' be the principal aim for migration for a person to qualify as a migrant worker. Thus, many migrants, in a very broad range of situations, qualify as migrant workers. Migrants and migrant workers can be placed in numerous, and often multiple, categories, as being in a regular or irregular situation, having migrated temporarily or permanently, as being low skilled or high skilled, or as being students, recruited workers, accompanying family, refugees or asylum seekers.[808]

It follows from this definition that in defining the term 'migrant worker' one has to take into consideration all the category of migrant workers be it those under regular and irregular migrations,[809] refugees working in the host countries, migrant students working in the host countries, asylum seekers working in the host country, among others. The choice of these categories of migrants is justified by the fact that the objective of finding a job and better living conditions is one of the main motivations for migration.

The ILO in its Convention 97 defines a 'migrant workers' as 'a person who migrates from one country to another with a view to being employed otherwise than on his own account and includes any person regularly admitted as a migrant worker.'[810] Some specific groups of workers, such as frontier workers, members of liberal professions and artisans who enter on a

---

806 See V. Chetail., *Code of International Migration Law*, Brussels, Bruylant, 2008, in C. Papinot., 'International protection of migrant workers,' PhD thesis *Paris West University* Nanterre, 2014, P. 19.

807 At this instance, the said migrant is considered as an alien until he/she acquired the nationality of the said country.

808 Global Commission on International Migration (GCIM). Report of the GCIM,' Migration in an Interconnected World: New Directions for Action', GCIM, Switzerland, 2005, P. 6. Among the many and complex reasons for such migration are the following: the conflicts and human rights violation, unemployment and/or lack of career opportunities in the country of origin, need for flexible labour force and/or low birth rates in the country of destination, as well as curiosity and entrepreneurship.

809 That is those who have a valid work contract in the said country as well as those who clandestinely entered the said country for employment.

810 See Article 11(1).

short-term basis, and seamen, are excluded from this definition, thus making it narrow and exclusive.

The ICPRMWMF offers us a more comprehensive definition, thus further developing this area. According to this convention, a 'migrant worker' is 'a person who is to be engaged, is engaged, or has been engaged in a remunerated activity in a State of which he or she is not a national.'[811] Commenting on this definition, Akamin[812] argues that it first limb (a person who is to be engaged) does not reflect who a migrant worker truly is. This to him is because for a person to be term a worker be it nationally or internationally, he/she must, first of all, attain the status of a worker. This reasoning is premised on the fact that a person who is 'to be engaged' is not yet a worker since as his/her engagement is still in due course, until when he /she must have concluded the employment contract (attaining the status of a worker), can we termed him/her a worker. This reasoning remains sound in labour relations in that a 'worker' truly as he/she is, is someone who has attained 'the status of a worker' (having a valid subsisting employment contract and working for a name employer).

Nonetheless, persons employed by international organizations, government employees sent to perform official functions in the host State, persons employed by a State or on its behalf outside the territory to participate in development projects, investors, refugees, stateless persons, students and trainees, seafarers and offshore workers are, for various reasons, excluded from coverage.[813] Whether or not the exclusion is justified, it has slightly limited the application of the Convention.

The need for international attention to migrants and migrant workers specifically is based on the presumption that they, as a category, share a common vulnerability, due to their migrant/migrant worker status. This vulnerability derives from two main factors: that of being a foreigner, with its consequences of cultural differences, language problems, legal gaps for border crossing, and that of being a worker, often employed in the most uncontrolled sectors.[814] For instance, migrant workers are often faced with exploitative

---

811 Article 2 (1) of the ICPRMWMF, 1990.

812 See Akamin *op. cit.* at P. 248

813 See article 3 of the ICPRMWMF. The reasons for exclusion and their impact on each specific category of workers have been discussed extensively by Cholewinski. See R. Cholewinski., *Migrant Workers in International Human Rights Law: Their Protection in Countries of Employment*, Oxford, Oxford University Press, 1997,P. 152, PP. 153-154.

814 P. Guchteniere and A. Pécoud., 'Introduction: The UN Convention on Migrant Workers' Rights', in P. de Guchteniere, A. Pécoud and R. Cholewinski., *Migration and Human Rights, The United Nations Convention on Migrant Workers' Rights*, Cambridge: Cambridge University Press, 2009, PP. 2-3.

working conditions, as forced labour, low wages, low levels of occupational safety, lack of social protection, denial of the freedom of association, discrimination, xenophobia[815] and social exclusion.[816] In this connection, Bustamante describes the vulnerability of migrants as the 'social condition of powerlessness ascribed to individuals with certain characteristics that are perceived to deviate from those ascribed to the prevailing definitions of a national,' being caused by discriminatory premises in national law and practice rendering social effects of human rights violations followed by impunity.[817]

9.2 The Protection of Migrant Workers in Cameroon

States primarily owes only their citizens an obligation to safeguards their rights and dignity. However, when States choose to ratify international instruments that mandate them to uphold the rights and dignity of aliens within their territories, it becomes incumbent on them to apply these instruments in law and practice. It is against this backdrop that we seek to examine the extent to which migrant workers are protected in Cameroon.

9.2.1 The Protection of Migrant Workers Under the 1996 Constitution of Cameroon

The Preamble to the Cameroon Constitution provides that 'Human person, without distinction... possesses inalienable and sacred rights, affirms the State's attachment to the fundamental freedoms enshrined in the UDHR, the ACHPR and all duly ratified international conventions relating thereto...'[818] The term 'human person, without distinction' according to this researcher, demonstrates the State's willingness to protect the human rights (labour rights inclusive) of both national and migrant workers.

---

815 Such as the one which occurred in South African commercial capital, Johannesburg in early September 2019 leading to the death of many Nigerians and nationals from other African countries. The main cause of xenophobia in South Africa as its supporters, claim is centered on the fact that most of the South African jobs have been taken by foreigners, while most nationals remain unemployed. See generally https://www.bbc.com/news/world africa-47800718, accessed on 15/9/2021.

816 See International Labour Conference, Report VI, 'Towards a fair deal for Migrant Workers in the Global Economy', 2004, P. 41.

817 J. Bustamante., 'Immigrants' Vulnerability as Subjects of Human Rights', *International Migration Review*, Vol. 36, 2002, P. 340, PP. 333-354.

818 See paragraph 4 of the preamble to the 1996 Constitution of Cameroon.

Paragraph five of the Preamble to the Cameroon Constitution states that 'all persons shall have equal rights and obligations'. A plain interpretation of the term 'all persons' in this preambular provision, seemingly suggests both nationals and migrants alike.[819] To conclude in the context of labour rights, that both national and migrant workers share similar rights and obligations may be a hasty decision as employment rules are *lex specialia* and so maybe interpreted differently[820]. Although it is incumbent on the State to safeguard the rights of migrant workers as demanded by the country's constitution, such migrants must satisfy entry, stay and exit conditions of Cameroon.

This legislative effort on the part of the State of Cameroon in curbing employment and occupational discrimination shows the country's commitment to its international obligation to protect the rights of those residing in its territory be they nationals or migrants.. In addition, In this light, this researcher commends this effort and generally argues that it can go a long way to safeguards the security of service for both nationals and migrant workers.

9.2.2 The Protection of Migrant Workers Under the Cameroonian Labour Code, 1992

Migrant workers' have several rights safeguarded in the Cameroon Labour Code. Prominent amongst these rights, is their right to Freedom of Association.

Their right to freedom of association together with its corollaries[821] is essential for sound industrial relations, and it is only through its protection that this category of workers can attain their security of tenure. The Right to Freedom of Association is a core Labour right. As Akamin[822] rightly put it, it is only through the protection of workers' right to Freedom of Association that their other ancillary rights can be attained. This analytical view is seconded

[819] By virtue of article 65 of the Cameroon Constitution of 1996 as amended in 2008, the preamble remains part and parcel of the constitution.

[820] For example see sections 10(2), 25(2) and 27(2) just to name a few.

[821] The rights to collective bargaining and strike constitute an intrinsic corollary of the right to freedom of association. Workers usually constitute themselves into trade unions to be able to better protect their economic and social interests through collective bargaining. The failure of workers to attain their interests through collective bargaining, will lead to an industrial action (strike).

[822] See Akamin *Op. Cit.* at P. 256.

by this scholar in that migrant workers' who are already in a vulnerable position[823] need trade unions that will better protect their rights as aliens in their host countries.

In upholding Migrant Workers' Right to Freedom of Association, and in conformity with Article 2 of ILO Convention 87,[824] Section 3 of the Cameroon Labour Code, 1992 provides that 'the law recognizes the right of workers... without distinction whatsoever, to set up freely and without prior authorization (trade unions)... for the protection of their interests, particularly those of an economic, industrial, commercial or agricultural nature, and for the social, economic, cultural and moral advancement of their members.' The term 'workers without distinction whatsoever' as captioned in this legislation is our point of focus here. A literal interpretation of this provision leads us to a logical conclusion that workers, be they migrants or nationals, have a right to form and join trade unions of their choosing without the necessity to seek and obtained any prior authorization in the country. This reasoning is informed by the fact that the term 'without distinction whatsoever' is taken to mean a total prohibition of discrimination on the enjoyment of workers' right to freedom of association, be it on grounds of nationality or any other.

However like the situation in other States,[825] the enjoyment of migrant workers' trade union rights is subjected to the fulfillment of certain conditions; the trade union must be registered like in the case of

---

823 Jorge Bustamante describes the vulnerability of migrants workers a 'social condition of powerlessness ascribed to individuals with certain characteristics that are perceived to deviate from those ascribed to prevailing definition of a national.' See generally J. Bustamante., 'Immigrants Vulnerability as subjects of human rights', *International Migration Review*, Vol. 36, P. 340

824 This Article provides that 'Workers.., without distinction whatsoever, shall have the right to establish and, subject only to the rules of the organization concerned, to join organizations of their own choosing without previous authorization.' The phrase 'workers...without distinction whatsoever' lends credence to the above position in that it does not differentiate between national and migrant workers. It follows from this view that both national and migrant workers have the right to freedom of association in Cameroon. This convention is relevant in the context of the Cameroonian legal framework in that it was ratified in 1960 by the State of Cameroon amongst other fundamental legislations on the protection of the rights of migrant workers, and by virtue of article 45 of the Cameroon Constitution, all ratified international instruments are domesticated in the country.

825 See for instance in the UAE, the 2007 Labour Law does not provide for freedom of association and collective bargaining. Also in Qatar article 116 of Law No. 14 as seen above, denies migrant workers the right to freedom of association, collective bargaining and strike. In Spain, the Spanish law of 2000 on the Rights and Freedoms of Foreigners accords trade union rights only to regularized migrants. See generally Keane and Mc Geehan *op. cit.* at P.144. The situation is not different in Malaysia. In Case No 2637, the Committee on Freedom of Association (CFA) examined a complaint against Malaysia with regard to the legal and practical barriers to migrant workers' right to freedom of association. This case was filed in 2009, alleging that the government

trade unions of national workers as per section 10(2) of the Cameroon Labour Code 1992, and the migrant workers seeking for the registration of their trade unions must have resided in the country for not less than five years. Though, in violation of article 2 of ILO Convention 87, the former requirement is same requirement to be fulfilled by national workers seeking to form trade unions for the protection of their interests, whereas the latter requirement is a unique requirement specifically adopted for migrant workers seeking to form trade unions in the country. The question that pre-occupies our minds at this instance is; what then becomes of the situation of migrant workers in the country from their first day till their fifth year of employment, bearing in mind that workers' rights can only be adequately protected if workers constitute themselves into strong trade unionism? In the light of this question, we submit that the restriction placed on the enjoyment of migrant workers' right to unionize in the country demonstrate the State sovereign right to determine the control of foreigners within its territory.

Section 2(3) of the Cameroon Labour Code, 1992 provides that 'forced or compulsory labour shall be forbidden.' Though this legislative provision is not specific to migrant or national workers, we opine that a literal interpretation of this provision will lead us to the understanding that it covers both national and migrant workers. This argument is supported by the fact that, it is incumbent on any State to respect the rights and dignity of persons within its territory, irrespective of whether such persons are of regular or irregular status.[826] It follows from this view that Migrant workers right to be free from forced labour in Cameroon is well cartered for within the prisms of Section 2 of the Labour Code above. Despite the above efforts, compelled labour continuous to be predominantly prevalence especially in the informal private sector employment.

---

were legal and practical barriers which limited the ability of domestic workers, who are mainly migrants, to join trade unions. Once again, the CFA reiterated that 'the right to freedom of association includes migrant workers', and subsequently urged the government to remove the barriers and to register the association of domestic migrant workers immediately. The CFA urged the government of Malaysia to take all necessary measures, including legislative measures where necessary, to ensure 'in law and practice that domestic workers, including contract workers whether foreign or local, may all effectively enjoy the right to establish and to join any organization of their own choosing.' See generally ILO, Committee on Freedom of Association, Report No 362 (November 2011). The case was previously considered in 2010. See ILO, Committee on Freedom of Association, Report No 356, paras 82 and 85.

826 See Article 9(4) of the ILO Migrant Workers (Supplementary Provision (convention No. 143), 1975.

The question that begs for an answer here is; what could be the causes of the persistent subjection of migrant workers to forced labour in the country? The answer to this question is premised on the fact that most migrant workers don't know their rights, most of them are in an irregular state and are employed in the private sector, where Labour Inspectors' visits are scarce.

Section 3 of same Labour Code, 1992 further upholds migrant workers' right to employment and occupational non-discrimination by stating that 'the law recognizes the right of workers...without distinction whatsoever...' The term 'the right of workers without distinction whatsoever' is literally interpreted in the context of this research to include both national and migrant workers.

However, despite the above commendable efforts in safeguarding employment and occupational non-discrimination for migrant workers in the country, migrant workers continue to be victim of discrimination in Cameroon. This view is informed by section 10(2) of the Cameroon Labour Code, 1992 which unlike the situation of national workers, limits the enjoyment of the trade union rights of migrant workers only to those migrants who have resided in the country for at least 5 years, in violation of Article 9(4) of ILO Convention 143 which specifically mandate States parties to treat migrant workers in a no lesser manner to their nationals.

9.2.3 The 2011 Law Relating to the Fight Against Trafficking in Person and Slavery

A more comprehensive protection against forced labour in the country is offered in the 2011 Law on Human Trafficking in Cameroon.[827]

Section 3(1) of this law provides that 'whoever subjects a person to debt bondage shall be punished with imprisonment for from 5 (five) to 10 (ten) years and a fine of from 10 000 (ten thousand) to 500 000 (five hundred thousand) CFA francs.'[828] The term person as contained in this provision is

---

827 Law No 2011 / 024 of 14th December 2011 Relating to the Fight against Trafficking In Persons and Slavery, 2011.

828 Since as immigrants usually faced exploitative situations especially those in an irregular situation, the state of Cameroon needed to enact such a legislation in a bid to uphold the dignity of a human person. The penalties provided for in Section 3 (1) above shall be doubled where the offender is either an ascendant, a guardian or a person having even custody over the victim. Sub-section 3 and 4 of this provision further intensify the punishment, by stating that 'whoever boards a person in debt bondage shall be punished with imprisonment for 10 (ten) years and with fine of from 10, 000 (ten thousand) to 1 000 000 (one million) CFA francs.' And 'whoever engages

generic. Therefore, if migrant workers constitute persons in the eyes of the law in the State of Cameroon, then they are equally protected like their national counterparts under this law.

9.2.4 The Protection of Migrant Workers Under Selected Domesticated International Laws in Cameroon

In *tandem* with Article 45[829] of the Cameroon Constitution, 1996, and also in line with the States' international obligations under ratified instruments, Article 6(1) of ILO Migration for Employment Convention (Convention 97) mandates the State of Cameroon to abide by the principle of non-discrimination and equal treatment.

In this regards, the State of Cameroon is compelled to treat migrant workers in a way no less favourable than that which it applies to its own nationals. Article 9(4) of the ILO Migrant workers' (Supplementary Provisions) Convention, (Convention 143) not only reaffirms that Member States have a general obligation to respect the basic human rights of all migrant workers irrespective of their status, it also prescribe more specifically the protection of equality of opportunity, which entails access to employment, trade union and individual and collective freedoms.[830]

Article 1 of ILO convention 143 mandate member States to respect the basic human rights of all migrant workers. Article 11(2) of same explicitly prohibits forced labour by stating that 'no migrant worker or member of his/her family shall be required to perform forced or compulsory labour.[831]

Article 20 of the UDHR safeguards the rights of everyone to freedomof association. Article 23(4) of same further provides that 'everyone has the right to form and join trade unions for the protection of his interests.' The term 'everyone' in the context of these provisions, covers both national and

---

even occasionally in the practice of trafficking in persons or slavery shall be punished with imprisonment of from 10 (ten) to 20 (twenty) years and with fine of from 50, 000 (fifty thousand) to 1, 000 000 (one million) CFA francs.' Section 5 on its part provides that 'whoever engages in trafficking in persons and slavery shall be punished with imprisonment for from 15 (fifteen) to 20 (twenty) years and with fine of from 100 000 (one hundred thousand) to 10, 000 000 (ten million) CFA francs'. Such exploitative situations according to section 2 of this law include amongst others exploitation of labour, or forced labour.

[829] This constitutional provision priorities international law to national laws in case of a conflict between the two.

[830] See article 10.

[831] These Conventions are particularly relevant in the context of this research in that the State of Cameroon ratified these conventions on 3rd of September, 1962 and 1978 respectively.

migrant workers. This is further supported by article 2 of same legislation which entitles to everyone, all the rights and freedoms outlined in this declaration.[832]

In line with the position in the UDHR, Article 22(1) of the ICCPR provides that 'everyone shall have the right to freedom of association with others, including the right to form and join trade unions for the protection of his interests'. Though this provision has not provided the kind of workers' interests to be protected as seen above, our point of focus here is on the terminology 'everyone.' The implications of the term 'everyone' as contained in this Article is to the effect that both nationals and migrant workers have the right to freedom of association for trade union purposes.

The ICESCR equally provides for the right of 'everyone' to form trade unions and join the trade union of their choosing, subject only to the rules of the organization concerned, for the promotion and protection of their economic and social interests.[833] The ICESCR provides for the kind of workers interests to be protected, and in line with the UDHR and the ICCPR, the ICESCR provides for the right to unionise for everyone irrespective of whether one is national or a migrant worker, documented or undocumented workers.

States Parties to the UDHR, ICCPR and ICESCR therefore, are under an obligation to ensure that all individuals, national or non-nationals enjoy the rights and freedoms set forth in these instruments, save the case when there is an express provision that permits the contracting parties either to limit the enjoyment of the rights and freedoms by non-nationals or where the provisions of the Conventions allow the contracting parties to reserve certain rights to their nationals.[834]

---

832 The term 'everyone here covers both national and migrant workers. Article 1 of same declaration states that all human beings are equal in dignity and rights. The generic term 'all' use in this article equally covers both national and migrant workers.

833 See article 8(1) (d) of ICESCR, 1966.

834 For instance article 21 (1), (2), of the UDHR states that everyone has the right to take part in the government of his country and has the right to an equal access to public services in his country. Article 2 (3) of the ICESCR permits developing countries to determine the economic rights of non-citizens by providing that 'Developing countries, with due regard to human rights and their national economy, may determine to what extent they would guarantee the economic rights recognized in the present Covenant to non-nationals'. The ICCPR implicitly allows distinction between nationals and non-nationals as seen in article 4(1) which provides that 'In time of public emergency which threatens the life of the nation and the existence of which is officially proclaimed, the States Parties to the present Covenant may take measures derogating from their obligations under the present Covenant to the extent strictly required by the exigencies of the situation, provided that such measures are not inconsistent with their other obligations under international law and do not involve discrimination solely on the ground of race, colour, sex, language, religion or social origin.

9.3 The Existing State of Migrant Workers' Rights in Present Day Cameroon

The above discussed legislative state of affairs of migrant workers' rights in Cameroon will suggest migrant workers are well catered for in the country. Indeed, this is far from reality. The respect, protection and fulfillment of migrant workers' rights in Cameroon is strongly hinged on the requirement of conditionality, consistent with the sovereignty of the State of Cameroon.

Though, paragraph 5 of the preamble to the 1996 Constitution of Cameroon provides that 'every person shall have the right and obligation to work.' The term 'every person' as mentioned herein in the above preambular provision, should not be misinterpreted as including both nationals and migrants. This provision is aimed at protecting Cameroonians' right to work. This reasoning is informed by section 2(1) of the Cameroon Labour Code, 1992 which provides that 'the right to work shall be recognized as the basic right of each citizen. The State shall, therefore, make every effort to help citizens to find and secure their employment,' and 'work shall also be a national duty incumbent on every able-bodied adult citizen.'[835]

For migrant to take up remunerated activities in the country, Chapter IV of Presidential Decree No. 2007[836] mandates such migrants to possess a valid resident permit.[837]

---

835 See section 2 (2) of the Cameroon Labour Code, 1992.

836 See Presidential **Decree No. 2007/255/PR** of 4th September, 2007 fixing conditions for the Application of **Law No. 97/012** of 10th January, 1997 laying down the conditions of Entry, Stay and Exit of Aliens from Cameroon.

837 A Resident Permit is an identification document given to a foreigner aged 18 and above, admitted to stay in Cameroon. Its validity is 2 years and 10 years renewable for a short and long stay Permits, respectively. For the issuance of a Resident Permit, the foreigner has to produce a certified true copy of his passport dating not less than 3 months, a certificate of domicile, a certificate of non-conviction, a tax certificate or an acquittal certificate, or a patent photocopy valid for the ongoing budgetary exercise. He shall also pay stamp duties provided by the law of finance; he shall give justifications of stay as stated by Article 31 of the Decree. The renewal of a Resident Permit for a short stay is subject to the production of the former Permit at least one month before its expiration and all justifications or proofs of stay. For the long stay Resident Permit, the foreigner will produce document depending on whether they are for a foreigner admitted to reside, for members of a religious congregation, or for the spouse of a Cameroon national. With regard to a foreigner admitted as resident, the conditions are same as those for a short stay. For members of a religious congregation, they have to produce an acknowledgement act from the Congregation, an identification document attesting the quality of the member signed by the head of the congregation, a certified true copy of a passport of less than three months of age, a certificate of domicile and a special police clearance. For the spouse of a Cameroon national, he/she shall produce a certified true copy of their Marriage Certificate, all documents required for a Resident Permit except the proofs of stay as laid down in Article 31.

In connection with the above reasoning, Section 25(2) of the Cameroon Labour Code 1996 subjects the employment of foreign workers to the prior approval of the Minister in charge of labour and social security. It is deemed that if after one month of filing the said application the minister does not give an opinion, the silence will be interpreted as an approval[838]. The implication of these legislative positions is to the effect that, for migrant workers to enjoy any labour rights in the country, they must first and foremost seek and obtained the fiat of the Minister of Labour and social Security.

The question that begs for an answer at this instance is: are the above obligations on the part of migrant workers consistent with international law? One may be tempted to answer this question in the affirmative. This position is grounded on the fact that Article 2(3) of the ICESCR provides that 'developing countries, with due regard to human rights and their national economy, may determine to what extent they would guarantee the economic rights recognized in the present Covenant to non-nationals.'[839]

This is in no way a waiver of States obligations under ratify international treaties. We therefore submit that the ratification of the Migration for Employment Convention,1949 and other related conventions, is an expression of willingness on the part of the State of Cameroon to stand by its obligations under these conventions, and as such she must respect, protect and fulfill the rights of migrant workers as contained therein.

---

838 See also section 27(2) of the Labour Code.

839 It has been observed that it was intended only to rectify situations in newly independent states where the influence of non-nationals on the national economy limited the enjoyment of economic rights by nationals. States are urged to interpret this provision narrowly, limiting its application to 'the notion of economic rights and to the notion of developing countries'. See generally D. Dankwa, 'Working Paper on Article 2(3) of the International Covenant on Economic, Social and Cultural Rights' *Human Rights Quarterly*, Vol. 9, No. 2, 1987, PP. 230–249. Also see D. Weissbrodt., 'The Protection of Non-Citizens in International Human Rights Law' in R. Cholewinski *et al.*, *International Migration Law: Developing Paradigms and Key Challenges*, The Hague, TMC Asser Press, 2007, P. 223.

INDEX